UFO
CRASH LANDING?

FRIEND OR FOE?

THE FULL STORY OF THE
RENDLESHAM FOREST
CLOSE ENCOUNTER

JENNY RANDLES

BLANDFORD

A BLANDFORD BOOK

First published in the UK 1998 by Blandford

A Cassell Imprint
Cassell plc
Wellington House
125 Strand
London WC2R 0BB

Distributed in the United States by Sterling Publishing Co., Inc., 387 Park Avenue South, New York, NY 10016–8810

A Cataloguing-in-Publication Data entry for this title is available from the British Library

ISBN 0–7137–2655–5

Designed by Chris Bell

Printed and bound by Mackays of Chatham

CONTENTS

PREFACE

IT WAS A DARK winter's night in one of England's most rural counties. Christmas celebrations were winding down, but as wisps of sea fog clung to the air a surprising number of people were still out and about in the early hours of Boxing Day morning.

Suddenly their peace was shattered by something plunging from the skies. It fell to the ground in a silent blaze of light and sent nearby Suffolk air bases into a frenzy. As the glowing object plummeted from above, woodland creatures scattered in its wake. Human eyes and protective radars peered upwards, seeking to determine whether the intruder was friend or foe.

The national defences of NATO – Europe's guardian against enemy attack – prepared to respond to this intrusion. Then reports flooded in of a large object that had come down amidst forestry land and of radiation spewing forth among the stately pines.

The US Air Force had to react swiftly to such an unlikely event. It was their job. But there was a problem – how does *anyone* deal with something as unconventional as this? The strange happenings were taking place just 8 miles (13 km) from the major town of Ipswich and much too close to London for comfort. Yet the public were to be told nothing. Secrecy was deemed more important than safety that night.

The thing that had dropped from the sky early on 26 December 1980 was not a Soviet spy plane. Nor was it a terrorist attack. Such eventualities are well described in official USAF manuals and trained military personnel know exactly what to do. But just what *can* you do when the cause of the panic is both unexpected and unexplained? When it is something, perhaps quite literally, out of this world.

A UFO had crashed to Earth in East Anglia that night – and many lives could never be the same again. Mine would soon be one of them and this book will tell you why.

INTRODUCTION

OUT OF THIS WORLD

I T IS MORE than 16 years since the Rendlesham Forest landings took place, yet they have haunted my life ever since. In some respects I do what I do today as a result of those perplexing events more than 200 miles (322 km) from my home and during which I was sound asleep, oblivious to them all.

Can I prove to you what actually took place? Can I explain what that UFO was and why the powers-that-be, in both the USA and Britain, went to extraordinary lengths to say nothing about it? That is the challenge this book represents and I know that it is far from easy.

This is not the first time I have put pen to paper and attempted to describe this remarkable case. Ordinarily I would not find it reasonable to dwell so much upon one UFO encounter. However, this story simply *demands* your attention.

Its focal point is a series of complicated events in connection with two major US air force bases, known as RAF Bentwaters and Woodbridge. Both were leased by the British Ministry of Defence to the American Air Force as part of their long-term NATO defensive duties. They sit within the enormous surrounds of Rendlesham Forest, a vast East Anglian pine wood near the coastal spit of Orford Ness, and they dominated the local area for more than four decades.

The twin air force bases operated as one unit and served as a rearward maintenance centre for troops on the frontline in Germany. They were large and important complexes which were ultimately vacated in 1993 as part of the USAF decision to pull many troops from Europe after the cessation of the Cold War. Ironically,

Bentwaters was then offered to the Maharishi Foundation to be developed as a site to train yogis in mystic flying, although they turned it down after deciding that the 'vibes' were not suitable. It has now been sold to a mysterious Middle Eastern investor, for a purpose as yet unknown. The intrigue of the area thus goes on!

I will allow the story to unfold gradually, so that you can see some of its convoluted background taking shape. These multiple layers are what make it so important. While I could just report what witnesses claim, or plunge straight in with an imaginative reconstruction, I will not do that. This case goes beyond sensationalism. It is a fascinating detective story just waiting for someone to find the truth.

For that reason, I will try to omit nothing that may be relevant. We shall start with seemingly innocuous happenings, look at odd features of the local environment, take in top secret experiments, meet shady characters from the intelligence services of both Britain and America and cope with all manner of clues, several of which are, no doubt, big red herrings, before digesting countless possible theories about what might have taken place.

In the end only you can decide what the true answer must be.

First, however, we must backtrack a little to see UFOs in their broader sense.

Strange things are undoubtedly going on all over the world and we have invented a magic word – UFO – to convince ourselves that we understand them. We don't. After 50 years of baffling activity in the skies above, we are little more than a few steps down the road toward comprehension.

I have been actively investigating UFOs since 1972. At first it seemed straightforward because the tabloid press told me that it was. Aliens from another planet were roaming the universe and there was a massive government conspiracy to hide the truth. Then it crossed my mind that if the US Government could not even cover up a burglary in the Watergate building then how the heck were they going to stop someone blabbing about the greatest story in history?

Also, if you think about it, why hide that secret anyway? It made more sense to share knowledge with scientists – joining forces in a quest to learn the truth. Can you imagine the astronomer who discovered a planet beyond Pluto spending billions of dollars on some international conspiracy to ensure that nobody ever found out about his or her achievement? What happens when someone less intent on silence makes the same discovery and goes public ? Any cover-up is ultimately futile.

Of course, there are other considerations, notably the inevitable interference by the somewhat inaptly named 'intelligence community'. However, misinformation, disinformation and downright incompetence apart, the truth about UFOs is far less easy to unravel from the dubious machinations of the CIA and MoD than pop media pronouncements would have it. Sadly, these are often fuelled by wide-eyed buffs and sensationalist writers in the UFO world – of which there is no shortage.

If it were as simple as an ET version of Neil Armstrong taking rocks home (to whatever distant planet home might be), then we would have proved this long ago. We haven't – so I think it's safe to say that the truth is rather less apparent than that.

As we grope towards the answers it turns out that much of the truth is perhaps disappointingly mundane. From the thousands of UFO investigations that I have carried out down the years I am certain that the vast majority – 95 per cent and rising – are explicable in completely Earthly terms. They are aircraft and weather balloons or laser light shows and freak mirages. The list is pretty big and always getting bigger as we find new ways to pollute our crowded atmosphere.

These countless reports describe what we call IFOs – *Identified Flying Objects*. They have been nowhere near any hypothetical planet circling a distant star. I find it part of the fascination of UFOlogy that we must solve the logic puzzle that most sightings become. You collect the evidence, sift the clues, shuffle hypotheses and try to identify the culprit. Then you finger the suspect and hope that Miss Marple doesn't walk in and make a fool out of you by proving that it was really someone else.

Of course, demystifying UFOs and showing that Mrs Brown – who thought she saw a spaceship above the Red Rec – was really watching a police helicopter chasing teenage joyriders – is not the stuff of which great newspaper headlines are made. I don't think that this is all there is to it, but I am not stupid enough to be dogmatic about that prospect. Human beings are very good at fooling themselves, and UFOlogists (their own inflated egos to the contrary) *are* human and so very prone to being led astray .

However, there are good reasons why I am convinced that not all UFO sightings will turn into IFOs even after considerable effort. Sober research by the likes of the Battelle Memorial Institute in the USA and GEPAN, a team of French atmospheric physicists in

Toulouse, has effectively proved to my satisfaction that there is a fundamental difference between the solved and the unsolved cases.

This research (for example, assessing the effects of clarity in the atmosphere against the number of unexplained sightings) shows that the unsolved reports would not simply disappear if more evidence came to light about them. That is a popular misconception emanating from pompous sceptics who have probably never even heard of Battelle or GEPAN. There *are* unexplained riddles within the hodge-podge that is UFOlogy.

Unfortunately, too many UFOlogists spend their time chasing trivial lights in the sky, which lack any solid evidence to back them up. With the best will in the world and the investigative prowess of Sherlock Holmes these could still turn out to be anything. It is far better, in my view, to pour years of effort into one case that has the potential to be more definitive.

That is why those events in that East Anglian woodland on a dark December weekend deserve to be considered in so much depth. There is little doubt that they represent the most important UFO case ever to occur in the British Isles, and very possibly in Europe. They would certainly rank as one of the most influential cases anywhere in the world if you ran a poll of serious UFO researchers.

This is not to say that an alien spaceship has to lie behind them. I suspect that many unsolved cases will eventually prove to have no more to do with visitors from another world than does the 5.15 train from London's Waterloo station. It is wise too to remember what those letters U-F-O stand for.

There are fascinating phenomena out there which are constantly pushing back the barriers of our knowledge. We are constantly learning new things about physics, meteorology, optical and electrical activity in the atmosphere and peculiar events which seem to be taking place within human consciousness. To me UFOlogy often represents progress for some branch of science, while, sadly, most scientists see only the media line that 'UFO' is synonymous with 'alien spaceship'. Unhappily, as scientists inevitably contend that alien spaceships do not exist, then, to extend this faulty application of logic, neither do UFOs.

In fact, UFO was simply a term invented by a particularly bright US Air Force investigative officer in 1952, aiming to get away from the overblown image of the 'flying saucer'. That man, Captain Edward J. Ruppelt, did not believe in alien starships and thought that calling this rag-bag collection of phenomena *unidentified flying objects* would be more down to Earth and less misleading in his (ultimately forlorn) quest to explain them all away.

He was right, of course, although it took the media and the vociferous UFO lobby little time to ensure that the term UFO simply replaced the term flying saucer and then came to mean much the same thing. This is a shame because a UFO is, quite simply, an *unexplained* phenomenon witnessed in the sky and for which no solution is immediately obvious. As already stated, most UFOs are not unexplainable and readily turn into IFOs after a reasonable period of investigation. The few that remain unsolved may still one day be deemed natural, not supernatural, following new discoveries about what makes the universe tick.

We are always making such discoveries and this process continues in the late twentieth century. Phenomena such as glowing balls that can enter sealed rooms and illuminate neon lights switched off at the mains were long reviled by science just as UFOs are today. Now, however, this so-called 'ball lightning' is the subject of major international physics conferences, although, unfortunately, the best examples tend to be misreported by their witness as UFOs. As a result, by debunking UFOs, science never sees the best evidence that is vital to its own research and so loses out on data that might enable it to comprehend an intriguing natural phenomenon. It is a wicked irony.

Some of the still unsolved UFO sightings will one day be resolved in scientific terms as a range of natural phenomena of this type, and which we do not yet recognize. After all, the Sun shone for a few billion years before scientists discovered the nuclear furnaces through which this comes about.

A UFO is a UFO, nothing more and nothing less. That statement, while simple, is, none the less, one of the most profound that I can make and it should never be forgotten. However amazing a case may seem, it is not immune to explanation, perhaps many decades after it has occurred. The purpose of any UFO investigation should be to try to find out what that UFO was. This is the motivation behind this book. It is emphatically not my purpose to prove that aliens landed east of Ipswich. As you will see in this case, appearances can be most deceptive about questions like that!

The world's favourite answer to the UFO mystery – that we share this planet with visitors from afar – may simply be an example of human gullibility. However, there are some cases where an alien interpretation, while hardly proven, is perhaps inferred as a reasonable contender. The crash landing in Rendlesham Forest is one of them, although we may well be led towards a far more fascinating possibility than that – one for which UFOs take a back seat and much bigger ethical questions appear.

This case merits serious attention for another excellent reason. No other similar event in UFO history has provoked so much political bluster. If it were nonsense then senior politicians would have avoided it like the Black Death because UFOs are terminally damaging to a high flying ministerial or civil service career. Here they had no choice but to get involved.

If there were some simple answer – a military incident relating to a slight mishap – a secret device (which would hardly still be state of the art so many years later) – or just some bureaucratic blunder, then by now we would surely know. To explain a case like this has got to be less damaging than for officialdom to maintain a far less credible denial of information. To say *mea culpa* over some minor military affair and silence the UFO activisits and tabloid hacks must be preferable to allowing the idea that Suffolk played host to visiting extraterrestrials to keep on gaining momentum .

Official silence speaks volumes – as does the involvement of political heavyweights, from Michael Heseltine to Merlyn Rees, from Lord Trefgarne to Senator James Exon. When we add senior figures in the Ministry of Defence, such as Lord Hill-Norton (once commander in chief), Ralph Noyes (who had equivalent rank of air commodore) and Nick Pope (who ran the UK Government's own UFO files for three years and is now a media star likened to Fox Mulder of the X-*Files*!), then you begin to see the problem. You don't get that sort of public commitment for a nonsense. Such a catalogue of public comment must suggest that something pretty darned important has taken place.

Not that this crash landing stands or falls merely upon what the bigwigs had to say about it. There is also a surfeit of hard evidence.

This is not simply a few civilians seeing something odd on their way home from a party. It is heavy data from trained military personnel – senior officers up to the rank of base commander – the people whose fingers were on the nuclear trigger and whose bombs could have wiped out Europe. We have to trust that they did not all go mad one dark night and presume that the authorities did not judge this to be the case either; because many of them subsequently received promotion and went on to run their own bases in the UK and around the world – with even more fire power at their disposal.

If UFO-spotting is a disease of the mind or an embarrassing error made by trigger-happy nincompoops, then it is worth noting that none of the military personnel whose stories you will read were judged harshly for such a thing nor punished for ineptitude. Moreover, would it not be every bit as disturbing to conclude that those who hold the fate of the Earth in their hands are prone to wild hallucinations and might shoot what they think are Martians first and ask questions of intruders later?

This case is not only about this kind of responsible testimony from more than 20 eyewitnesses to the events in the forest. There is hard evidence to back it up – from radar trackings of the UFO to high levels of radiation scattered in the woods and kept secret until a shameless government was forced into the open – radiation worse than any left in Britain after Chernobyl went critical!

Some of the incidents were even captured 'live' on a tape recording of stunned words and shaken emotions spoken by human beings facing something for which none of them was ready .

The first time I wrote about this case was in 1984, in a long out-of-print book called *Sky Crash*, with two brave colleagues (Brenda Butler and Dot Street) who had sacrificed a great deal to collect stories from local folk and who alone ensured that the authorities could not keep a lid on this sequence of events.

I admire Brenda and Dot greatly but they were enthusiasts not methodical scientists. They made few notes and collected little systematic data and it was a struggle to figure out what had actually taken place. Moreover, when we put *Sky Crash* together there was too little information about the case. A few civilians had talked. One military witness had gone public with a story that seemed to many to be dubious and was even disputed by some of the other witnesses. Even that man wanted anonymity, although his tale is now the basis of a book called *Left at East Gate*. As frustrated researchers, it was really very difficult to put together any sort of coherent account.

Thankfully, that situation has much improved. Most of the witnesses are now on record. Hard evidence has been secured. The amazing 'live tape' of the events unfolding in the forest is in place. I have travelled the world chasing the data and it is possible to tell the story of this famous case while in possession of probably as much accurate information as we are ever likely to get.

As the UFO subject has now reached its fiftieth anniversary, this is the right moment for me to put an important encounter into its proper context and free it from the hype and hysteria.

I also want to address some of the deeper questions that emerge from such an extraordinary case, such as the reasons for the so-called 'cover-up' and the attitudes and responses of the British and American Governments to the UFO mystery. In the process I will tackle a number of other claims of military involvement with UFOs, which throw some light on the events in Rendlesham Forest.

In recent years I have spent much time researching such questions under contract to BBC Television and wrote and presented my own documentary (*Britain's Secret UFO Files*) which gained a record audience for the department with which I worked. Inevitably, there was a vast amount of data that I could not make public— and the quest for answers has continued unabated.

This book offers the chance to show you what I learned from the murky world of the secret service and their involvement with UFOs. The incident in Rendlesham Forest is a highly reflective case that I have lived with for many years. It has come to possess me and I have often struggled to fathom its meaning.

In writing this book I not only have the chance to report on events that are pivotal to the UFO mystery, but an opportunity finally to exorcise that ghost.

Jenny Randles
Derbyshire, August 1997

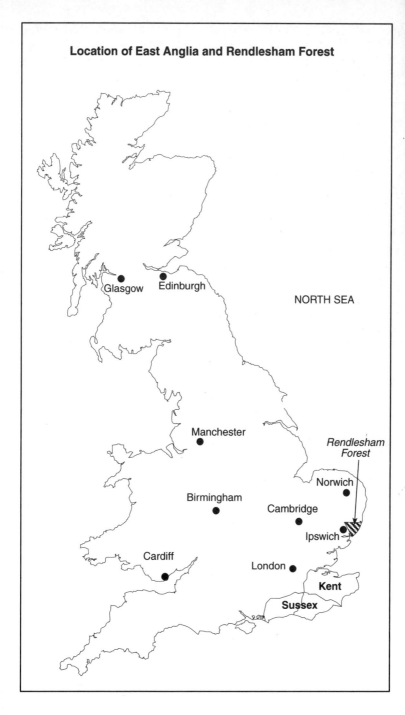

Location of East Anglia and Rendlesham Forest

NORTH SEA

Glasgow

Edinburgh

Manchester

Rendlesham Forest

Norwich

Birmingham

Cambridge

Ipswich

Cardiff

London

Kent

Sussex

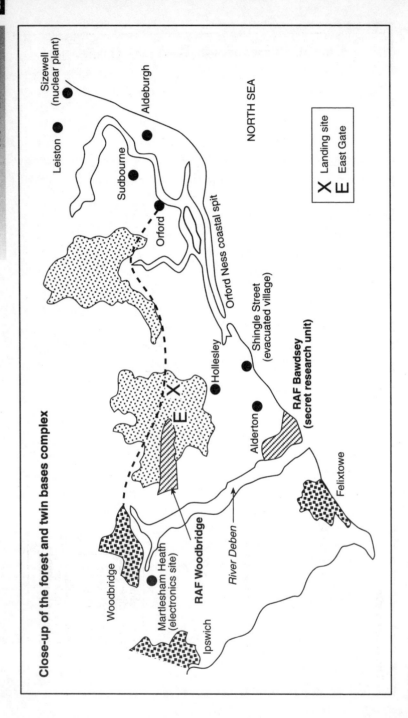

Close-up of the forest and twin bases complex

Ipswich

Woodbridge

Martlesham Heath (electronics site)

RAF Woodbridge

River Deben

Felixtowe

Alderton

RAF Bawdsey (secret research unit)

Hollesley

Shingle Street (evacuated village)

E

X

Orford

Orford Ness coastal spit

Sudbourne

Leiston

Aldeburgh

Sizewell (nuclear plant)

NORTH SEA

X Landing site
E East Gate

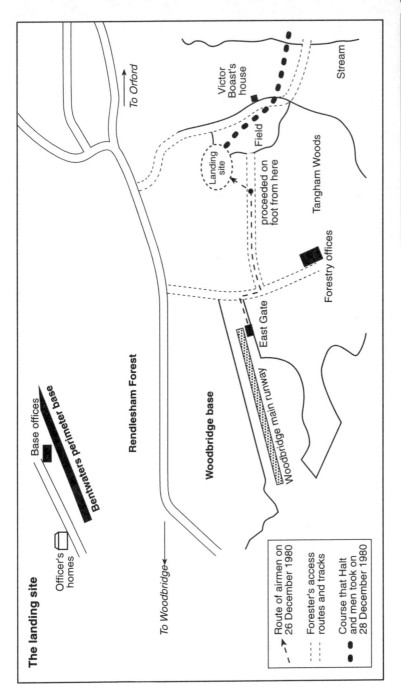

The landing site

Officer's homes

Base offices

Bentwaters perimeter base

To Orford

Rendlesham Forest

To Woodbridge

Woodbridge base

Woodbridge main runway

East Gate

Forestry offices

Tangham Woods

proceeded on foot from here

Landing site

Field

Victor Boast's house

Stream

— ▶ Route of airmen on 26 December 1980

---- Forester's access routes and tracks

●●● Course that Halt and men took on 28 December 1980

1

CHRISTMAS ANGELS

A T 9.07 PM on the night of 25 December 1980 northern Europe was suddenly illuminated as if by a giant fireworks display. The sky glowed with numerous sparkling fireballs like a Christmas cake sprinkled with candles. Santa Claus had really come to town.

The records of BUFORA (British UFO Research Association) show the events very clearly. A number of sightings were made from Kent and the Thames Estuary. Witnesses eventually concluded that they must have seen a UFO and described what they had observed in consistent terms.

'A formation of six lights emerged from one dazzling object, like babies being born from a whale,' explained a poetic witness near Folkestone. Another, near Dartford, told how a trail of blazing matter, like an aircraft on fire, passed eastwards towards the North Sea and appeared to be breaking up as it moved along.

These people were mystified, and understandably so. Of the half dozen reports from south east England, four initially presumed they were witnessing an aircraft exploding. Only the eerie silence and the fact that the trail of burning debris did not fall out of the sky dented that conviction, resulting in their decision to contact one of the many UFO groups that are found in most major towns.

However, to a seasoned UFOlogist this case was not remarkable. It had all the hallmarks of a brilliant meteor or blazing space debris, although its long passage across the sky (witnesses estimated that it was in view for more than two minutes) would provoke some discussion. Meteors are rarely more than a brief flicker and even the biggest and brightest tend to disappear inside a matter of seconds.

More long lasting and spectacular are the re-entries into our atmosphere of 'space junk' – the metal parts of rockets and satellites that burn up stubbornly as they meet the intense friction of the upper levels of our atmosphere on their downward spiral from an unstable orbit.

That option seemed a good bet here and, when press reports commented that the booster stages from a Russian military satellite were expected to have met their fiery doom that same night, it appeared safe to conclude that one more UFO had been successfully resolved.

Unfortunately, things were to prove more complicated than that.

Collecting the evidence has taken many years, but a coherent picture has been drawn up. It may seem peripheral to the main events in Rendlesham Forest a few hours later, but it is not. According to the sceptics, it is the key to the whole mystery. Even some witnesses who insist that a real close encounter unfolded in that Suffolk wood say that this Christmas light show is very significant.

Indeed, one of the most persistent stories that I heard during my years of investigation of this case was that I should 'remember the comets in the sky that night'. We were first told this curious thing by an electronics engineer working at Martlesham Heath, a major telecommunications research centre on the fringe of Rendlesham Forest. I later heard it independently from other sources, offered up in a knowing manner which suggested that these sources were aware of something which they were not at liberty to discuss, but which I might be able to work out for myself from such an obvious clue.

John Burroughs, a crucial US Air Force eyewitness at Bentwaters on that December night, said much the same thing when I first met him in Arizona nine years later. 'Those "meteor" events in the sky that night are important,' he told me, refusing to be drawn into further explanation.

However, the first solid evidence that something unusual was afoot regarding the Christmas 'comets' came when it was reported by the press that civil aircraft may have witnessed this phenomenon from mid-air. It took some time for UFOlogists to track these stories down to source, but it was established that a passenger jet outbound from Stansted airport in Essex had radioed to air traffic control that they had seen a brilliant 'explosion' in the eastern sky out towards Felixstowe.

More importantly, air traffic advised the Boeing's crew that radar at Heathrow had picked up the object as an unidentified target heading east above the Thames. If the Russian space junk was responsible then it must have been surprisingly low in the atmosphere, and not up to 40 miles (64 km) high as anticipated. Otherwise it could not have been recorded on civilian aircraft radar. In other words, it had been a real threat to people on the ground and not simply a spectacle high above the Earth.

More strange things were to follow. On 16 January 1981 I received a letter from Michael Pereira and subsequently obtained a more detailed report from him because his story sounded most intriguing. Superficially, it appears as if he also saw the rocket re-entry, but if his story is true (as I found no reason to doubt) then it raises many problems that cannot be explained quite so readily.

Michael was on holiday from London at a place called Paco de Arcos near the town of Santo Amaro in Portugal. He was on the waterside with a local friend called Pedro enjoying the pleasant winter's evening, which was mild with wonderfully clear skies. Many stars were visible amidst a calm, almost breezeless environment.

As near as they can recall the time was about 9.15 pm, but it could have been a few minutes either side and so was very probably coincident with the purported burn up of that Soviet satellite – code name Cosmos 749 – which was officially reputed to have re-entered at 9.08 pm.

The Portuguese UFO was first seen by these two young men heading in a slow arc towards the south west. Although, visually, it resembled both things, Michael insisted that it was 'moving too slow to be either a comet or a meteor'. It was oval in shape with a trail of light behind it, not unlike the tail of a comet. The colour was pink and quite beautiful to look at. Indeed, it made the sea underneath glow and the witnesses were adamant that it was possible to see a wake of turbulence trailing beneath, as if the UFO were churning up the water as it passed by.

I questioned this because I realized that it was impossible for debris from a satellite burn-up to do any such thing. In their passage over Portugal the blazing metal fragments would have been far above sea level and could not possibly create a disturbance on the water below. If this effect was real, rather than an optical illusion, then either this object was not Cosmos 749 or something very peculiar was going on in connection with its re-entry.

However, the problem with the turbulence was by no means the only difficulty. After initially heading out over the Atlantic, the witnesses told me that this object suddenly altered direction quite sharply some 30 seconds into their observation. Now it moved inland – eastwards – and made directly for the two young men standing open-mouthed on the quayside.

Needless to say, re-entering space junk cannot make such radical changes in direction. It comes in at a steep angle, burns up as it plunges downward, and is gone. If this account was not another illusion then, again, it left me in some doubt as to the Cosmos 749 explanation.

However, the description of the object given by these two witnesses fitted a space junk re-entry so well and their timing was so close to that of the officially logged 749 burn-up that it was difficult to imagine they could have seen anything else.

The easy way out would have been for me to reject their story as fanciful and assume that they did see space debris and somehow imagined the rest. Yet their accounts were sober and well documented and did not have the appearance of confabulation. Furthermore, there was yet another problem which they had to report. The two men claimed that the UFO had burnt them!

Both Michael and Pedro insisted that as the object crossed directly overhead they felt a sensation on their skins like prickly heat. Their exposed shoulders and heads were tingling. Of course, the weather in Portugal was a lot warmer than the sub-zero temperatures a few hundred miles north in Britain, but it was nothing like warm enough to create sunburn, especially as Pedro was a local man and therefore well used to the sun. Michael had also had several days to adjust to the warmer climate.

Moreover, the witnesses were positive that the heat sensation occurred precisely as the object passed directly overhead and at no other time. In any case, even in Portugal you cannot suffer from sunburn in the pitch dark several hours after the sun has set.

The object headed over mountains to the north east and was lost to view after about another two minutes, making the sighting some two and a half minutes in duration all told. It never made a sound, and as the surroundings at Paco de Arcos were fairly quiet, the two men should have heard a noise had it been present.

That night both men had much difficulty in sleeping, experiencing an itchy sensation on their skin, watering eyes and a pounding headache. These are identical symptoms to those that I have heard described many times by witnesses to UFOs during what are known as car stop cases.

In these instances, the force generated by the passage of a UFO stalls the car's engine and blocks out its electrical lighting system. These cases are surprisingly common, around a thousand cases having been thoroughly documented from all over the world since the 1950s. Some researchers believe that the symptoms described result from exposure to ionizing radiation which may be a by-product of the UFO, which, in turn, could well be some type of natural atmospheric energy in the form of a plasma. Note that this is not a wild leap to conclude that UFOs must be alien craft, zapping people in cars with 'death rays', which is another myth of media UFO reporting. On the whole, serious researchers seek more restrained options.

Needless to say, re-entering space junk cannot possibly burn people – at least not according to any process that we understand. Yet both Michael and Pedro claimed to suffer from a red rash, like sunburn, in the days following their close encounter. Pedro's skin, perhaps being more used to the sun, showed the effect for only 48 hours. However, it lasted four days with the less fortunate Englishman. This suggests irradiation – but irradiation from what source?

I had no idea what to make of all this. To accept that they had seen what logic told me they must have seen (the death throes of Cosmos 749), I would have to reject all of the central features of their story. But if these were nonsense then why believe anything the two men said? Except, of course, they were describing an object that we know was real because many other people also saw it on that same night.

So, was I justified in believing only the bits of their story that I wanted to believe because they fitted my preconceived explanation? Or should I judge it all together? However, by doing so, how could it possibly have been the space junk re-entry that I so firmly believed them to have seen?

The next step was to ascertain what astronomers had to say about the spectacular space phenomena encountered on that Christmas Thursday night .

The BAA (British Astronomical Association) did publish a report on the events. This was compiled by director George Spalding and assistant director (now president) Dr John Mason. It was to prove something of an eye-opener because even the professionals in the field were intrigued by what was taking place. Nor did the story simply revolve around Cosmos 749. It seems that 25/26 December 1980 was a bumper night for fans of fireballs and space junk. The sky was literally full of them. Although they are not especially rare, so many on one night is certainly unusual.

There had already been two fireball meteors (i.e. big lumps of rock burning up in the atmosphere) by the time that Cosmos 749 came along. Both of these earlier events (at 5.20 pm and 7.20 pm) were witnessed from south-east England. The biggest of the lot was at 2.50 am into 26 December. This was a most spectacular fireball, brilliant like the full moon and visible for four seconds. It would surely have made a few eyes pop among witnesses on the ground, although there was less potential for people to see this final incident because of the unearthly hour.

Then there was the problem with Cosmos 749. It was a problem even to George Spalding and his team. Reported by astronomical observers on the ground as 'a fireball of extremely long duration', it was seen to fragment and disintegrate. Over 300 sightings were described to astronomers from both southern England and northern France. The episode in Portugal was at a site much further south but with a good northerly perspective across the Atlantic. Of course, that anomalous sighting so far south was not reported to astronomers and there were probably others like it.

However, even without the Paco de Arcos case, the BAA had concluded that there were strange things about this re-entry. Indeed, astronomers commented that the early identification of the fireball, reported at 9.07/9.08 pm as being the re-entry of Cosmos 749, was now thought 'extremely unlikely'. Their report justifies this scepticism by arguing that the sightings measured an orbital inclination (re-entry path) at 55 degrees – whereas Cosmos 749's was known to be 74 degrees.

There were further riddles, according to the BAA report. The track of the disintegrating fireball suggested that it burnt up just off the east coast of England (pretty close to Rendlesham Forest, in fact). Yet there were more reports of a contemporary bright fireball over Holland, Belgium and Germany, well to the east of this location and at times after the rocket should have been utterly consumed. Bits of metal found on the ground at Maldegem near Bruges were initially thought to be from the Cosmos 749 rocket, but now that prospect was in some doubt.

In conclusion, the BAA noted that a second space junk re-entry might have occurred at almost exactly the same time and burnt up over the same part of northern Europe. This double coincidence (of both time and space) would be improbable as re-entries are fairly uncommon and they can burn up anywhere along their orbital path which forms a circle around the planet. Of course, there may have been yet another big fireball meteor, which would be almost as unlikely.

Either way, the fact that the professionals dealing with space debris phenomena found the events of 25/26 December 1980 peculiar was most intriguing. When matched alongside the Paco de Arcos sighting and the frequent mentions during investigation that the 'comets' seen over East Anglia throughout that night were somehow important to the UFO landings, the puzzle could only deepen.

In 1994 Dr John Mason described in more detail the findings of the BAA. He feels that the unusual plethora of fireball events must explain what went on in Rendlesham Forest. No UFOs were therefore seen, he argues. These naturally occurring fireballs triggered the whole drama.

Unlikely as I find that explanation, for reasons that will become clear as our story progresses, his comments on the fireball activity are authoritative. He explained how the BAA were able to track the course of the Cosmos debris from Beachy Head in Sussex across the Thames to its point of disintegration above 'the North Sea off the coast of East Anglia'. He further suggests that a fragment from the blazing rocket booster may have 'landed, or fallen in the sea off Orford Ness'. He notes how civilian air traffic control picked it up on radar (and heard of it via pilot sightings) and, therefore, speculates that military radar in East Anglia would have detected it as well.

It is not hard to understand why a scientist would assume that these unusual events must have been the cause of the UFO activity. One, possibly two, rockets burning up alongside several fireball meteors, all in the same geographical area and within a few hours of each other, would be a huge coincidence if they had nothing to do with a spectacular UFO episode that also took place that night. However, an important rider should be added to this very reasonable conclusion.

What if the spate of fireball activity was far from 'normal'? This is implied by the events in Portugal and the orbital anomalies recorded by the BAA, aside from the large number of events that seem to have occurred during such a short space of time. In any case, the Cosmos event precedes the major UFO landing in Rendlesham by five or six hours – too long to be simply an error in timing.

Dr Alan Bond, a specialist in advanced physics and rocketry propulsion, has done contract work for the MoD. Years after the event I saw his name associated as a leading light with the HOTOL space plane project – an extraordinary cross between a jetliner and a rocketship which could fly in sub-orbital space from London to Sydney in just a couple of hours. Dr Bond's arrival on the scene was crucial.

The physicist phoned my home in November 1984 and told me that he would not normally read about UFOs but a mutual contact had advised him to look at what I had to say on this case. He told me he had a few ideas about what might really have happened in that forest and that, if true, it was political dynamite. He would now check them out. Some days later he called me back.

This time he was more defensive. He explained that there was something wrong with the orbital figures regarding a second Russian military satellite that was said to have re-entered the atmosphere on 26/27 December 1980 and was coded Cosmos 1226. Nobody was really sure what kind of device it carried as the USSR kept quiet about its military space missions. Bond then ventured his own speculation as to some incredible things that might have happened to that satellite.

It sounded like a plot from a science-fiction novel but raised the idea of the re-entering 'comets' and their concentration on southeast England. Indeed, it explained why the wave of objects that night may be relevant to the Rendlesham landings but explicable in very terrestrial terms. We shall look at that in more detail later in the book.

'I am heading off for a conference in the Netherlands,' the rocket man told me sombrely. 'When I get back I will not be taking this any further. You do not know what you have got yourself into. You are messing with something for which you can end up at the bottom of the Thames.'

Needless to say, I was stunned by his words. I am used to critics telling me that I am too credulous (or even too sceptical) but it is not every day a reader of your work says something like that. Of course, I had no way to judge his theory. What did hit home, however, was that, yet again, somebody in an undoubted position to know was telling me that the key to this case revolved around those amazing 'comets' seen in the sky immediately before the main events in Rendlesham Forest. He was also indicating that there was a problem with the computer figures regarding another Soviet satellite re-entry, just as the BAA had done about Cosmos 749. So what on Earth was going on?

This has since made me look at other situations where spectacular UFO sightings have been blamed upon satellite burn-ups and so been quickly written off by most researchers. Had the same situation happened on other occasions?

On 31 December 1978 – a holiday period just like Christmas night in Rendlesham Forest – there was a classic example. Indeed, I was able to make a close study of over 100 sightings from around 7.05 pm that evening, which came from all over Britain and were made by witnesses including police officers and air traffic controllers. I thought that this case offered a great example for statistical research in that we knew exactly what these witnesses had seen (film of the re-entry was taken even in Morecambe) and so we could compare the truth with the witness descriptions.

The blazing trail of debris that was in view for between two and three minutes that New Year's Eve was quickly attributed to the re-entry of a booster rocket from Soviet satellite Cosmos 1068. Because many people were out and about on a clear, starry night, travelling to or from family reunions or party celebrations, the number of witnesses to this incident was considerable.

My study found many interesting things but two stand out. First, there were no wild exaggerations of what was up there. Nobody spoke of the re-entry churning up the sea, or changing direction completely or giving them physical symptoms like burns, as at Paco de Arcos. There could not be a clearer example of how people faced with an unusual phenomenon and in a situation where one might expect fantasy to run riot (thanks to the convivial mood and the effects of alcohol consumption that night), none the less displayed no such tendency.

However, there were also some reports – notably a major spate in Ormskirk, Lancashire – which looked on the surface to be further sightings of Cosmos 1068 and yet, upon investigation, appeared to be of a quite different phenomenon. The oval object described here emitted a loud humming noise and did other things that the space junk could not have done.

J. Bernard Delair of Contact UK suggested a theory to accommodate this, which seemed even more outlandish than the weird hypothesis Alan Bond was now proposing to me. Delair wondered whether not all of the sightings made around 7 pm that New Year's Eve in 1978 were the result of the Cosmos re-entry. What if someone out there had used that event as a smokescreen?

The UFOlogist had noted that, with our own technology, we could predict more or less when and where this naturally occurring spectacle would take place. So what about an advanced civilization with far greater technology at its disposal? Maybe they saw the burn-up as a perfect opportunity to roam our skies, safe in the knowledge that, if spotted, their activities would just get swallowed up amidst all the sightings of space junk? What better time for UFOs to fly completely unhindered?

More recently, there was another example that may provide even better evidence of that possibility. For this one has now got some official backing from the MoD!

The events occurred on the night of 30/31 March 1993 and were well investigated by Doug Cooper, then with my investigation team at BUFORA and running DUFORG, his own local group. He was first alerted at 2.20 am on 31 March by a call from Sergeant J. Furneuxe of the Devon and Cornwall Police, describing a sighting made by himself at 1.10 am that morning while on patrol at Liskeard. Two bright lights were at first seen stationary. Then, as he stepped out of his patrol car, he watched them move away to the south east, emitting what seemed to be self-luminous trails of vapour.

In a superb piece of dedicated investigation and with wonderful assistance from his local police, Doug spent the next few hours tracking down and interviewing no fewer than 11 police officers in Devon, Cornwall and Gwent who had witnessed something very similar and had called their central control room in Exeter to back up the report they had heard Sergeant Furneuxe transmit on the radio. This focus on police witnesses is explained by virtue of the fact that few other people would have been out and about in the rural West Country at that hour of the morning.

Meantime, I was discovering that there were witnesses far and wide to this same event – all talking of two bright lights and a trail of other lights moving majestically across the sky. In Ireland, a military transport plane heading from Baldonnel to Donegal saw them cross its path. Air traffic controllers at Shannon saw the lights as well, as did a Garda police patrol in Churchtown, County Limerick. Again, this case had all the hallmarks of a satellite re-entry.

Ultimately, we were able to establish that there were sightings as far away as the south of France and northern Italy. This proved that the object had to be many miles high in the atmosphere in order for it to have been witnessed simultaneously over such a wide area.

Interestingly, NORAD (the North American radar defence system in Colorado, which tracks both incoming ballistic missiles and high orbital satellites) told the Irish military 'air miss' enquiry that there was no space junk passing overhead at the time. In fact, there was a re-entry in progress, which NORAD had somehow missed – one of the boosters from Cosmos 2238, which the Russians had launched only about an hour earlier. Having been so recent, this launch may explain why the NORAD computer log did not yet feature the event, although they are usually aware of such things.

In any case, Cosmos 2238 was indisputably the cause of most – if not all – of the sightings at around 1.10 am throughout Europe that night. Doug Cooper did come to agree with this conclusion. However, he had two quite legitimate reasons to feel that there was more to it than that.

The first concerned highly anomalous sightings that were 'trawled in' along with other reports of the burn-up. These came thanks to Doug's tenacity and a major PR campaign via the local media. It is tempting to presume that these new reports are just rogue sightings of the re-entry, but that is difficult because they would entail many serious errors on the part of the witnesses.

A good example came from a Somerset police officer, PC Filer, at 9 pm – that is, three hours before the Russian rocket was even launched and four before any bits of it returned to Earth in a blaze of glory. He was on the Quantock Hills with a group of scouts, co-ordinating a field exercise. This police officer described how he saw a series of lights with a craft dimly outlined between them – 'like two Concordes flying side by side and joined together'. The whole thing passed over on a south easterly course and, in many ways, duplicated the Cosmos debris. It was almost like a precognition of that event, displaced several hours ahead of itself. If it was simply a sighting of the Cosmos debris then this police officer got his timings spectacularly wrong, which seems hard to imagine.

Filer's description of what he saw was eerily similar to an account given by two fishermen (Vernon Rolles and Mervyn Kelly) who were on the River Parrett near Bridgwater at just before 2 am. They also saw two lights approach and pass silently overhead. Rolles described a superstructure linking the lights which he said resembled 'a large catamaran'. As they moved off towards the south east, two beams of light were thrown out of the rear of this object. One might question why the fishermen did not also report the 1.10 am re-entry if what they saw was something else. However, Doug feels that they witnessed a genuine UFO and that it was timed 50 minutes after the Cosmos re-entry.

Interestingly, the fishermen had initially presumed that the lights were helicopters because at about 1.30 am they had seen three military helicopters dropping flares in the area. It has been speculated that this activity was in response to some of the UFO sightings, such as that somewhat earlier on the nearby Quantock Hills. Of course, we cannot know for sure what these helicopters were doing.

Other military activity was reported by a retired airline pilot who contacted Doug to say that he had seen 'two jet fighters travelling at thirty thousand feet (9,144 m), heading in a westerly direction and at a very fast speed – about 1,500 mph (2,400 kmph). They had after-burners on, which indicated that they may still be climbing.'

We could again stretch this data to fit in with the Cosmos re-entry, especially as two lights with trails figure in this man's story as well as in the re-entry. But could an airline pilot be so mistaken — getting the time wrong and having the phenomenon head in en-tirely the opposite direction to the known course of the space junk? Moreover, he would also have to identify blazing lights wrongly as two very specific military jets, the type of which he was able to rec-ognize, according to his evidence.

I have to say that the sceptic in me feels that all of these reports must surely have referred to the space junk and that their distor-tions were just serious errors made somehow by witnesses (e.g. pilots and policemen), even though we would normally expect such witnesses to be accurate. However, I can see why doubts nagged at Doug Cooper. He must have felt fully vindicated when he phoned up the MoD in London and spoke with Nick Pope, the man then in charge of their UFO data collection centre – Air Staff 2A.

Even then, a year or so into his new job, Nick Pope was known to UFOlogists in Britain as a breath of fresh air because of his own per-sonal interest in the subject. Pope's predecessors at Air Staff 2A (or Defence Secretariat 8 as it was formerly known) had been saddled with the job and had no enthusiasm for doing it. UFOs were an unwelcome headache, rife with potential PR disasters. The MoD were always getting letters from nutty UFO buffs accusing them of a cover-up and the 'chosen one' at Air Staff 2A was the clerical officer who had to respond with a set formula of noncommittal words. Not surprisingly, they preferred to keep a low profile.

Nick Pope was different. Not only was he interested in the sub-ject but he came to believe that UFOs were extraterrestrial through his personal studies while working at the MoD. He had private meet-ings with top UFOlogists. He talked volubly to all who asked for his views. By 1996 (having now been promoted out of Air Staff 2A into a new job at the Ministry), he had published a book proclaiming alien reality and was on a lecture/TV interview tour that took him all over the world, enjoying the label of Britain's Fox Mulder (the FBI agent in the hit TV series *The X Files*).

Working on cases in conjunction with UFOlogists was unheard of before Nick Pope came along but, following the March 1993 events, his sortie with Doug Cooper was not the first and would not be the last. However, it was to be one of the most extraordinary.

Using his official contacts, Nick responded immediately to Doug Cooper's call the same morning within hours of the events. Pope found that there were no jet aircraft airborne over the West Country when that airline pilot had made his report. The logs simply recorded no flights by RAF or other NATO aircraft and the MoD man was at a complete loss to explain his sighting of two jets.

There are really only two possibilities here. One is that the witness saw the re-entry and mistakenly thought its lights were from aircraft. The other is that the jets were on a secret, unlogged mission, perhaps to intercept the UFO that had alerted the MoD to its presence. Indeed, the MoD would probably not have identified the space junk solution before any intercept mission was sent.

Caution forces me to suspect that mistaken identity is the most likely answer but it appears as if both Cooper and Pope concluded that real jets may have been up there that night. Given Nick Pope's unique access to official information, his views on that matter have to be taken seriously.

Moreover, Pope advised BUFORA in writing three weeks later that the MoD had received so many reports for the night of 30/31 March 1993 that he had to include a map of their distribution. Of course, many of them were almost certainly the Cosmos re-entry, as the MoD had concluded. However, one object, witnessed by military personnel and a meteorologist passing between RAF bases on the Welsh Borders, projected a beam of light toward the ground and seems very hard to interpret in this way (see page 217).

For the first time in my experience I found myself as a UFOlogist in an odd position. I was trying to explain the events of 30/31 March 1993 as the product of the Cosmos re-entry. As Director of Investigations with BUFORA I considered it my duty to try to solve cases. Yet I was being actively dissuaded from that very possibility by the man from the MoD.

I still cannot eliminate all thought that these rogue events are somehow extreme misperceptions of the space junk re-entry. However, I do recognize that it is difficult to argue that opinion without challenging a great deal of seemingly reliable testimony. Which means, of course, that if I am wrong and witnesses such as the Bridgwater fishermen and PC Filer on the Quantock Hills were not watching the Cosmos burn-up, then they were watching UFOs that seem to have known all about the imminent re-entry. Indeed, these UFOs were mimicking that natural event with clear evidence of an intelligence. Natural phenomena could not have behaved in this way.

Read that last sentence again and absorb its meaning. It stuns me every bit as much as I trust it will stun you. For, if it is true, then these particular UFOs were capable of toying with our air defences and of using predictable natural phenomena that they knew about in great detail. These served as camouflage to let them go about their operations.

It is also worth noting how all three of our examples for these puzzling re-entries occurred on public holidays. Nick Pope went further and noted the proximity of the 1993 case to 'April Fool's Day'. Was the anticipated low level response of the media a factor in the choice of these dates? If so, then who did the choosing?

There were further inklings of something odd taking place in January 1995 when a British Airways crew reported a UFO that nearly hit their passenger jet as they were on their final approach to Manchester Airport. Many familiar sounding 'fireballs' were in the sky that week. I thought this had to be what the crew had seen, but they insisted it was a wedge-shaped craft. The CAA investigation report agreed with them. Was this another smokescreen operation by some unknown source?

Whatever the truth, we can now see that the 'comets in the sky' above Rendlesham Forest on that Christmas night are of much more significance than one might imagine at first sight.

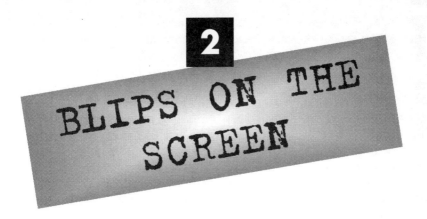

2

BLIPS ON THE SCREEN

EAST ANGLIA is alive with radar screens. They glow in eerie shades of green and orange, with fuzzy blips and clusters of dark images revealed every few seconds as their ceaseless sweep continues.

The system is vital. It scans the heavens eastwards from the military bases that dominate these flat lands – forever vigilant for possible attack. The radar also fulfils the peacetime function of controlling a never-ending logjam of air traffic that traverses the skies.

In late December 1980 there were still a dozen radar stations sited throughout the three counties of Cambridgeshire, Norfolk and Suffolk. On Christmas night – when the comets flew – several of them were active. Although it was a holiday period and traffic was light, the job of radar control is a 24-hours a day, 365-days a year occupation. Indeed, a few military exercises still took place, mindful of the motto that the enemy never sleeps.

Malcolm Scurrah was one of the air traffic controllers at work beside his tiny screen, just a few inches in diameter. I met him in 1989, thanks to UFOlogist Philip Mantle, and he had quite a story to relate. It fitted perfectly with my then growing knowledge about the events that winter weekend.

Scurrah is not absolutely certain of the date or time, but it was very late at night during December 1980 and would appear to have been during the few day period when Rendlesham Forest was buzzing with UFOs. He was based at RAF Neatishead near Norwich and his task that night was to operate the 'nodding height finding radar'. As the name suggests, this nodded up and down and gave information about the height at which an aircraft was flying. Parts of it were strictly classified because the MoD did not want enemy intelligence to know how high above the ground it could successfully track. Any holes in radar coverage might have been exploited .

That night Scurrah's prime concern was several RAF Phantom jets which took off from various bases in the area, notably Wattisham. Air space had been cleared for them over the Wash and out into the North Sea, to allow them to take part in a night exercise at speeds of over 500 mph (800 kmph). However, as this was proceeding, another of the radar controllers at the base was picking up a target on his scope that ought not to have been there.

The blip was clearly a problem because it displayed no IFF (identified friend or foe). This is a computerized electronic signal which tags any aircraft on the radar, be it a civil or military flight, and thus identifies precisely what it is. An enemy invader will not have been allotted an IFF, of course, nor would any unidentified object. Therefore, this blip was readily spotted as a threat, hovering as it was in a zone that should have been free of air traffic to give the Phantoms room for their dangerous exercise.

For a moment there was measured concern in the radar room as procedures were put into motion. Out in the North Sea there are a number of oil rigs and it was speculated from the apparent lack of speed of this object that a helicopter might be making an unscheduled flight. This was soon disproved. Local weather stations also reported that there was no activity under their supervision.

It was a genuine and potentially deadly mystery.

The senior control officer now contacted 'Eastern Radar' – the nearby centre at RAF Watton. This joint RAF and Civil Aviation Authority unit co-ordinates that busy region of air space. They confirmed that there should be no target where this blip appeared to be hovering.

By this point, two of the jets had been vectored by RAF flight command to head out on an intercept course and investigate the intruder. Scurrah thought that he was tracking one of these jets as he watched a blip appear on his screen and when the intercom barked out a request for height information he began to describe details of the target on his scope as it climbed from 5,000 ft (1,524 m).

Within moments Scurrah realized his mistake. Whatever he was monitoring was unlike any aircraft and was climbing far too rapidly. This was confirmed by the voice over the intercom. One of the Phantom pilots was now reporting a visual target – a brilliant light dead ahead. Another radar controller added that the jet was closing fast on the radar blip and was now under 1 mile (1.6 km) from intercept. As the jet approached the blinding light shot upward at phenomenal speed. This transition from standing still to rocketing skyward had been done in the blink of an eye. The G-forces alone would have killed any pilot who had been inside the cockpit if this target were just an aircraft.

Amidst growing amazement at the information he was passing on, Malcolm Scurrah continued to perform his duty, calling out heights and coded information in response to the RAF pilot's request. Almost before he had uttered one sentence the radar swept around to reveal that the blip had climbed yet again. He found himself reciting a litany – 'Level one zero zero, level one five zero, level two zero zero . . .' and onward, recording the height changes through 10,000 ft (3,048 m) and upward at a staggering pace.

When the blip got to 90,000 ft (27,000 m) in under five minutes the radar operator was certain that this was without precedent. No aircraft, except perhaps the USAF spy plane – the Blackbird – could go so high nor could they stand such a rate of ascent. The chatter in the radar room from officers recording other information was every bit as shocking. Nobody had a clue what this target could be.

The Phantoms had long since pulled out of their pursuit. They gave it their best shot, streaking up at maximum speed to give chase to the glowing light, but it outflew them as easily as if they had been biplanes from an aviation museum in a futile race against supersonic technology.

Eventually, the UFO vanished off screen somewhere to the south and at an amazing height. Now that this radar system has been upgraded from its 1980 performance levels, Scurrah is willing to state the details about that height. It was out beyond 100,000 ft (30,480 m) that they lost the target. Even then the UFO was still climbing almost vertically upward toward the stratosphere.

There was much discussion about this matter afterwards. All RAF personnel understood the need for secrecy, as this was not the first time an unknown object had been tracked. Indeed, Malcolm Scurrah recalls that when a report was entered into the 'UFO log' for the base there were several other recent events already included, although he had not been on duty when they had occurred. One was very probably the Cosmos 749 episode which seems to have been tracked not only by Heathrow radar on Christmas night but also by the military. Another had followed this incident with the Phantoms.

Scurrah later heard that the radar recordings and station logs for several consecutive nights around this period were taken away for analysis by an intelligence agency. It seemed that the skies above East Anglia had been full of UFOs that week and someone was desperate to find out why.

Neatishead was not the only base to receive unexpected visitors that Christmas. RAF Watton had them turn up on its own doorstep the following Monday, 29 December 1980.

When I first learned this fact in late January 1981 it was to be my earliest contact with the still top secret goings on around Rendlesham Forest. There had been no press stories, not even in the local papers in Suffolk. The few references to the 'comets in the sky' on Christmas night had all been written off as a space junk re-entry. We had no idea that amazing UFO encounters had supposedly occurred on the ground in Rendlesham Forest or in the skies above East Anglia the preceding weekend. Such evidence would only emerge very slowly through many years of research – research that began when I became aware of an episode described by the radar officers at RAF Watton .

My first source of information on the incident was Paul Begg, a sceptical writer on paranormal matters whom I knew slightly via a mutual friend. Paul phoned me to say that he had just met a man in his local pub which at that time was in a village near Norwich. Begg had been there with his wife and they both knew this man as no more than an acquaintance. From occasional drinks together, they were aware that he was a civilian operator based at 'Eastern Radar' but that was about it.

Feeling the urge simply to tell somebody of his remarkable story, the man had seized on Paul Begg because of his background as a writer (having penned a pretty sober account of various unexplained disappearances). The radar man reported what had happened but Paul was at a complete loss to know what to do with the news, having no real interest in UFOs. However, he suggested to me that I might like to follow it up and contact this radar operator whom I will call David Potts. Potts is not this man's real name. While other witnesses in this book have allowed themselves to be correctly identified, I must still protect this radar operator from being recognized by his present employers.

David was very forthcoming about the events he had witnessed, explaining that they began for him on 29 December 1980 when a group of intelligence officers from the US Air Force arrived at Watton and required access to both the log books and the film of radar recordings for a several-day period surrounding the previous weekend. As Watton was not a USAF base this was unusual but, of course, quite acceptable. Radar recordings were always kept for a few days in case of an emergency – for instance, if there was an air crash and investigators needed to study data for their accident enquiry.

However, David had heard about no accident and, in any case, these intelligence operatives were giving a quite different and truly fantastic reason for their request. They said that a UFO had crashed in woodland near RAF Bentwaters and that Watton may have tracked it on radar.

As it happened, Potts was not on duty on either of the nights in question (it seems the period 25/26-27/28 December were the two nights that were involved). However, another officer who had worked during that period explained to him what had taken place.

One of the incidents detected on Watton radar was probably the Cosmos 749 event. The more intriguing incident, however, was an incident on the night of 27 December moving into the early hours of 28 December (i.e. the Saturday/Sunday night of that fateful week-end). This involved an object that was first detected over the Wash, just as the radar at Neatishead had reported in their own encounter.

The unidentified target was tracked by Watton heading south on a descending path. It cut the coast somewhere near Lowestoft. Eastern Radar lost sight of it as it fell below their coverage to the east of Ipswich, that is, somewhere above Rendlesham Forest and in the vicinity of the twin NATO bases of Bentwaters and Woodbridge. The object appeared to have been heading toward a possible crash landing and the USAF suggestion that it struck the forest seemed not unreasonable, given what the radar at Watton had picked up.

I discussed the matter with a friendly senior air traffic controller at another air base (who was discreetly sending me copies of 'secret' UFO reports that his team was compiling for the MoD). He noted that the distance between Watton and Rendlesham Forest (about 35 miles or 52 km) indicated that any object passing below 3,000 ft (914 m) would vanish from radar coverage.

David Potts was also told by the visiting USAF intelligence men that during the night of this second incident tower radar operators from Bentwaters had phoned Eastern Radar to describe strange lights that were under observation and to ask if Watton had anything on their screens that might coincide.

The radar tracking at Watton had, of course, been fascinating enough, but nothing could have prepared Potts and his colleagues for the extraordinary claims made by the visiting American intelligence agents. As part of their explanation for taking the recordings, they gave an account of what had supposedly happened after the UFO went down into Rendlesham Forest .

I still have my notes, written during my first conversation with David Potts in late January 1981. This was long before I obtained information from any other source to confirm or deny the Rendlesham case. It is amazing just how accurate the story was that Potts had been given. In fact, he was able to provide nearly all the key features during that very first conversation. It would take me another 15 years to verify most of them!

Ground sightings were made by airmen in the vicinity of Woodbridge and Bentwaters, Potts was told. The UFO had first been spotted about 4 miles (6 km) east of the Woodbridge runway. After discussing what to do, as the light had appeared to come down in the forest, senior officers were withdrawn from a Christmas party underway on the base, for consultation. They went out to the site by jeep and found the UFO landing zone. Both the jeep's engine and VHF radio sets suffered interference, as did battery arc lights being used by the military to illuminate the forest. The whole remarkable episode was recorded on a battery-powered portable tape deck as the drama was unfolding. Anomalous radiation traces and marks on the ground were also found in the woods.

Before they learned of this fantastic sequel to their radar tracking, Watton had called West Drayton in Middlesex immediately after the target was lost. West Drayton is the MoD command centre where air traffic radar are co-ordinated and reports of UFO activity are channelled en route to Whitehall. The unit set up to collate all data at the MoD is known as Air Staff 2A. Police, airports, coast guards and various other sources have all been issued with instructions and an official report form in order to supply Air Staff 2A with details of unusual sightings via West Drayton.

The MoD told RAF Watton that there had been other radar observations that weekend and referred to an aircraft on flightpath Red One that had already filed a UFO sighting form. This was almost certainly a reference to the Cosmos 749 affair which, by then, was some 48 hours earlier.

However, one intriguing thing that West Drayton did reveal was that another radar report had been received for this second night (i.e. 27/28 December). That report had come from Ash in Kent, just south of Margate and only a few miles across mostly open sea from Rendlesham Forest.

All of this begs the question as to why the USAF intelligence officers felt the staff at Watton had any 'need to know' about the landings in the forest. The matter was successfully hidden from the public by the British and American Governments for another two years. Telling anyone about it risked that secrecy. The radar film could simply have been confiscated with official approval and no questions asked. So why tell the personnel at Watton the story that they did?

David Potts says that he was never asked to keep this amazing yarn confidential, although, as a signatory to the Official Secrets Act, he was aware of the situation. The real reason why he spoke, but requested anonymity, was because he did not want to implicate his colleague who had reported to him details of the radar from first-hand observations. However, there is still something vaguely suspicious about the way this information was so casually fed out to these radar staff by US intelligence.

Moreover, the intelligence officers had been even more explicit about what had supposedly taken place in the woods after the initial landing. According to the story they told staff at Watton, the USAF base commander from Bentwaters had gone out that day into the forest and established direct contact with small alien creatures who had emerged from the UFO. Their craft had been damaged but was repaired while the US Air Force stood guard. Eventually it took off again.

I was utterly bemused by this bizarre tale, particularly the last part. It seemed hard to imagine any USAF intelligence officers sharing such information with British radar personnel. If it were true, then surely these people would simply never have been told such a fantastic secret. If it were a tall tale from the USAF, what did they hope to achieve by telling it?

Certainly, I found it hard to shake the belief that a deliberately wild UFO story had been given to the staff at Watton in expectation that it might become public. Was this in order to hide something else, perhaps a military accident which had occurred that night? The more absurd the story about aliens and crashed spaceships that was spun, the less likely it would be that anyone would launch a sober, public enquiry. Rather, talk of aliens would ensure that nobody threatening to national security would take the matter seriously. As disinformation it was a masterstroke because the UFO community had a decided penchant for believing in- and telling the whole world – the wildest things.

However, time was to prove that much of what the intelligence officers had told the staff at Watton was supported by solid evidence. The basic tale was definitely not an invention. The only element in serious doubt was the reputed alien contact.

If disinformation games were being played, they were subtle in their nature. However, as I was to learn from a senior MoD figure, the best misinformation is always based upon the truth so perhaps this is what we face – a story we should believe part of the way. But which part?

Of course, it would be years before I came to realize most of this. In January 1981, when I was first told about the Watton story, it was a completely unsupported tale which proved impossible to verify. Potts would not go on record in writing. His colleague would not talk to me first hand and attempts made to verify the story via the base or MoD hit a brick wall of denials.

The radar trackings during that weekend still remain controversial. There has never been any official confirmation about them, either from the MoD or from the US Government via numerous Freedom of Information Act requests to try to vindicate the stories. What happened to the confiscated radar films also remains unknown. The US Government has lied under Freedom of Information before about this case and the British MoD covered up everything they knew about it until absolutely forced to confirm data bit by bit after it was squeezed out through other means. So any denials about the radar evidence cannot be taken as proof that nothing happened.

In any event, years later official MoD and USAF data confirmed much of what Potts told me on that January night. It must be reasonable to assume that if the story given by the visiting USAF intelligence officers was essentially valid, then the claim about the radar trackings was also genuine. One seems contingent upon the other as the intelligence officers would not even have been at Watton to tell this story unless there was some radar evidence there for them to take away.

The continued denial, by both British and American Governments all these years later, is both curious and significant. You do not need to hide an absence of evidence, but if you are avoiding the issue for more sinister purposes then the evidence being covered up must be something that you do not want people to see. There are, however, several further clues about the radar data.

The first comes from a visit that I made (with Brenda Butler and Dot Street) to the Ministry of Defence main building in Whitehall, London. This took place one afternoon in August 1983 when I took with me a copy of solid documentation verifying the sightings in the forest. This explosive document had just been obtained via the

American Freedom of Information Act. It was devastating stuff and proved that the MoD had conned the British public since December l980 by choosing to hide the truth.

The power of this document was sufficient to gain an audience with the then occupant of the MoD's UFO hot seat. Her name was Pam Titchmarsh. By simply turning up unannounced, holding these papers and threatening to go to the press with them, we threw the ministry off guard and it gave me the perfect chance to ask probing questions, face to face, inside the MoD bastion.

Naturally, I asked about the radar trackings. Pam Titchmarsh was quite forthcoming. She said that some film from radar units had been checked out for that weekend but none had correlated with the sightings from Rendlesham Forest. No records about this checking process have ever been made public. To her knowledge nothing existed in writing on the matter. Nor had any unidentified radar recordings in any other situation ever been tied in with visual UFO sightings.

Specific as these comments were, there seemed to be a real problem. Pam Titchmarsh had just stated quite assuredly that she had not consulted any file on this case before agreeing to meet me. She did not know we were coming so had no time to prepare beforehand. The case was not well known publicly in August l983 as all press revelations had yet to happen. In any event, as we later confirmed and the MoD have always insisted, the only data they claim to possess on the case in their records was the report by Colonel Halt which I had brought to show to a rather worried MoD official after its Freedom of Information Act release in the USA. That report makes no mention of radar trackings.

So – I put to this MoD officer – how could she possibly know so much about the radar trackings and their lack of correlation with the Rendlesham UFOs, given the fact that there was no source on file for her to have consulted about the matter?

She seemed a little put out by this logic but answered swiftly. By coincidence, she and her staff had been given an official briefing a short while before our surprise visit to Whitehall. This had been from RAF radar personnel, discussing how to deal with cases where radar was allegedly used to track UFOs. As there had never been a real case of any actual correlation, the failed sightings in Rendlesham Forest more than two and a half years earlier were used as an illustration during that briefing. By good fortune, therefore, Ms Titchmarsh was well versed about the details I was requesting.

I found this a rather convenient explanation.

A few years later a second lead to the radar trackings was offered by American researcher Benton Jamison who, in 1986, was put in contact with an A-10 pilot (Major Everett) who had been stationed at Bentwaters during December 1980. The noted aviator John Lear, whose family ran the Lear Jet business, had been the go-between who had set up this contact.

The major had not been directly involved in any of the sightings on the base but had attended a 'stand-up' meeting the day after the final landing in the woods. Everett was uncertain of the date but it may have been Monday, 29 December. In any case, at this meeting were senior base personnel, including the overall commander for Bentwaters and Woodbridge (Wing Commander Gordon Williams), as well as one of the key witnesses to the encounters, deputy base commander Colonel Charles Halt (the author of the report that I had taken to Whitehall to confront the MoD). These men had discussed the incidents of the previous weekend extensively at that stand-up meeting.

Major Everett recalled that a tracking of the UFO by radar at a place called RAF Watton was referred to by senior staff. He later became unsure as to whether this statement was made at the stand-up or in later conference. However, he is adamant that this base and its radar tracking were a reality.

A third clue has come from Colonel Charles Halt himself, who, as mentioned above, was deputy base commander at Bentwaters at the time of the events and who we now know was the man who made the battery tape recordings in the forest as the second batch of landings occurred on the Saturday/Sunday night. This was the evidence that I had first heard about, only five weeks after the encounters, via David Potts at Watton, but which would not surface in public for several more years.

In 1994, after leaving the US Air Force, Colonel Halt finally went public with his own testimony. In his account he confirms that there was contact between the control tower at Bentwaters and Eastern Radar at Watton during the sightings on the second night. By inference, he suggests that this was early in the morning of 28 December, while he himself was in the forest watching UFOs. This fits precisely with the story given to me by Potts 13 years before Halt's revelation.

Finally, thanks to a new climate of open government, where further information about UFOs is being offered quite unsolicited by the MoD, Eastern Radar at last relented in late 1992. Following a written request by UFOlogist Nick Redfern, their Squadron Leader, E. E. Webster, agreed to issue a statement.

He noted: 'Our log book for the period does indeed say that a UFO was reported to us by RAF Bentwaters at 03.25 GMT on 28 December 1980 . . . All radio and radar recordings from that time have long since been disposed of; consequently, we can provide no more information.'

However, Squadron Leader Webster added a verbatim transcript of the log entry, viz: 'Bentwaters command post contacted Eastern Radar and requested information of aircraft in the area – UA 37 traffic southbound FL 370 – UFO sightings at Bentwaters. They are taking reporting action.'

This is fascinating in that it establishes for the first time documented evidence that Bentwaters did attempt to obtain radar verification of an unknown object heading south at 3.25 am on that Sunday morning. However, the references to Upper Amber 37 (an air route east of Bentwaters and out over the North Sea) and a flight level of 37,000 ft (11,277 m) imply a rather distant and fairly trivial incident. The claims about what really happened in the forest that night were – as you will see – considerably stranger than that. This tepid 'admission' by Watton is, I fear, more problem than solution.

You will also notice that there is no reference at all to whether Watton tracked anything themselves on this night, or at any other time during that holiday weekend. However, if there was no prospect that the base had tracked something then why would USAF intelligence officers have gone there immediately afterwards and taken away the radar recordings for analysis?

Importantly, Watton do not deny that any radar tracking *might* have happened – they only say that they no longer have the records to comment on the matter. This is classic MoD evasive tactics. One senior MoD figure, Ralph Noyes, who was of the equivalent rank of air commodore and an under-secretary in the civil service, has explained it to me this way. 'Suppose you are asked whether there are British nuclear weapons on some Mediterranean island. You cannot lie, so you do not deny it, even if you know that it is true. Instead, MoD officers are taught to avoid the question skilfully, by saying something like: "Figures are not available on this matter ",or "It is not policy to discuss the deployment of nuclear weapons at British bases".'

Much of what the MoD says about this case seems to be skilful evasion. But just what are they trying to evade?

Rendlesham Forest in East Anglia is a fascinating place. It is not just a vast pine wood, but its fringes contain more scientific research facilities than any comparable location within the UK. That alone makes the intense UFO activity and radar trackings reported here more intriguing than ever.

From as early as 1949 – as once secret data, now released by the US Freedom of Information Act, reveals – the American Government had noticed a worrying trend. UFO sightings focused on sites where scientific research was at its peak. This pattern was partly responsible for the intervention of the CIA who gathered a research panel of top scientists in Washington during 1952 in order to debate the UFO evidence. It was kept very secret, of course, and employed rocket scientists and physicists. There was not a psychologist or sociologist in sight on this so called 'Robertson panel' (named after relativity physicist Dr H.P. Robertson who was chosen to supervise the team). That alone shows very clearly how the US Government judged the UFO matter – not as an illusion, but as a physical reality.

This panel was convened in the wake of numerous reports from around White Sands, Sandia and Los Alamos in New Mexico where the nation's top minds were then perfecting rocketry and atomic weapons technology – and still do. Most of the major UFO events in those days – from the Roswell crash in July 1947 onwards— seemed to 'home in' on this hotbed of scientific activity.

Serious debates about this matter were held at Los Alamos on a regular basis between 1948 and 1952. They involved big names in American science, such as astronomer Dr Lincoln La Paz and one of the 'fathers of the atom bomb', Professor Edward Teller. These men were primarily concerned by the spate of UFO events surrounding top secret facilities, notably fuzzy green fireballs that acted like reconnaissance devices and a startling number of 'bright meteors' whose trajectory 'coincidentally' took them over the labs. Scientists feared that the Russians might be using missile technology of advanced design. However, it was soon obvious that the USSR could not have built craft that behaved like the things being observed. Indeed, these were not wide-eyed mystics seeing lights in the sky. Witnesses were often the scientists themselves, as few others were allowed into these well-guarded locations!

Lincoln La Paz was a meteor expert and he struggled to prove that the 'fireballs' were natural events. Of course, that could not then mean space junk burning up because the first artificial object was not put into Earth's orbit until many years after the sightings. But the astronomer failed to find any natural cause for the fireballs, despite government funding for a secret experiment known as

'Project Twinkle'. This deployed various sophisticated detectors to record hard evidence from the overflying UFOs.

La Paz concluded that the objects were not meteors, but the Freedom of Information Act supplies us with no data on research after 1952. None the less, CIA documents from the 1970s hint at top secret work into 'propulsion systems' that was based on UFO activity long after these green fireballs flew.

Unsurprisingly, the CIA team ordered secrecy to dominate the UFO mystery. They demanded that the US Air Force 'cook the books' to make it look statistically as if UFOs had simply gone away, in order to curtail public interest. They ordered monitor programmes to keep an eye on civilian UFO investigators who might influence public opinion. They even proposed cartoons be made to make UFOs look ridiculous and steer any serious attention away from the subject.

These plans were forced upon the US Government by its own secret service in response to their escalating worries over UFO activity. These extreme tactics certainly worked. A year after the panel had met, a memo (released only a quarter of a century later) reveals the US Government's pleasure that its moves were having the desired effect on public attitudes towards UFOs.

Those who are understandably sceptical of UFO reality would do well to ponder these extraordinary government initiatives in response to a clearly disturbing act of 'intelligence' displayed by the phenomenon. Would naturally produced lights in the sky, or cases of mistaken identity, show preference for the most sensitive locations in American scientific research?

Perhaps you have also noticed the intriguing parallels. In 1950 strange fireballs concentrated around the home of America's most sensitive post-war research facilities, designing rocketry and nuclear energy research. Thirty years later, exactly the same thing was going on above Rendlesham Forest, England where modern top secret research was being carried out. Once again we are drawn to consider the importance of the 'comets in the sky' which sound disturbingly similar to those fireballs that so concerned 'Project Twinkle' three decades earlier.

Around Rendlesham Forest there are even quite a few sightings of 'green fireballs' eerily similar to those that plagued the scientists in New Mexico. For example, postmaster Thomas Meyer was on the beach near Sizewell with his dog at 6.55 pm on 24 February 1975. Suddenly a green pumpkin-shaped object floated at head height from over the sea and seemed to 'inspect' them both. The dog fled in panic but Meyer felt a tingling sensation on his skin and smelled what he called 'acid drops' as if the object was ionizing the air. That evening, houses in nearby Leiston village suffered an unusual amount of static interference on their TV sets. Meyer also felt tired and nauseous after the event and was unable to work for some time.

There are quite a few other examples. We heard from fishermen at Sizewell who had often seen these green fireballs over the Orford Ness spit just off the coast by the forest's edge. On 15 October 1983, one was seen to plunge into the North Sea near here and was still glowing as it dropped beneath the waves. The lighthouse keeper at Orford Ness confirmed to me that he has heard similar stories from fishermen regarding phosphorescent glows on the surface of the water.

Dorothy Whymark, who lives in the village of Eyke, recently recalled for me one event from 20 years before which had occurred in March 1974. She had been taking her dog for a walk, just like Thomas Meyer, when the ball of light appeared and seemed to send a beam down towards the ground. She rushed home to get her daughter but the UFO had disappeared.

Dorothy chose to report this matter not to the police or to the MoD but to an RAF site at Bawdsey and asked them if they had tracked it on their 'secret radar' (a local in-joke). Predictably, they said no but they did send a flight lieutenant from their intelligence staff to ask probing questions about the UFO. Mrs Whymark notes that this officer took the event seriously. Military intelligence very rarely pursue civilian witnesses and their stories. That suggests there was something special about this one.

Dorothy Whymark's story is not the only time that I have been told by a witness that the MoD made a personal visit to follow up a sighting. However, the visits do seem to be rare and the MoD is very selective about which cases to pursue. It is certainly interesting that something going on in Rendlesham Forest should get the attention of RAF Bawdsey and speed them into action. It makes you wonder whether Bawdsey's 'secret radar' was not so quiet after all.

This RAF experimental unit located at Bawdsey is just one of the facilities in this area that is subject to great secrecy. I have heard many stories about it, particularly from those who work at the near-by remand centre in Holleseley. Indeed, one of the warders claims that they were given preliminary orders by the RAF at Bawdsey to plan an evacuation from here on the weekend of the Rendlesham Forest sightings in December 1980. However, the final order to quit never came.

There is also an electrical engineering facility, which was operated by Marconi Industries for some years, and British Telecom have a research site at Martlesham Heath, from where, if you recall, came the first suggestion that we should take note of the 'comets in the sky'.

In 1983 I also spoke with an engineer who worked at this research site and who claimed to have heard an 'intercepted' version of what was then a 'holy Grail' of this case – the long-sought tape recording supposedly made in the forest as the UFO sightings took place. Could Martlesham have had facilities that allowed this recording to be 'picked up' and 'intercepted', just as those with scanners can listen in on mobile phone conversations today? Either way, that tape was real. We now have it.

Other oddities include the evacuation of a village called Shingle Street – for the testing of what was termed 'a revolutionary weapon'. According to the MoD, both here and on Orford Ness they tried out detonators for British nuclear weapons. So this was a hotbed of early nuclear weapons' research as well. Not that you can discover much. Shingle Street data is still covered by the Official Secrets Act.

There are also the highly sensitive nuclear facilities to be found at Sizewell, the small coastal village around which most of the green fireball sightings have concentrated (just as they focused around Los Alamos during the 1940s and 1950s).

Indeed, the Sizewell nuclear plant was subjected to many strange events while under construction during the 1960s. By chance, I met one of the builders before the Rendlesham Forest case occurred, so he was certainly not influenced by that event when we were talking. He told me that many of the staff refused to go back to work because power tools would repeatedly energize themselves and lights kept switching on and off. They thought the site was haunted, but it sounds like another example of some kind of latent energy field at work. This is a common theme in the vicinity of Rendlesham Forest and cropped up repeatedly throughout this investigation.

All of these places are within a few miles of one another and turn this forest into a hive of well-hidden scientific research. The locals speculate widely that far more odd things are taking place, beyond the knowledge of the general public. For example, there have always been stories in the area about power cutouts and cars mysteriously stalling, which tend to be blamed on these scientific experiments.

These tales actually go as far back as the 1930s when rumours were rife that a 'death ray' was under development locally! Aircraft more than once just 'dropped from the sky like stones' when passing over the forest, it was alleged. Of course, in those days aircraft were probably a lot less reliable than now and would be early prototypes flying from the local bases, so this may have a simple explanation.

However, press stories from the time reveal that fishermen out in boats around Orford Ness also claimed to develop blisters on their skins which they blamed on strange experiments that were said to be taking place on the island. You must remember that this is where the MoD now admit they were starting experiments with nuclear detonators – to the extent they had to evacuate an entire village!

Even today it is not hard to find locals who blame frequent power losses and car malfunctions on such unknown research. Barry Bridges has told me how his car failed twice when he was out with a girlfriend on the beach at Shingle Street. The garage crew that came to rescue him asked immediately: 'Were you driving near Bawdsey, then?' Apparently, it is well known that cars 'conk out' for no reason when near that secret RAF base. In this case it was found that the newly charged battery on Barry Bridges's car had been completely drained for no obvious reason.

Behind these seemingly ridiculous (and unconnected) stories there is something very real, a heritage unique to Rendlesham Forest. It was, in fact, the birthplace of radar during the 1930s. Here, on Orford Ness itself, the first primitive experiments were successfully carried out by Dr Watson Watt of the National Physical Laboratory and by February 1935 he had persuaded the Air Ministry to fund even more detailed research.

Radar was the weapon that did so much to win the Battle of Britain in 1940 and it was, of course, a closely guarded secret. It was undoubtedly the source of local rumours about a secret weapon and death rays, but did the research really cause any of the physical symptoms described?

After the early experiments on Orford Ness, the expanded operations were moved to Bawdsey Manor (now RAF Bawdsey) where the first working radar models were developed by 1938. Coincident with all of this came the start of local claims about car stops, electrical interference, strange glowing lights and mysterious physical illnesses – stories that have persisted ever since. It is difficult to imagine that this is all mass hysteria or coincidence because both the radar and the nuclear research were perfectly real, even if they were top secret when the stories began.

The gossip about 'death rays' under test was an extreme speculation of the early days but one not entirely without merit. It is known that original research by Tesla and Marconi into the newly discovered radiation emitted by subatomic particles had provoked initial attempts by physicists to develop killer waves. It was hoped that they could destroy electrical systems by a blast of powerful energy. Indeed, these might literally knock aircraft out of the sky by fouling up all of their controls.

Thankfully, it was discovered that such weapons, while not impossible, required huge energy output to be in any way practical. Even so, the failure to progress with these destructive forces pointed the way towards radar which used similar energy beams in a rather more beneficial manner.

Radar, of course, is the system whereby an invisible net of energy beams sweeps across a vast area of space (perhaps hundreds of miles in diameter) and detects anything that passes through, because it changes the field pattern and records its presence on a radar scope. This is an oversimplified description, but what is important is that radar has always depended upon an energy beam being emitted from a central point and thus saturating an area under its coverage with an intensity that is strongest near the point of emission. During both of those early experiments and the later, more sophisticated research, that emission point was on Orford Ness and at nearby Bawdsey Manor – the focal points of the area's intense UFO activity.

While radar waves are widely regarded as being harmless to and undetectable by the humans in their path, they inevitably have possible side effects that may still go unrecognized. Moreover, in the early days, when nobody knew what field strengths to use, it is perfectly possible that too much energy leaked out from primitive equipment and harm resulted accidentally from the preliminary trials.

Researchers today are rightly fearful of electronic pollution, caused by saturating the atmosphere of our planet with broad-band radiation, e.g. high-tension power cables and microwave beams. There are growing fears among a number of scientists that these 'harmless' emissions may produce both physical and psychological illness among some humans, notably those who are subjected to very high dosages because they chance to live at focal points of this invisible network of energy. The matter is highly controversial and is still being debated but more thought is now being given to the possible side effects of artificial radiation exposure than was true just a few years ago.

UFOlogist Albert Budden has even produced a fascinating

theory, drawing together research into physical ill effects from electromagnetic radiation and pollution of the atmosphere. He argues that this may extend to the point where it triggers hallucinations because it stimulates parts of the brain. This can result, he proposes, in visions such as alien encounters. His thesis has growing support from some, e.g. Canadian neuroscientist Dr Michael Persinger and American psychologist Dr Kenneth Ring.

Whether Budden's theory is ridiculous or trailblazing (the jury is still out) it shows that we cannot discount a possible link between UFOs and the extraordinary research into radar and energy beams that was undertaken in the vicinity of Rendlesham Forest. Could it also be connected with the other strange phenomena, such as power cuts, car stops, energy surges and fuzzy green fireballs smelling pungently of acid drops, that have all been reported here in some abundance?

Nor did the experiments end with the success of radar. Land on Orford Ness was occupied for many years after World War 2 in secret research programmes known as 'Cobra Mist' (during the 1970s) and 'Cold Witness' (throughout the 1980s). The nature of these projects is not fully known even today as they remain official secrets, but they were said to involve 'experimental over-the-horizon radar projects'. The CIA was involved, as was the NSA (National Security Agency), one of America's most secret intelligence organizations, primarily concerned with satellite and electronic surveillance techniques.

Indeed, the NSA has many questions to answer about its UFO associations. When the Freedom of Information Act became law in the USA in 1976, the NSA initially denied having any UFO data. As time went by, it was forced to admit that it did have some but said that these files could not be released 'for security reasons'. In the meantime, other agencies, such as the FBI, CIA and US defence and air force intelligence units, were all reluctantly making reams of data available to the public concerning their 50-year battle with the UFO phenomenon. Not so the NSA. They had to be taken to court even to consider releasing any of their evidence at all.

After several years of court battles – presided over by some of the highest security-cleared judges in the land – the NSA agreed only to produce a 21-page affidavit explaining why it could not make its UFO files available. The judge was allowed to read this but not to see the files themselves! Nevertheless, based upon this memo, he agreed that the NSA was immune to the Freedom of Information Act in so far as releasing its UFO records was concerned.

At first a perfectly reasonable suspicion was that the NSA files could not be released because they might reveal the electronic surveillance methods used by this infamous body – believed to include the ability to record any phone conversation in the world if a computer recognizes a key word being spoken. In response, UFOlogists suggested that the NSA should simply release the messages that had been intercepted, rather than the means of obtaining them. However, the NSA refused and the judge upheld that refusal, implying fairly clearly that it was the UFO content of the data that they did not want made public.

Eventually the 21-page affidavit itself went through the courts. After much soul searching, the NSA released it – or, rather, a censored version of it. Virtually the entire set of pages vanished under a sea of black censor's ink, with only the odd paragraph or two left readable. Even so, this still allows us to see that the NSA did things like attend UFO conferences, commission papers speculating on UFO origins and used the interesting phrase 'surprise material' to describe its data gathered about the subject.

One has to wonder why one of the world's most secret intelligence agencies was so fascinated by UFOs and, of course, why they went to such phenomenal lengths to ensure that what they have learned on the matter is out of bounds in a land where there is supposed to be 'freedom of information'.

Although the NSA is an American organization, it operates worldwide. Aside from its secret 'over-the-horizon radar' research on Orford Ness, it has a massive complex called Menwith Hill in the Pennines, near Harrogate, which is surrounded by golf ball radar domes hiding top secret electronics. This is, allegedly, the focal point of NSA electronic surveillance across much of Europe.

The area around Menwith Hill has a long history of some very interesting phenomena – such as (you may well have guessed it), coloured fireballs, car stops, electrical interference and one of the highest levels of UFO activity anywhere in the world. Indeed, since the 1950s these moors have been considered the biggest UFO hotspot in Britain. Most of the major close encounters – including alien abductions of police officers in their patrol cars – are concentrated thereabouts.

That the two known sites in Britain where the NSA is operating should also be such hotbeds of dramatic UFO activity seems to me to be well beyond the realms of coincidence.

In February 1995 the National Trust magazine reported on their purchase of Orford Ness from the MoD. Planning to open it up step by step as a tourist attraction, it pointed out that bunkers and underground complexes were left intact and cited the role of the island in the testing of nuclear weapons, ballistic missiles, radar and the more recent NSA experiments – all officially terminated here when the US Government pulled out of the area by 1993. The National Trust even noted with a smile that Russian spies were constantly mystified by the weekly visits of a truck from Aldermaston, Britain's top secret site for nuclear and chemical research, which promptly disappeared into a sand dune!

Can it really be pure chance that Britain's biggest UFO case occurred in this remarkable spot?

In December 1980, when the Rendlesham Forest case took place, fascinating secret research projects were still underway at RAF Bawdsey and on Orford Ness. They involved agencies like the NSA whose involvement with UFOs is notorious .

These are certainly matters that we cannot afford to ignore.

3

ARTHUR SMEKLE was a travelling salesman from Essex. He had stayed with friends in Butley, Suffolk during Christmas 1980 and, early on that fateful Friday, 26 December, he was finally heading home. It was pitch dark as he drove along the little B-road that snakes through Rendlesham Forest and separates Bentwaters and Woodbridge Air Bases. Then he spotted something very strange.

'Suddenly, I saw a mass of lights in the sky through trees, which seemed to be heading across the sky very low down. I watched with interest, assuming it was an unusual aircraft but the thing was covered in light and looked a bit triangular in shape.'

Upon arrival home, Arthur told his family about the curious incident but there were no press stories reporting any UFO encounters and he was reminded of his proximity to the air base. As a result, he simply dismissed what he had seen as an odd military aircraft and did not recall the matter until months later when claims of UFO sightings at the twin bases came to his attention.

This man was by no means the only civilian witness. The Webb family from Martlesham had been for a Christmas night out in Ipswich and they were on their way home along the A 1214 at about 2. 30 am. RAF Woodbridge was dead ahead, a short distance away through the forest.

As his wife was taking her turn at driving, Roy Webb held his young daughter, Hayley, who was perched half asleep on his lap. Through tired eyes it was Hayley who first saw the UFO.

'Look at that star – it's following us!' she cried. Sure enough, a huge glow was illuminating the forest. Stopping at the first opportunity, in a lay-by in the road, they took a closer look at the object.

'It was hovering close by and completely silent,' Roy Webb pointed out. Then, 'It accelerated from a standing start and shot across the sky. It disappeared in a couple of seconds.'

Another witness to this blinding light above the forest early that Boxing Day morning was Gerry Harris who owned a small garage near Woodbridge. Although he pointed the object out to his wife, they took little notice at the time as they were used to all sorts of aerial activity connected with the twin bases. However, this was not to be the end of the story as far as the Harrises were concerned.

Some hours afterward, late on Saturday 27 December, more spectacular sightings were to follow. 'I was returning to my house after locking the shed door,' said Tony Sorrell, a food production manager a few miles away at Thetford, across the border into Norfolk. He may well have seen the object that was then being tracked on radar by Neatishead or Watton.

'The night was still, bright stars everywhere,' he continued. 'For some unknown reason I looked up into the air above my house (towards the north east). I saw this triangle-shaped object moving along. It was like lightly frosted glass. As it moved the stars above it dimmed . . . It made no noise and was very sharply defined. It was really amazing and not moving very fast.'

After about 20 seconds it just disappeared.

Something similar befell a man who was then much nearer to the forest and situated a few miles along the southerly course of this triangular object.

Gordon Levett was very tired that night after the Christmas celebrations and was putting his dog into a large outdoor kennel. His home in Sudbourne was on the very rim of the forest. It was a fairly remote house and the dog served not only as a family pet but as a valuable guard against intruders. However, both animal and owner were to get a real shock that evening.

'My attention was aroused by some unknown means,' Gordon states in a sworn declaration that he insisted on signing. This 'intuitive' starting point for his encounter is remarkably similar to that of Tony Sorrell a few miles to the north west at what appears to have been the same time. Something alerted the senses of both these men.

Gordon explains how his dog was also apparently looking skyward towards the coast in the north east. He followed its eyes and both animal and owner were soon focused on an extraordinary object that glowed with an eerie phosphoresence. He likened the thing to an overturned mushroom, although his sketch shows it more akin to a shallow triangle or a bell tent.

The UFO descended and headed right towards the man and his dog before hovering for a few seconds directly above the garden at about twice the height of the rooftops. However – as if seeming to tire of this moment's observation – the UFO quickly sped away and, as Gordon notes: 'disappeared over the woods in the direction of Butley, Rendlesham Forest and RAF Woodbridge'.

The next day, Gordon Levett's dog was still showing signs of great distress. It cowered in its kennel and was not interested in coming out. This was very unusual behaviour for the normally fierce and protective animal. The dog never fully recovered. A few days afterwards it was quite ill. A week or so later it was dead. A vet suggested some sort of poisoning as there was no obvious illness to be seen.

As the object disappeared from Gordon Levett's view that night, it plunged into the depths of Rendlesham Forest. Meanwhile, inside those same dark woods David Roberts and his girlfriend were enjoying a few romantic moments out of sight from prying eyes. They had parked their car just off the same Orford to Woodbridge B-road that Arthur Smekle had travelled 40 hours before.

The Earth was certainly about to move for this courting couple.

'Suddenly we saw this massive white glow coming from above the trees,' David explained. 'It was like a big oval but made absolutely no sound. My girlfriend was terrified and insisted we get out of there. So I drove off fast. The object was still shining through the treetops as we headed out of the area.'

Another witness was actually inside Bentwaters Air Force Base at this time, but he was not part of the military. This was Michael Simms, the teenage son of a USAF officer stationed there. He was with two of his friends that evening when they spotted the glow above the forest.

'It was an enormous object and was covered by lights,' he reported to us later. 'It was mesmerizing. Then it flew away from us, picking up speed. We tried to chase it towards the forest but it went too quick. Then it split into three parts, each light flying off in different directions and disappearing.'

This is a very interesting account. Similar splitting lights have often been reported from villages such as Menston in Yorkshire in and around the NSA site at Menwith Hill. The NSA, as we saw earlier, were also very active near Rendlesham Forest during late 1980.

Compare Simms's report with the case of a woman in the

Yorkshire Pennine village of Walsden (although she now runs a children's home elsewhere). These two sightings are completely independent and neither witness had any knowledge of the other. Jenny's encounter occurred on 30 November 1978, just over two years before the Rendlesham Forest case.

Jenny had been horse riding on a rural hillside and was about to return to her village with her dog. As she told Roy Sandbach and me when we went to visit her at the site: 'That night still haunts me to this day . . . I had my whippet with me as the Yorkshire Ripper was on the prowl and you had to be constantly on the alert . . . As we walked down the track my dog literally slid to a halt. It had been frolicking about. Now it was just staring up at the sky. I looked up too and there was this amazing thing, no higher than the rooftops might be. It was lens-shaped and surrounded by a misty glow.

'I had to do a double take and look away,' she continues. 'But when I looked back it was still there. Inside it was like a neon glow. I was utterly transfixed by it. In fact there was a spiritual bond between us. I felt divorced from myself. It was as if that thing drained me – all my essence went into the UFO. I know this sounds terribly subjective but it was as if I were a computer terminal and data was being exchanged . . . It gets so frustrating, visualising it but not being able to put it into words.'

Jenny paused to try a metaphor, suggesting that if you were walking over the moors and the QE2 liner materialized in front of you, then you might face a similar dilemma. You would *know* that you really saw the thing, but would equally appreciate the futility of trying to persuade anybody else because the idea of its appearance was absurd. That was exactly how she felt after this encounter.

'I always believed before that night that if I saw a UFO then I'd tell the world. But it wasn't like that,' she added. 'It was so impossible I could not believe that I was seeing it for myself. But I was. And so was my dog.'

As she watched the object, Jenny tried to rationalize its problems. It was blinding and low down but it did not cast a glow on the ground. But how? The 'mist' that surrounded it was greenish silvery yellow and seemed to thin out towards the edge. There was what she termed a 'communion' between herself and the cloud, which turned this sighting into a highly spiritual encounter. She even referred to her thoughts and life memories being 'sampled'.

There are intriguing similarities with the experiences of people who have come close to death after an accident or during surgery and who recall seeing bright lights and becoming disassociated.

Jenny further describes how her encounter with the glowing object ended that night. 'I knew that it was going and I felt terribly sad. It seems ridiculous. I feel embarrassed about it now. But I stood there on the moors crying. It was as if I were losing my best friend. I pleaded with it to stay but it left. It shot away like a stone zapped from a catapult, with a shower of sparks and splitting into two. One light sped off towards Bacup. Another headed towards Manchester. And it was gone.'

There are many points worth noting here. If UFOs are imagination, a common defensive claim of the sceptic, then it is hard to explain why dogs would suffer from the same hallucination at the same time. Yet we have already seen three cases where dogs apparently alerted their owners to the UFO (at Sizewell, 1975, Walsden, 1978 and Sudbourne, 1980). They are very common.

This reference to witnesses 'just looking up' is also another frequent aspect – perhaps suggesting that they are instinctively aware of some energy field or aura associated with the UFO. Many people, myself included, can often estimate when a thunderstorm is imminent. They sense the electrical changes in the atmosphere and this alters their own body electricity to manifest as an 'intuition'. If UFOs have electrical fields around them then this could also lead to witnesses 'sensing' their presence before they look up .

In fact, the glowing cloud reported at Walsden and Sizewell (as well as in many other cases) may have been formed out of ionized particles attracted from the surrounding air by such an electrical field. The ionization might also stop car engines and switch off headlights, as is often alluded to by close encounter witnesses and as has been widely noted by locals living near Rendlesham Forest.

Of course, if humans can sense this change to the local electrical field then so could dogs and other animals. It is well known, for example, that certain creatures seem to detect atmospheric changes and ionized gaseous particles emitted by the ground prior to an earthquake. In this way they act as rather better early-warning devices than any that science has yet perfected (see the research by various scientists in the excellent book *When the Snakes Awake* by Dr Helmut Tributsch).

The green glow surrounding the UFO and its electrical field were both also major elements of the Sizewell beach encounter by the postman and his dog in February 1975. Indeed, there are more than a few interesting links between that Suffolk case and the UFO seen by Jenny in Yorkshire.

Finally, Michael Simms and Jenny both refer to the way in which the previously large, cohesive object split apart and – as quite separate lights – rocketed away from each other across the sky. We might suggest that the collapsing energy field gives these glowing lights different electrical charges and that they then repel one another just like similar poles of a magnet.

There has been much scientific research into many strange lights at a remote site in the Hessdalen valley in Norway. Here very similar effects were seen and photographs taken of what measurements suggest to be some sort of atmospheric plasma. It was described by local witnesses, of course, as being a UFO.

Whatever the case, you can see from the study of these close encounters that there is evidence waiting – not in the 'X-files', as a certain TV drama might have it, but in the ex-files of UFO research groups that describe sightings such as these. If we examine such data with a scientific mind, we can try to fathom out the physical causes that are behind UFOs.

Together, such cases may prove that something real is flying about our atmosphere. Specifically, the concentration of encounters above Rendlesham Forest in late December 1980 surely demonstrates that a real object was present in the skies. It would be difficult to dismiss all of this interlocking testimony as fraudulent or mistaken.

However, let us return to that Saturday evening, 27 December, when the likes of Gordon Levett, Tony Sorrell, Michael Simms and David Roberts were seeing the strange thing that descended into Rendlesham Forest. There was another report, which came from garage owner Gerry Harris and his wife, who had previously witnessed the first night's events during the early hours of the Friday.

'The wife and I had been out for a drink. It was Christmas time,' he points out sardonically. 'We were coming home and I saw lights. She said, "It's just the lights from aircraft and the airfield." But they were not quite right.'

Gerry explains how he stood watching them from his hall window puzzled as to what was going on inside the forest. For they were not over the runway but well off to the east of there and amidst the trees themselves.

'Being more curious, I went outside into the yard and stood watching by the gate. I thought, If they are aeroplanes they are going to crash into the trees.' He observed closely as three separate lights moved up and down and around in circles. Then, 'all of a sudden one of them went down behind trees. Then, after a few minutes, it went up again like a bat out of hell – just like a rocket. Then it was all just gone like that . . . The whole lot just went.'

Gerry described in detail how he watched these huge lights zoom up and down for between 30 and 45 minutes. They were bigger and brighter than he had ever seen on aircraft connected with the bases. They certainly moved unlike any aircraft he knew. If they were aircraft, he noted, then they would have smashed into the trees, given the amazing manoeuvres they were making. All of the time there was no sound, which is very unusual for aerial activity connected with the two bases.

After the lights had gone he heard Bentwaters and Woodbridge spring into life.

'I could hear it from here – the lorries and people shouting and vehicles starting up. At that time of night it was unusual.' It was now after midnight into the early hours of Sunday, 28 December.

However, Gerry was not the only one baffled by these odd goings on in the woods. Sarah Richardson, then just 12, gave a detailed account of her story some 14 years later when we were making an LWT TV documentary about the case. At the time, she was at her mother's home in Woodbridge. It was between 1 and 3 am into Sunday, 28 December.

'From (Mum's) house you could see the river and the forests and the bases. You could hear the revving of the engines. You became familiar with all the spotlights and other activity.' This night was different. Three bands of light appeared over the woods to the side of the runway.

'They were star-like and they were bright, coloured red, blue and yellow. One was in the north and two were in the south. At the time I thought that someone was having a party and these were fireworks. It was cold and clear and there were lots of stars in the sky and a constellation (*sic*) that had been pointed out to me – Sirius. These lights were different. They were low.'

Sarah recalls putting her head out of the window for a better view. She says the light was so intense it was 'kind of unreal'. She had later thought about helicopters but having seen many of these in the area rather doubts it. Also, helicopters hovering that low in the middle of a dense forest on a dark winter's night seemed rather improbable, she had concluded.

However, she adds of the lights: 'They were solid. No moon was shining on them, but they were kind of metallic. But the oddest thing was the colour changes. Blue, green, yellow, so on'

She claims they were present for two hours, until well after 3 or 4 am. Then they just 'shot straight off'. Had they been aircraft there would have been some sign. These just disappeared.'

Over the years Sarah has met many others from the area who saw strange things that night. Most witnesses have never spoken out. 'I know for a fact that there are more people who have seen things but they won't come forward because they are scared . . . I know a lot of people who are very worried about this. Very worried indeed.'

By Monday, 29 December, several customers had arrived at Gerry Harris's garage with their cars. He knew that they were servicemen from the twin bases as they were regulars. Not surprisingly he asked them what on Earth had taken place over the weekend, assuming that there had been some sort of military accident or an exercise. He was told that they were 'not allowed to say'.

Unwilling just to leave it at that Gerry spent some time trying to quiz the clearly disturbed USAF personnel. Over the coming weeks he noticed that quite a few of them never came back. Some had been customers of his for years and had not been scheduled to move bases. Taking the opportunity to enquire as to their whereabouts from a friendly USAF patrol man, he was told discreetly: 'Anyone who saw anything that night has been shipped out. You won't be seeing them again.'

After his failure to get answers from his USAF customers on that Monday, Gerry admits he was nosy. Later on 29 December he got into his own car and set off down the little track heading for the woods. He then got out to walk toward the point where he estimated the lights to have been.

'There were English policemen there and military police with guns. I was told to go away. I explained that this was a public footpath,' he recalls .'Not today it ain't', came the reply.

A few days afterward, Gerry noticed that a large area of trees in the nearby woods had disappeared almost overnight. He asked a forester who called in at the garage why this curious event had occurred, asking if it was connected with the UFOs he had seen.

'Those trees were radioactive. They had to go,' the woodsman insisted with a stern face that indicated nothing more was to be said.

4
WOODCUTTERS' TALES

ET US BRIEFLY review the mounting evidence. This comes
from radar and the civilian witness testimony discussed in
more depth during the preceding chapters.

The area of rural East Anglia surrounding Rendlesham Forest
is rich in interesting scientific activity. From nuclear energy to state
of the art electronic telecommunications research, things have been
going on here for many years. Aside from the presence of the US Air
Force at the twin bases of Bentwaters and Woodbridge, the NSA
(National Security Agency) was then a major player on Orford Ness
alongside the ubiquitous British MoD, most visible at Bawdsey.

Indeed, in many ways one can sense a conflict of interest between
these various British and American power-brokers. Presumably,
through the NATO alliance, these interests would ordinarily coincide. However, it is tempting to wonder if the events of that weekend
in late 1980 strained the so-called 'special relationship'. More than
one contact in the British Government has told me 'off the record'
that this is a key reason why this case has become so contentious.

The very act of taking the radar film from RAF Watton by USAF
intelligence staff, following the sightings, has even been likened to
me by one senior air traffic control officer as almost criminal. He
said that he could conceive of no situation in which the analysis of
any such evidence would not first have been conducted by British
intelligence (and then, quite properly, shared with the USAF).

So, did Uncle Sam act prematurely because his boys found themselves in the thick of things? Bear in mind that the main encounters
took place well off base and inside a wood owned by the Forestry

Commission. This was strictly British territory – unlike the air bases themselves which had been leased by the MoD to the Americans. That US Air Force staff were commandeering events inside that forest suggests this may conflict with their agreement with the British Government.

But then, according to Gerry Harris, when he went out into the woods on the Monday, British police were supposedly mingling with USAF personnel to clear up and control the mess. Several sources have further alleged that MoD personnel (presumably coming from Bawdsey) were out there during the encounters themselves that weekend. This claim has never been supported by the British Government. Their position has always been that there was no official MoD involvement in this case until notified about it by the USAF more than two *weeks* later. However, in June 1997 deputy commander Charles Halt assured me that this was simply not true. He told me, 'The MoD were informed about the events from the start. The British liaison officer on base was on the phone to London that first weekend. An investigation into the case began well before I submitted my report.'

So were the Brits happy about the US Air Force tramping all over their land, mounting investigations that should have been outside the jurisdiction of Washington? Why did the Americans take this risk? Were the NSA experiments on Orford Ness a factor in their decision? You will recall that the US intelligence services had been very worried about UFOs appearing above secret scientific research complexes since the green fireballs had buzzed New Mexico in 1948. The CIA had also convened a panel to try to deconstruct any serious public interest about UFOs as long ago as 1952 – although the link with scientific research centres was an issue about which they themselves were rightly perturbed.

There appear to have been three distinct phases to the UFO activity that weekend.

It began at 9.08 pm on 25 December, with the re-entry of the Soviet satellite Cosmos 749. However, this, and subsequent 'comets' in the sky during the next six hours, are sufficiently odd to cast doubt on that precise identification. All we can say is that something was going on in the skies and it was witnessed by numerous people on the ground, tracked by civil and military radar in East Anglia and was peculiar enough to attract attention from both the military and astronomers.

At some point towards the end of this six-hour 'window' there were sightings of a brilliant light plunging into the forest. It was seen by civilians in the vicinity of the woods going home after a party or having their own *very* close encounter in the bushes. Was this one of the numerous fireballs or satellite break-ups? Was it the object tracked on radar at Neatishead and chased by RAF Phantoms? Either way, as we shall see later, it fired up the local air bases. USAF personnel saw it too and followed its trail into the woods. Here they reportedly got a very good perspective on the fallen object.

By breakfast on Friday, 26 December, the site of the landing a few hours before had been identified. USAF personnel from the base have told us that an A-10 jet, using infra-red detection equipment, scoured the woods from low level at daybreak to pinpoint the spot. The USAF officers who had seen the UFO also knew the general location, although they had been in a forest in the dark and so were fairly disorientated. At the site some physical evidence was reputedly found, according to what the radar staff at Watton were told by the USAF intelligence team who took away their radar film.

The next night, Saturday, 27 December, there was an officers' party on base. It was from here that senior personnel were called away to investigate reports that UFOs were back above the forest. Several hours of nocturnal manoeuvres followed into Sunday, 28 December. This concentrated on the landing site from two nights before. It was during this second set of encounters that the infamous 'live tape' was made by Colonel Charles Halt, photographs were taken and much else occurred. It was this subsequent woodland encounter that was to generate most of the attention grabbed by this case.

Civilians seem to have witnessed this latter activity. The arrival of a triangular object heading for the woods is well evidenced in sightings from Thetford to Sudbourne. Watton seems to have tracked something on radar. As Gerry Harris records, the object above the woods sent the local bases into turmoil – involving countless personnel, jeeps and equipment, despite it being the middle of the night. Other witnesses also appear to have seen strange bands of light changing colour and behaving oddly, which hovered in the sky above the woods for several hours during that second night.

The denouement came on Monday, 29 December, when Harris is but one person who described the frenzied scene of investigation in the forest where no civilians were allowed to go. The stand-up meeting on base also occurred that day, to debate how to contain the situation, and radar film was then being secured by the USAF intelligence from Neatishead and from Watton.

The testimony of the military witnesses, who were generally much closer to all these events than any civilian, will provide a much more detailed picture of them. We shall come to that in the next few chapters. Already, however, we can see the sheer strength of support for this encounter.

In the meantime, there is some evidence to be considered from one other group of civilian witnesses, those who, by the very nature of their work, were closest of all to the incidents in Rendlesham Forest. These are the men and women who work for the Forestry Commission.

The only forestry worker most casual observers link with the case is a young man called Vince Thurkettle. He gained prominence during October 1983 when he 'explained' the case to the satisfaction of the more highbrow British media. We shall look at his involvement shortly, but he was not the most important forester to appear in connection with these events.

You may recall that garage owner Gerry Harris says that a woodsman visited him a few weeks after the encounter and claimed that a group of trees in the area were felled unexpectedly because they had been found to be 'radioactive'. We have no way of judging the truth of this story as that man has never been traced. In any case, it seems difficult to imagine that a radioactive area could be made safe just by knocking down a few trees. However, this story can be judged alongside what we do know from several forestry commission witnesses who have gone on record.

The first to do so, during January 1981, was James Brownlea, one of the team from the little wooden headquarters in what is known locally as Tangham Wood. This is under a mile from the alleged landing site. He recalls the day when a colleague pointed out a strange area of forest. It was about two weeks after the encounters – i.e. during the first few days of 1981.

'I noticed that the pine trees well above the ground were broken as if something heavy had fallen through from the sky,' Brownlea reported. 'Branches were also torn off lower down. There were signs of scorching and burning on the forest floor and a series of indentations which indicated that something solid had come down there. There was also evidence that an object may even have been dragged along the ground to remove it from the area.'

Brownlea and his colleague thought it a little odd but merely reported the finding to their boss when they returned to the offices that lunch time. He said that the commission had heard stories about a crash in the trees involving some craft from the air base and would 'take care of things'. Next morning James Brownlea arrived for work to learn that this part of the forest was to be cut down immediately. Indeed, when he reached the site felling was already in process and the stumps were ablaze.

Brownlea adds, 'I have to say that this area was due for felling at some point in the near future. The trees had score marks on them to indicate this fact. However, the way in which this spot was reduced so quickly after our report about the damage we had found did strike me as odd at the time.'

James did not pursue the matter, assuming that the base simply wanted to hide an accident to one of their aircraft. Talk around the Forestry Commission offices that January was that the crash had involved a small experimental helicopter. Then, a few weeks afterwards, Frank heard the now blossoming local rumours about UFO activity and so decided to tell his story.

He was not alone. Another local, called Ron Gladwell, describes how 'around Christmas' he came upon a group of USAF men in the forest. They were surrounding what looked like an impact crater in the ground and were rapidly filling this in with earth. Taken together it suggests that efforts were quickly set in motion to remove any sign of what had occurred in the forest.

Another story, coming to light during early February, was from a USAF airman on Bentwaters base. He reported that a false trail had been set in the woods for anyone who might hear about the landing site and go sniffing around. While the original area was by then already destroyed, thanks to the efforts of both the USAF and the Forestry Commission, a giant arrow had been scratched into the earth to direct nosy airmen or snooping locals towards an area of rough physical damage on the ground. It was anticipated that they might then assume this to be the 'landing site' of local legend. However, it was bogus and contained nothing unusual except for a few animal scratches in the soil.

Throughout January and February 1981, while all of the above was going on in secret, I was chasing up the alleged radar tracking at RAF Watton which had just come my way. Over 250 miles (400 km) south, at Leiston on the edge of the forest, ghost hunter Brenda Butler was hearing stories about the UFOs in the woods from villagers and friends on the air bases. By mid-February she had brought in colleague Dot Street (a member of BUFORA) and together they started asking locals what they knew. This led to them finding quite a few stories, from people such as Ron Gladwell and James Brownlea. Indeed, it seems probable that their methods of investigation – asking anyone and everyone (often in pubs) – came to the attention of the US authorities. This may even have been responsible for the destruction of the trace evidence and the seeding of the bogus site with its giant arrow.

Eventually, on 24 February 1981, the duo felt it was time to visit the Forestry Commission offices in Tangham Wood. Brenda had by then already been told by one of her many USAF acquaintances that the ground and trees in the area had supposedly 'glowed' after the encounter – perhaps the origin of stories about irradiation. The impact site was reputedly cordoned off for several days and civilians turned away. That certainly seems to fit the claims by Gerry Harris. Anyone who demanded an explanation for the existence of a US military guard on British civilian land was told that an aircraft had crashed and such precautions were necessary for public safety.

That so many rumours and second-hand claims about the episode were circulating around the twin bases in those weeks after the sightings was probably inevitable. There were simply too many people who were aware of the encounters to keep the lid on a big story like this. Much of the talk was no doubt speculative, based loosely on the truth, but it was certainly another reason why the seemingly extreme move of planting false evidence in the forest and destroying the original site was conceived by USAF intelligence. They may have seen this as a necessary containment operation.

With this is mind, Brenda and Dot felt sure that the Forestry Commission would have to know something. Their land could not have been sealed off by the USAF, even for just a day or two during the slack period between Christmas and New Year, at least not without them being told why.

Sure enough, the two foresters in Tangham Wood that day were aware of the story. They had been told about an accident by the USAF but found it very hard to believe that this could have occurred without leaving any physical evidence behind. In mid-January forestry workers had visited the spot and found no sign of an air crash. In fact the area was bare of trees. They described the landing spot as being precisely where Brenda and Dot had also been directed by a contact on the base. He had even sketched it for them on a little map which he photocopied and sneaked out.

The two women had already been into the woods looking at this spot. By then only seven weeks had passed since the close encounters, but a scene of total devastation had greeted them. A huge area of trees had been felled and the ground laid waste, just as the foresters claimed. It was hard to imagine the scene as it had been during the UFO encounters less than two months before.

Brenda asked the forestry workers why these trees had been cut down. It had nothing to do with the UFO stories, she was assured. The Forestry Commission existed to provide wood and this part of Rendlesham Forest was next on the list for chopping down. It was all just a coincidence.

In October 1981, out of frustration, as the case otherwise seemed to be at an impasse, Dot and Brenda tried to interest the local BBC Anglia region in pursuing this case. There was a limited response at the time because of the lack of any documentation or a military witness who was willing to go on record.

Needing permission to film on Forestry Commission land, Dot and the TV crew were escorted around the site by a forester named McDonald. He recalled a visit to the Tangham Wood offices on New Year's Day 1981. This was made by a well-spoken British man who seemingly knew all about the case. Other sources have mentioned this curious event as you will see in a moment.

Reporter John Kiddy filmed a short item with Dot at the site, which was still denuded of all trees. The BBC also contacted the Forestry Commission head office in Cambridge and were told candidly that they had been: 'informed by Bentwaters of an incident which had caused slight damage to some trees. We were asked to keep it quiet because the story might otherwise have got out of hand. The felling of the trees in this area was unconnected. It was a scheduled operation.'

Bentwaters's public affairs office was equally co-operative with the BBC researchers, confirming the story, but adding that the episode was not an air crash, as they told the foresters at the time, but a sighting of 'a few unexplained lights – a minor incident – nothing serious'. All claims of aliens and crashed spaceships were nonsense, said the air base. They were trying to play it all down.

Understandably, in the face of this underwhelming story, the BBC lost interest – at least until the case gathered serious momentum some years later.

When Brenda and Dot had first visited Tangham Woods in February 1981 the foresters had other stories to relate. They told how a local farmer had come into the office and reported that a colleague had found his land bathed in a huge flood of light. His cows had also been scared by a strange noise that had filled the area in the early hours of one December morning. USAF personnel had come out to investigate and told the farmer to keep quiet. However, he could not resist telling his friend who had inevitably wondered whether the forestry offices knew what had taken place.

They also described how two men had visited the Tangham Woods headquarters, asking detailed questions similar to those being posed by Brenda and Dot. This was before the farmer had come in to see them so the foresters were in the dark and could not be of help. The two strangers asked the foresters if they had heard about a 'crash' or seen anything for themselves. They truthfully answered no, but directed the visitors to 'local farmers' as they were requested to do.

These visitors wore civilian clothing and were definitely British – so not from Bentwaters or Woodbridge bases. It was presumed by the men on duty at the commission that they were journalists sniffing out the reported air crash, although they had never identified themselves as such.

Whoever these men were, they seem unlikely to have been reporters as no story ever featured even in the local press. The date of that visit was easily remembered by the Forestry Commission – Thursday, 1 January 1981. This was less than a week after the sightings and long before news surfaced about the case. Brenda first heard the story from her contact on base about a week after that. My own initial knowledge, from the radar at RAF Watton, was a couple of weeks later still. According to the MoD their first awareness of the case came via the forwarding of an official report from the USAF deputy commander at Bentwaters – and that was on 13 January 1981, although Halt disputes this fact. So who were these men and how did they know about the sightings as early as 1 January?

One of the 'farmers' to whom the forestry offices directed the men that day was gamekeeper David Boast who lived near the landing site. Brenda and Dot went to see him, and father Victor Boast, after leaving the forestry offices and he told them of two men who asked a lot of questions on New Year's Day 1981. He later denied this story when I asked him about it two years later, saying that he only remembered Brenda coming to visit. However, I also once chanced to speak to his young daughter on her own before her father intervened. She was eager to ask me about the huge object and how it had got through the trees without flattening them. Perhaps she was just being curious.

I also visited the offices in Tangham Wood. Head forester Donald James was quite insistent: 'Something definitely did happen in the forest that night.' But he would not be drawn into surmising what that something might have been, which was fair enough.

Another interesting character I met that winter was Vince Thurkettle who, in October 1983, had appeared in *The Times* and on

BBC television explaining the physical evidence in so simple a way that many were persuaded he had dismissed the whole issue. I found Thurkettle an honest, likeable and unassuming man, but think it is a considerable exaggeration to presume that he solved this case. Indeed, I think he adds an important element to its mystery.

According to the reports by the media, Thurkettle had seen the 'landing site' back in 1981 and he was adamant that the damage was natural. The only traces on the trees were the score marks put there by the woodsmen to indicate that they were due for felling. The only marks on the ground beneath the trees were three holes in a rough triangle, dug by rabbits burrowing for shelter and warmth as was quite common in the forest during winter. As such, he argued, the physical evidence was a nonsense.

Vince Thurkettle showed me examples of similar marks all over the woods. They looked odd but were so widespread that I doubted that anybody would consider them to be significant for very long.

Thurkettle added that he decided to come forward after reading the first big media stories about the case in October 1983. These hailed the events as a crash landing by a spaceship, in typical media sensational manner. This was something he found 'amusing and ridiculous'. He recalled what he had seen at the time and decided to speak out 'really just to suggest an alternative. I wanted to offer ideas, that's all. To show there was another way of looking at things.'

So had Thurkettle seen the landing site and established from his indisputable expertise that the 'damage' was not caused by a crashing UFO (or helicopter) but was simply the result of natural causes? I do not think so. There are strong reasons for my doubt.

For one, he found the site 'about a month' after the late December sightings – i.e. around the end of January 1981. From what we know of the chronology, via James Brownlea, the woodsman who talked to Gerry Harris, various stories given to Brenda and Dot and the testimony of the forestry workers in Tangham Woods on 24 February, this date comes *after* the USAF destroyed the site.

We do not know exactly when that event occurred, but on 1 January – when the two British visitors went to the forestry offices – men were also seen at the site, taking plaster casts of the indentations. I suspect these men were from the same British intelligence source. Brownlea found the site approximately ten days later, after which it was immediately felled and burned. This implies that Thurkettle's discovery came a couple of weeks after the real site had disappeared.

There are also two significant clues which I believe establish for certain that the young forester did not see the real landing spot. Firstly, he did not recall seeing any damage to the pine tree canopy above the ground. Yet this was a most important feature which instantly caught the attention of James Brownlea. In addition, on the tape recording made 'live' at the site by Colonel Halt and his officers early in the morning of 28 December, there is a very clear description of this damage: '*Looking directly overhead one can see an opening in the trees plus some freshly broken pine branches on the ground underneath. Looks like some of them came off about fifteen to twenty feet up (4-6 m).*'

Halt also refers to the damage on the ground as being like a 'blasted or scruffed-up area' with traces of a heavy object having imbedded itself in the earth and rotated. These traces were in addition to three 'indentation holes' in an equilateral triangle. This sounds much more like the remains described by James Brownlea than what Thurkettle reports. It is hard to imagine that a woodsman such as Thurkettle would have missed the gaping hole in the pine tree canopy that was so obvious to Halt and Brownlea.

However, the real proof that Thurkettle's solution is built on sand comes with his reason for his assurance that he had found the correct landing site of local legend. He felt he was at the right place because there was a big arrow in the ground pointing it out, yet three years before Thurkettle reported this discovery, we were told by a source on base that a bogus 'landing site' was created by USAF intelligence. This was put there to lead outsiders astray. They were guided towards it by a very unsubtle arrow scratched into the ground. Surely it was this location that Vince Thurkettle stumbled upon *after* the true landing site had been obliterated.

5

EAST GATE PATROL

T AROUND 2 AM on 26 December 1980, 20-year-old USAF airman John Burroughs was in a police cruiser. With him, in a jeep, was his watch supervisor, Budd Parker. They were driving inside the perimeter fence at Woodbridge, close to the east gate of the air base where the runway ends and the thick Corsican pines of Rendlesham Forest dominate the horizon.

Burroughs was a tall, sober man with a steely gaze, who had been stationed at the twin bases (Bentwaters and Woodbridge) since July 1979. He knew the area well, having spent some time in the forest on picnics. He loved being in Britain. As he pointed out, the culture shock of coming from the USA to Britain was not as great as it could be for those unlucky enough to be posted to some far-flung corner of the planet.

The American worked for the law enforcement branch – the cops of the USAF – and progressed to the rank of sergeant before he left the service in 1988. I first met him a year after that, in Arizona. We talked for hours and it was very exciting for me finally to meet one of the two original witnesses to the Rendlesham Forest encounter. I had known of his existence for seven years and his importance to the case was stressed to me by almost every military contact with whom I had ever spoken – from the base commander Colonel Charles Halt, downwards.

Burroughs had bided his time while still with the USAF, choosing not to talk in public and having been relocated from Bentwaters only a few months after the incident. Now he was willing to tell me everything that happened that night, although his companion –

Parker – is one of the military witnesses who has yet to come forward.

'I was patrolling with my supervisor,' the airman began. 'He noticed something before I did and asked me: "Have you ever seen anything like that before?", pointing towards the forest. At first I didn't see anything. Then I did. I looked back at his face and he was staring at these lights, mystified, just repeating: "Have you seen anything like that?" and I could only truthfully tell him – no.'

Baffled as to what they were looking at, the two policemen decided to go off base to investigate further. Burroughs got down from his cruiser, opened the gate, returned to the vehicle and they drove off towards the end of the base approach road where a Forestry Commission track headed deep into the woods.

'I got out of the vehicle again,' the airman continued. I just stared forward into the trees. I was scared, I don't mind telling you, and had this very weird feeling. I looked back at Parker. He was still sat there and I could tell from his expression that we should get out of there. He probably looked to me just like I did him to him – dumbstruck. So I returned to my cruiser and we took off back towards the base.'

What was it about the lights that so scared these two men? Burroughs says that at first there was just one big light, low in the sky. This changed as it fell and now resembled Christmas decorations – as if someone had put fairy lights in the forest. There was a large white glow and a bank of multi-coloured glowing lights, mostly red and blue. As Burroughs stood at the rim of the forest, the white light had suddenly become much brighter. This contributed to the rise in tension that decided their next move.

Back at the gatehouse, Burroughs called through to report the incident. He had great trouble persuading the man on the other end of the line to take him seriously. The police officer had to keep stressing that the report was genuine and they really could see weird lights through the trees.

Burroughs pointed out: 'The law enforcement desk sergeant was having a hard time understanding me, I guess. It was Christmas so he probably thought I was joking. I was also babbling. My supervisor then came on the line and together we convinced the sergeant that something really was going on out there. Then he transferred me to CSC.'

CSC is Central Security Control. Whereas law enforcement (i.e. base police) would look after routine misdemeanours involving airmen, CSC was more specifically concerned with any security threats or intrusions on to base territory. The CSC controller was sufficiently worried to tell Burroughs and Parker to stay where they were and await the arrival of a security patrol which he would despatch.

The man chosen to mount this investigation was Jim Penniston. He had spent all his time in the USAF serving in England, first arriving at RAF/USAF Alconbury in 1975, reputedly the original home of then top secret stealth jets. He asked for the transfer to Bentwaters and Woodbridge because he had heard a great deal about the friendliness of the Suffolk locals. This was also a quiet posting, with the main action focused on USAF headquarters in Germany – the expected front line in any future war. He could get on with the job he loved in reasonable security at Bentwaters.

Penniston, an intense man used to scrutinizing problems and assessing incidents from many perspectives, remembers the call. He had been eating when it arrived.

'They told me that there was a non-emergency of critical importance – which I guess meant that it was important but non-life-threatening. I responded by code two, which meant using lights and sirens at crossings. I set off for the east gate.'

In fact, Sergeant Penniston was being driven by an airman called Herman Kavanasac who was to play a small part in the unfolding story. He also has not yet told of his involvement – as, indeed, is the case with most of the airmen and officers who remain in the USAF. Only bit by bit, year by year, as the numerous eyewitnesses have left the forces, have they felt it possible to come into the open and share their memories of that extraordinary weekend 17 years ago.

Neither Penniston nor Kavanasac saw anything on the way towards the east gate, but on arrival they met Burroughs and Parker standing by their vehicles and staring at the woods, talking in awed tones. Burroughs saw the arriving CSC officer and pointed immediately towards Rendlesham Forest.

Penniston notes, 'I observed multiple coloured lights out there. They appeared to be a fire – the sort of thing you might get from chemicals burning after an air crash. Based on my experience that's what I assumed it was. They were just on the edge of the forest inside the trees.'

Indeed, Jim Penniston had already handled more than 30 incidents involving A-10s and other jets crashing and burning in more or less serious circumstances. It was part of his job. He was sure that this was another example – hopefully a minor scrape, but potentially a fatal accident – and immediately began to debrief Burroughs and Parker – 'Did they see the plane go down? Did it make any unusual sounds?'

Burroughs was shaking his head in response, just repeating, 'It didn't crash. It landed.' Penniston was completely unable to accept such a statement, especially given the dense woodland at which they were looking, which made any controlled landing improbable. He was sure that the plane must have crashed.

Unable to get either Burroughs or Parker to agree with this diagnosis, he went to the gatehouse and called back to CSC – his training dictating that set procedures should be followed. On the line to the CSC controller, Jim began the routine checklist of things to do in the wake of an aircraft going down.

Jim Penniston confirms that the two airmen beside him were visibly shocked. Burroughs, who is normally very animated, was waving his arms about but was otherwise unexpectedly quiet and it was obvious that he had seen something inexplicable. The men were both still well in control of themselves and behaving as calmly as their training allowed – but you could see that this thing had got them spooked.

At this point, as Penniston notes: 'My concern rose sharply. They were not behaving at all as I expected them to. Both had seen air crashes. They should not have been affected like this.'

Burroughs also recalls the first moments of that meeting with Penniston. 'I think (Jim) saw the disbelief in our eyes. We were just trying to show him that something really strange was going on. I did not care whether he believed me. I was just glad that somebody else was seeing what I was or else all the onus would have fallen on Budd and I.'

'At one stage Penniston walked up to the gate and stared into the woods at the lights. Then he went back to the gate house.'

The patrol officer admits to a few twinges of guilt about his interaction with the CSC man, feeling that he ought to be a little more professional in this situation. However, Burroughs adds, 'It was hard. I rather doubted what I was seeing because I could not explain what was going on. But I knew I wasn't crazy.'

As Penniston went through the checklist on the radio phone with the CSC office, the concern level back at base clearly began to rise. The night duty flight sergeant even came on to ask what was happening, having monitored the radio traffic.

Penniston asked the control tower to check for any radar returns, but was not hopeful. The base was very quiet. It was Christmas and the middle of the night. No air traffic was up at all. He doubted that radar would have been operating. Burroughs mentioned something about having heard that the Brits were to stage a naval exercise off the coast near Felixstowe and over to the north towards the Wash, using both ships and aircraft. Could one of their planes have come down, Penniston half-wondered?

However, the problems with the air crash theory were mounting. Burroughs and Parker were both adamant that the lights descended gently and silently into the woods and were initially seen as just a big white light that had then sat on the ground for 15 minutes in the multi-coloured form that all four USAF men were now observing. The CSC man had to agree that this did not sound like any air crash with which he had ever been associated.

Penniston only officially came forward to tell his side of the story under his real name in 1994 when he agreed to participate in the LWT TV documentary that we put together. However, Brenda, Dot and I feel that we had several dealings with him much earlier than that.

A witness approached us in October 1983 and remained in touch (rather infrequently) throughout the next few months, always insisting upon anonymity. We fully appreciated his difficult situation, still being in the USAF and feeling tied by loyalty. We gave him the pseudonym of Jim Archer. This man was always concerned about a breach of security but was torn between his duty and the desire to tell the truth. He was an excellent witness, the only one of the numerous military personnel who called from the base during those early years whom I came to believe truly was involved. Many other callers, I suspect, were simply conveying second-hand stories that they had heard from colleagues.

While it has never been confirmed that this man was Jim Penniston and I might be mistaken, their two stories are closely similar. A glance at our book *Sky Crash* (written in 1983/84) will show that 'Archer's' testimony is by far most like the truth as we now seem to have it direct from Burroughs and Penniston. It therefore seems reasonable to suspect that Archer probably was Penniston.

Returning to that fateful night beside the east gate, Jim Penniston quickly decided that investigative action was the only appropriate course to follow. He got permission to take one law enforcement and one security officer out to the 'suspected crash site' and chose Burroughs and his driver Kavanasac. Parker was to stay behind at the east gate. Before leaving him there, the three men checked in their weapons with the law enforcement supervisor, securing them in his police cruiser. This was standard policy when leaving the base and entering British civilian territory.

They had only driven a hundred yards or so past the east gate towards the forest when their radio contact with base began to break up. Penniston ordered Kavanasac out of the vehicle to stay on the road as a relay. He thought that the trees might be blocking the signal and this precaution would ensure that he and Burroughs could maintain a direct link with help should it be required.

Reaching the point where Burroughs and Parker had stopped a few minutes before, the lights were still plainly visible through the trees but the logging track was proving difficult to negotiate in the dark as it was full of ruts in the frozen soil. The temperature was hovering around freezing point and the muddy earth was rock hard.

They decided to continue towards the 'crash site' on foot. Jim Penniston says that he still had few doubts that they would be confronted by a downed aircraft. In fact, they were heading for a close encounter that the two men would never forget.

6

CLOSE ENCOUNTER

A S JIM PENNISTON walked into the forest at around 2.30 am that Boxing Day morning, his assurance as to what he and Burroughs were facing was still holding firm.

'Part of the woods was brightly lit by a mass of fluctu-ating light – like an aircraft engulfed in flames. I'd seen that many times before. Inside the tree line it appeared larger than we expected. The illuminated area was approximately 164 ft (50 m) across.'

Burroughs says that he was in two minds as they proceeded into the woods. On the one hand he did not want to be out there, but on the other he needed an answer as to what they were seeing. Of course, he had watched the thing come down and was well aware that Penniston was mistaken. This was not an air crash. Indeed, the policeman rather envied Budd Parker and Herman Kavanasac who had been left behind somewhat out of the firing line and, as he put it to himself, now 'safe'. So he was not too distressed at the next development.

The radio communications back to base – even back to Kavanasac at the relay point – were by now deteriorating badly. Some sort of unusual static interference was blocking reception. It was more than just the proximity of the trees. The nearer they came to the light, the worse it got.

Penniston began to fear that they would lose all contact with the outside world and decided to hold Burroughs back just on the perimeter of the 'crash site' – about 164 ft (50 m) away from the now brilliant illumination.

The glow seemed to be coming from beside a small clearing within the trees.

However, Burroughs did not stay on hold for long. It was soon evident to both men that they were facing something way beyond the crash of an A-10 jet, and protocol went out of the window. No military training could ever have prepared them for this moment.

Temporarily separated from his colleague by a few yards, Penniston proceeded forward towards the area of forest where the glow was now pouring out. Burroughs, unwilling to stay on his own as things became progressively more weird, soon followed his superior officer to the rear.

Penniston recalls, 'When I got within a hundred feet (328 m) of the suspected aircraft crash, what appeared to be five or six multi-coloured lights, like a flame appeared. Then it all started to become more clearly defined. A definite form – some sort of image – was emerging from the glow. I knew at that moment that this was not an air crash.'

At about 30 ft (9 m) from the patch of trees beside the clearing, the men could see that some utterly fantastic object was sitting there just waiting for them. The men threw themselves on to the ground as the glow increased in intensity. As Burroughs put it bluntly: 'We ate dirt.'

What stood only 30 ft (9 m) in front of them was beyond mere words. It was completely astonishing. As Jim Penniston reported with irony: 'This thing was definitely not in the *Jane's Book of World Aircraft*.'

Burroughs also describes what he saw: 'The lights seemed to get brighter and more defined. There was more colour behind them. The best way I can describe the object that emerged from this background is that it was a very brilliant white light with multi-coloured lights inside.'

He was unsure if it could be termed an object in any conventional sense. While somewhat triangular, it was also only vaguely solid. There was a transparency associated with it, allowing you to see lights *inside* it or *through* it. Meanwhile, a huge white glow was pouring from underneath and this lit up the entire forest. 'Words are useless in this context,' the airman told me.

Either because of the shock of this close encounter, or some other effect, John Burroughs's memory of the next few minutes is vague. He only has recall of a couple of minutes before the object left. He also rejects all the stories that later emerged (such as from the radar site at Watton) which claimed that alien beings were seen near the UFO.

'I never saw any aliens,' he insists. 'That is nonsense. But this thing felt like it was under control. Someone or something might have been inside there.'

Jim Penniston says that they were watching the object for much longer than Burroughs recalls. His account is also more descriptive of the object.

'As I was walking through the woods, the closer I got the more defined the shape appeared. There was absolutely no sound despite our proximity. It was the size of a tank and was triangular. It had a very smooth surface – almost like glass.'

He was baffled by the strangeness of the lights and says that the red and blue glows were not like aircraft strobe lights. They did flash, as do running lights, or, rather more correctly, they 'alternated' between red and blue colorations, but they appeared to have a function – as if more than just aircraft lights in use for a visual display.

Just as John Burroughs struggled to relate the sheer weirdness of this object Jim Penniston had similar problems, noting: 'There were no sharp edges. It seemed like there were no ninety-degree turns on it. The fabric of the craft was moulded like black glass, but opaque or misty. It moved from the black fabric of the craft into the coloured lights imperceptibly. It just blended together.'

Penniston is also insistent that he saw no aliens, but said there were indications of shadows or movements inside the misty opaqueness of the object. Perhaps these were the men's own reflections against the strong light. That could possibly have given the impression that there was something inside, but it was too vague and uncertain to determine the status of such imagery.

The two men were still flat on the ground and about 20 ft (6 m) apart. By now the CSC officer had regained enough composure to realize two things. Firstly, if the craft before them had any hostile intent then they had been sitting ducks for several minutes. He began to suspect that they were not under obvious threat. Penniston also remembered that he was the senior investigating officer now face to face with something totally unknown. It was his job to determine what to do next.

However, there were thornier problems than simply witnessing this bizarre object sitting there, floating just above the ground. For both Burroughs and Penniston had been experiencing physical sensations that were intensifying all that happened. The closer they got to the object, the more severe these had become. It was as if an extraordinary wave of physical energy had washed across the forest.

As John Burroughs remembers: 'The nearer we got to that thing the more uneasy I felt. This was more than just apprehension. It felt almost like static electricity in the air and was terribly uncomfortable. I had never felt a sensation quite like that before. I do not really know how to phrase this but it was as if I was moving in slow motion. I felt really hot and as if the hair was standing up on the back of my head. Yet all around me everything was moving so slowly. I was not even sure that I had any control over my body.'

Penniston's description of this effect was made independently but is closely similar.

'The air was filled with electricity – like static. You could feel it on your skin as we approached the object. There was also a sense of slowness, like time itself was an effort.'

He later elaborated a little on this point because he regained the ability to raise himself from the ground and edge towards the object. He was not prepared for how difficult that would prove. The air was like glue, holding him back. Everything was slowing down and it took enormous effort of will to make those final few steps towards the object. This seemed to take forever.

Burroughs added that it was as if time and space were distorted in the close vicinity of this object – as if it was surrounded by some barrier that defended it from anyone who might attempt to get too near.

Unbeknown to these two men, they are describing a classic effect of UFO literature. It has been widely reported but only in very close encounter situations – never in long-range sightings or reports of distant lights in the sky. The term 'Oz Factor' has been defined to cover this effect, as witnesses frequently allude to how time stretches out and space is disorientated, rather as if they have been suddenly taken out of normal reality and have emerged in a magical land (such as Oz) where all the normal rules of physics break down.

There are two schools of thought as to what the Oz Factor means. One argues that it is a mental phenomenon, perhaps a product of an altered state of consciousness being stimulated in the witness during proximity to a UFO. The other argues that some real physical energy – perhaps a defensive shield or a by-product of a propulsive system – creates an effect that literally warps time and space in the immediate surroundings of an object.

Either way, the Oz Factor is clearly an important feature of close encounter cases and has been so reliably recorded from all over the world that it is fundamentally significant to any interpretation of the evidence.

In Rendlesham Forest on that December night the well-described nature of this little understood phenomenon came from two men who had no background in UFO phenomena. It surely establishes beyond reasonable doubt that they were truly in the presence of a genuine UFO – whatever a genuine UFO might be!

Penniston had fought his way towards the craft, struggling through the treacle-like barrier that was distorting time and space. Burroughs had followed and reached even closer to the object. He appeared intent on trying to touch it, although he does not recall any details of these moments.

The CSC officer says that from his new vantage point – a few feet from the object – its incredible nature was most apparent. On its upper left side he could now see a marking about the size of a car licence plate – maybe 3 ft (90 cm) long, with symbols or writing that were a few inches high.

'What fascinated me', Penniston recalls, 'is that this was on the glass-like surface of the craft. Almost as if it were etched there.'

He reports an odd feeling as if the symbols seemed somehow familiar. He could not put his finger on that belief. Certainly he did not actually recognize them. They were a bit like mirror writing.

There is some evidence that during this phase of the encounter a period of time may not be accounted for. Burroughs thinks they were there only a couple of minutes, while Penniston says it was maybe twenty. According to the personnel back on the base, the two men were out there for about an hour.

The final departure of the object was recalled by both witnesses. John Burroughs says, 'One minute it was there. Then it climbed sky-ward and was gone like a blur. There was no sound and I felt no blast of air from any exhausts.'

With the departure, the Oz Factor disappeared and the surroundings returned to normal.

The deadly silence that had hung over Rendlesham Forest was shattered in a moment. Local wildlife exploded into a cacophony. Deer ran from cover and fled. Birds screeched out of trees and scattered into the air. This unexpected event struck the two airmen with such force that they stopped dead.

Some sceptics (e.g. forester Vince Thurkettle in association with science writer Ian Ridpath) have bravely suggested that these two men simply watched the Orford Ness lighthouse, 5 miles (8 km) out on the coast near the NSA research site. Its sweeping beam can be seen from the forest.

Burroughs laughs this speculation away, saying, 'I have never seen a lighthouse that can fly,' and adding that he clearly remembers looking around as they stood in the forest immediately after the object had vanished. Everything was back to normal and he saw the lighthouse pulsing away as usual to the south. Having lived in the area for 18 months, he was completely familiar with it. It is difficult to believe that two experienced airmen would be so readily fooled.

Jim Penniston is more specific about the disappearance of the UFO. They had both approached it by now and felt that they had it cornered. But then it seemed to retract what looked like three legs or protrusions amidst the white glow on the underside – not unlike shafts of light. The object then shot up a few feet and edged backwards.

Then: 'It started moving back, weaving in and around the trees. It got about forty feet (12 m) away and just raised above the clearing and the treeline. It hovered there for two or three seconds and shot away at extreme speed – faster than any aircraft I have ever seen.'

It left in a silent explosion of light, leaving the two men all alone amidst the pine trees. They stared at each other for long moments and desperately tried to comprehend what had just taken place.

7

AFTERMATH

THE CLOSE ENCOUNTER of John Burroughs and Jim Penniston must rank as one of the most extraordinary on British soil. It has some quite amazing details but it is not unique.

Stories about Oz Factor distortions of time and space are barely known by the general public but are extremely well documented in numerous cases. The same is true of the peculiar opaque, semi-transparent and colour-blending nature of the UFO itself. Here are just a few examples from my personal case files. There are many more in the UFO archives around the world.

At the small mining town of Fencehouses, County Durham on 3 September 1976, two women (aged 18 and 63) came upon a small object landed on a mound of earth. It was the size of a car and appeared to be formed from some kind of smoky glass or material like Perspex. The witnesses felt hypnotized and found themselves walking towards it. As they did so, they report: 'All noise around us stopped. The traffic sounds vanished. Even the wind went silent. Then it felt as if time stood still. We were suspended in a sort of field of energy that surrounded this thing.' The women had a strange close encounter inside that weird 'cocoon' which is only dimly remembered. Far from being eager for publicity, they ran away from all attempts by UFOlogists or the media to follow up this sighting – scared witless by what had happened to them. However, they do recall seeing strange little beings with pale faces and huge round eyes, who seemed somehow connected with the object. One of the women was also wearing a watch. After the UFO disappeared this worked perfectly but was found to be ten minutes slower than 'normal time' – that is, running behind the time found in the world that had never been inside that cocoon. It was correct before they had walked towards the UFO.

Another event at Livingston, Scotland in November 1979, like Rendlesham, involved a wood and a forester. Bob Taylor encountered an object in a clearing and experienced strange sensations in close proximity to it, including some loss of time. However, the most intriguing feature was how the object appeared to blend in and out of reality, becoming translucent and even transparent as if it were not there, with the background scenery sometimes visible through what, at other times, was a perfectly solid surface. Taylor even had similar difficulties to those of Burroughs and Penniston when trying to conjure up the right words to describe these peculiar effects and has never been interested in publicity, although he suffered severe psychological trauma in the aftermath.

Not far away, at Harperriggs Reservoir in Scotland's Pentland Hills, a more recent encounter took place in August 1992. Two men, Colin Wright and Garry Wood, drove directly underneath an object shaped like a bell. It was dark black and fuzzy; almost like a cloud. As they passed beneath it a dark shimmering curtain of light surrounded them and their car, while time and space became distorted. This occurred in such a way that they had no idea where they now were or how long things were taking to happen. The Oz Factor completely replaced the normal space-time environment. Again the encounter profoundly affected the routine flow of the men's lives. Seeing UFOs is no pleasure cruise. Most who encounter them very close up dearly wish it had never happened.

The experience of teachers' resources manager Elsie Oakensen at the Northamptonshire village of Church Stowe on 22 November 1978 is also significant. She was driving home when her car was surrounded by balls of light and all electrical power (engine and lights) rapidly failed. These balls of light acted weirdly and created both physical symptoms in Elsie and an Oz Factor state within the environment. When she was finally freed and the world about her returned to normal, some 10 or 15 minutes in time was unaccounted for. Shortly afterwards four other women in a car at nearby Preston Capes also suffered electrical interference in the presence of odd lights during an aborted repeat encounter. Both sets of witnesses were completely unconnected with one another and did not know of each other's existence at the time. Subsequently, Elsie recalled vague impressions about witnessing shadowy forms during her encounter – possibly intelligent beings who were within or behind the misty light.

An even more extraordinary case occurred on 22 July 1975 when a teenager called Trevor was on holiday with his family at Machynlleth in rural Wales. Climbing up Wylfa Hill he had a shocking close encounter in which an object hovered close to the ground, with lighting very similar to that of the object in Rendlesham Forest. The colours were so strange that Trevor said he could not describe them. There were indefinable shapes moving about behind an opaque smoky surface. The colours all ran into one another and the object vanished – not by flying away but by merging with the background – becoming grass green, sky blue, earth brown and then running together like paints on a canvas in a thunderstorm. The whole episode terrified Trevor so much that he had to be cared for by doctors and a psychiatrist for several months and suffered severe symptoms of what they considered to be post-traumatic shock, such as hysterical blindness and dumbness. These were, thankfully, overcome but, again, publicity was the furthest thing from Trevor's mind.

In addition to many cases such as these, there is an interesting photographic event, filmed by a team of scientists and Brazilian naval personnel setting up a meteorological station in the Atlantic during the IGY (International Geophysical Year). They were on board the *Almirante Saldhana*, then moored off the uninhabited rocky outcrop of Trindade Island in January 1958. The Saturn-shaped object which flew around the island was composed of dark fuzzy particles that seemed to form a cloud. A strong electrostatic field was also reported – indeed, the ship's mechanical winch stopped working during the encounter. From study of the resulting photographs (confiscated and analyzed by the Brazilian Government but released once they were satisfied that they had no idea what was on them!) one can see that the object was blotchy in parts and that it was possible to view the sky through its surface in some places.

It is possible that such fuzzy objects involve dust particles attracted to the surface of the object by the powerful electrostatic field that seems to be generated. An artificial cloud then surrounds, and effectively camouflages, the object. If that is true, then many other examples of cloud-like UFOs can be found in the records and these should be studied with renewed interest.

Of course, John Burroughs and Jim Penniston knew about none of these other encounters when they came face to face with their own nightmare. UFOs were a big mystery to them and they had no idea that anybody else had experienced what they had just confronted in Rendlesham Forest .

As they left the woods that night, they were confused and disorientated and also felt defenceless. Indeed, they were even beginning to doubt their own memories, although sure that they had seen evidence of indentations on the ground where the three 'landing legs' had been sitting before the UFO departed.

Back at the base, senior personnel had not been idle. Penniston's request to the control tower had been followed up by the watch supervisor and it was learnt that an object had indeed been tracked on the Bentwaters radar at about 2 am – coinciding with the initial sighting by Burroughs and Parker. The tower then checked with Eastern Radar who confirmed their own tracking that night. This combined evidence had suggested that the object was real and was heading south east towards Rendlesham Forest before it vanished off scope – presumably when it went below radar coverage about 5 miles (8 km) from the end of the Woodbridge runway.

Because of this confirmation, the 'funny lights' under investigation by the airmen inside the forest were now being taken more seriously at the USAF base. Concern grew slightly when the problems with radio communication first began. When, at around 2.45 am, all contact was lost with Burroughs and Penniston deep inside the woods as they closed in on the landed UFO, a decision was taken to mount a search. This soon became imperative when an airman in the control tower saw something behind the east gate at about 3 am. Described as a bright white light, it shot upward from the trees and was presumably the UFO on its way skyward.

Burroughs and Penniston were discovered emerging, shaken, from the forest about 45 minutes after this sighting and were taken back to the base for a debriefing session. Burroughs seemed agitated, almost as if he expected more to happen. Neither witness was sorry to be leaving the scene.

In the debriefing with their supervisor, a lieutenant, the airmen were understandably worried.

Burroughs says that he hoped the commander would believe him and could provide some sort of explanation and let him forget the encounter as a mundane phenomenon.

He admits, 'I knew people were going to have questions that I could not answer and I expected it to have an adverse effect on my career.' In fact, he notes, quite a few people who would normally have spoken to him avoided talking with him during those first few hours back on base. Despite the time of day, there were people about. It was as if many airmen were awake knowing that something big had just taken place.

Jim Penniston was several years more senior and in command. He had more to lose as a result of the coming investigation, but says, 'John and I decided that we could not tell them everything that had happened. It was too fantastic. Arriving at the lieutenant's office we just told him that we had seen some lights in the woods and found impressions on the ground. We felt it best to leave it at that.'

As he gave his official report in these wholly inadequate words, Penniston says he asked himself: 'What in the world am I doing here?' He felt certain that he had just ended his career.

Thankfully, the shift commander knew things of which Burroughs and Penniston were yet to be aware. He informed them of the radar trackings and the sighting of the UFO heading skyward, made by the control tower. Burroughs says that the lieutenant offered this evidence kindly, clearly trying to build the men's confidence. There was no sign that he disbelieved them.

Penniston recalls how the debriefing officer was holding his pen and tapping it on the table as they spoke, urging them to go back out there in daylight and look for physical evidence.

He told them: 'If you find it, then secure the area and report back.'

However, even as this briefing was taking place, the base commander, Colonel Ted Conrad, had decided to take further action himself. Mindful of the fact that this incident was on British soil, he determined that the civilian police would have to be called. A phone report was lodged with police headquarters in Ipswich, who directed a patrol car from Woodbridge police station. At 4.11 am Conrad met with two police officers on the logging road outside the back gate of Woodbridge and just a few hundred yards from the landing site.

The involvement of the British police in this case has been puzzling. In February 1981, when there had been no publicity (not even locally), Brenda Butler and Dot Street followed sensible procedure and tried to discover whether the constabulary were aware of the then recent events.

They had spoken with police headquarters at Ipswich (who simply told them that any UFO sightings would be referred back to the air base) and then actually visited the little Woodbridge police station. Here the UFOlogists asked the Suffolk force to check whether any reports of UFO sightings had been entered in their log during the week after Christmas – giving the date of 27 December, as was believed to be correct – plus a several-day window after that. The police officer on duty looked at the log book and sniffed: 'Nope – we have no records – try Ipswich HQ.' It was a dead end.

Of course, the date of 27 December was wrong by 24 hours for this initial incident. However, it seems unlikely that this small police station would have so many UFO encounters reported by the local base commander that they would not recall one that had happened only seven weeks beforehand.

Be that as it may, the Suffolk police only admitted to receiving the call from Bentwaters that night when we broke the story via the *News of the World* two and a half years later. Then they issued a statement confirming that local police officers had gone into the forest at the request of the air base but were unimpressed by what they had found. Indeed, the Suffolk constabulary informed the media, that their men saw only the lighthouse and thought that the ground traces had been left by rabbits – the very same conclusions that had already been reached by science writer Ian Ridpath and forester Vince Thurkettle as we shall see later.

Ridpath attempted to get written confirmation from the police and they issued a statement affirming the content of the Woodbridge station log. The science writer told us that the chief constable, realizing that the media would demand some kind of comment, given the major press attention, had advised his staff at Woodbridge station to have some sort of response prepared on the Sunday when our front-page newspaper story appeared in front of 4 million readers and shot the cover-up into tiny little pieces.

If so, then it is interesting that the police denied such involvement in February 1981 and only spoke when forced by this press furore. Given that they thought they had resolved the case from the very start, surely it would have made sense to produce this log entry when Brenda and Dot first visited the Woodbridge station soon after the sightings. We might legitimately wonder if they would *ever* have told the public had UFOlogists not forced this story into the open when they did?

Despite Ian Ridpath being an obvious ally – he and Thurkettle having solved the case in exactly the manner the police say they did – he was still denied permission to speak with the police officer concerned. His written request was flatly rejected in November 1983.

Brenda, Dot and I also made an attempt to talk to the officer concerned, a month before Ridpath did so. I spoke directly to Woodbridge station and asked for the officer in question to tell us what had happened when he was called into the forest by the airbase. Woodbridge desk admitted that the relevant officer (whose name was then unknown to us) was available that evening but was presently out on his patrol. In very friendly terms I was advised that this man would soon return and would call me back 'within the hour' when he got back to the station. He did not do so.

So I phoned Woodbridge again, but this time received a much more hostile response. I was, curiously, warned not to tape record the conversation and given very short shrift before the police officer simply slammed the phone down on me after saying that I was wasting my time attempting to get them to speak about this matter. Yet I had not been uncivil. Nor was my name associated with the press story about the case, so there was no reason why I should have been treated like this. Something had evidently happened in the two hours between these two conversations.

One man did, however, get to speak with the police officer. He was Chuck de Caro, a fascinating American journalist who flew over to Britain on behalf of CNN (Cable News Network), the world-renowned 24-hour cable and satellite station. During early 1985 Brenda, Dot and I spent several days in Woodbridge, showing him around and filling in the background to the case to help CNN make a film. However, then our relationship with de Caro became inexplicably strained. Every time a significant interview came up, the reporter seemed to want us out of the way, to the point where we complained and were promptly told we should let him be and go home. He insisted that he had his story anyhow and was now returning to the USA .

Frankly, I suspect that he perceived us as a nuisance, always posing awkward questions fuelled by our four years' work into this case. Perhaps he surmised that these might restrict his interview potential. In any case, de Caro was photographed by the local press the next day at the landing site, talking to the police. The 'lighthouse and rabbits' theory was given yet another airing following this session. De Caro had, at least, become the first reporter to succeed in talking with the police officer called to the landing site.

De Caro told us thrilling tales about his special relationship with the US Government and how he covered stories on nuclear energy and flew in prototype aircraft. He clearly knew how to push the right buttons to make big stories happen. Indeed, we considered him a valuable ally for that reason, particularly as he took seriously our opinion at that time that something more sinister than an alien spacecraft might lie behind these events – perhaps an accident tied up with nuclear weaponry.

In 1996 de Caro even played himself in an episode of the hit American TV series JAG, a fictional saga about lawyers who fight to expose cover ups and injustices among the US military. There he was, acting out the sort of influential investigative military role that we saw him adopt in real life back in Rendlesham Forest.

One day Chuck de Caro may have more to say regarding the events in Rendlesham Forest. I hope so. He is the sort of investigative journalist who could succeed in unravelling the mystery.

However, it was July 1994 before the Suffolk police finally allowed Officer David King to come forward to tell his story more openly. He did so for LWT cameras when we made our *Strange but True?* programme on the case. King says that he had a junior officer with him that night but this man has since left the police force and has not gone public with his opinions.

The Woodbridge patrolman told LWT how he was met at the east gate in Tangham Wood and taken by security police (and, we believe, Colonel Conrad) to a spot 'some half a mile to three quarters of a mile (800-1,200 m) from the back gate, in an easterly direction towards the sea'. After taking the patrol car as far as it could go, they walked the rest of the way and throughout this trip 'the only light that we saw shining through the trees or even in the area' was that of the Orford Ness lighthouse.

However, it is worth noting that none of the airmen present in the forest was apparently excited by this light or seeking to convince these two British bobbies that this light *was* a UFO. To me that fact is critical. Either one would expect the lighthouse misidentification to continue – if it had been the cause of the close encounter two hours before – or else the realization of this mundane truth, as now pointed out to them by the police, would have ensured that the story was officially killed back on base. That did not happen. The sightings escalated to involve more airmen and an official report was filed. Clearly nobody from the US Air Force that night thought the lighthouse *was* a UFO.

David King is well aware that by the time he and his colleague reached the forest the UFO had allegedly disappeared. All he could report on arrival back at the station was that they saw nothing unusual out there. He really was not inclined to take the matter much further, although checks were made with the MoD at West Drayton, as was standard procedure with UFO stories. From this the police learned about the 'comets' in the sky earlier that night and the radar tracking at Heathrow (probably of the Cosmos re-entry at 9.08 pm). They were also officially advised that the RAF knew of no aircraft that should have been above Rendlesham Forest at 2.30 am that morning.

Quite amazingly, UFO debunker Nicholas Humphrey adopted the visit by this police patrol as a way to solve the case during a Channel 4 TV documentary in October 1987. Quite incredibly, he was even praised for doing so by New Scientist magazine in one of their dumbest hours. Given how UFOlogists are often criticised for sloppy work, this 'research' by respected media sources is stunning.

Humphrey argued that the UFO seen by the airmen was the satellite re-entry (although this occurred five hours earlier).The landed UFO was the police car lights behind trees. However, the UFO was seen between 2 and 3 am and the police were called out in response to this event, arriving at 4.11 am – that is, over an hour after the UFO had departed and with Burroughs and Penniston now safely back on base. So the logic behind this scientifically 'respected' theory leaves me utterly confused.

This was not to be the end of police involvement with the case. Woodbridge constabulary were called again – at about 10.30 am in the morning of 26 December. King was not on duty by that time and another (lone) officer was sent to investigate the new report. His identity has not been revealed and he has not come forward. We must rely upon David King's evidence about how this second report was handled at the police station as well as the comments of Burroughs and Penniston, both of whom met this other police officer at the landing site inside the forest.

The two airmen had, of course, been ordered to go out at first light and look for the indentations which they thought they had spotted before leaving the forest. Burroughs, in particular, had reservations.

He hoped to find nothing, he admits, because solid evidence would confirm that the events had really happened and he was trying hard to persuade himself that it was just a crazy dream. He desperately wanted to put it all behind him, and finding evidence would not help him to do so.

Unfortunately, it was not possible to forget it. Daylight revealed more extensive physical evidence at the site than they expected. Not only was there a gap in the trees ('where it looked like something had flown up through them' Burroughs noted) but there were three holes in the ground where it seemed something had dug into the soil and twisted the ground.

John Burroughs remembers that the police officer who met them at the site that morning was pretty dismissive, saying that marks like those could be seen all over the forest because rabbits dug into the soil to find warmth during winter. The airman pointed out that these holes seemed to be in a triangle and were at the exact spot where, hours before, a UFO with three legs had been sitting. Then there was the gaping hole in the tree canopy directly overhead. However, the police officer was not impressed by any of this.

Penniston recalls being quizzed by the officer about the sighting – being asked if what they saw was a UFO. Unflappably, the CSC officer replied, 'I'm not saying it was a UFO. I am saying it was an object out here in the woods last night and I can't explain what it was.'

To this the policeman responded, 'Well I'm not putting that in my report. I am going to say that it was likely burrowing animals that did it.'

Both airmen tried to persuade the police officer to the contrary but it seemed clear that his mind was made up. As Jim Penniston notes, the ground at the site was frozen solid and even in the cold winter's daylight the temperature was hardly above zero. These marks were fresh and could not have been dug by any rabbit during the last couple of days because of the rock-hard soil.

Woodbridge station soon chose to dismiss the incident – possibly explaining their subsequent unwillingness to talk. Perhaps, with hindsight, it was suspected that they ought to have taken the evidence more seriously than they did. Indeed, they even failed to respond to a third call from the base later that weekend after further UFO sightings in the woods, although this time the police could justify such disinterest because a more urgent call to attend a crime scene came up at the same time.

Colonel Conrad was not pleased with the attitude taken by the civilian police, although one can perhaps understand it, especially in the light of the natural reserve the British have when it comes to swallowing UFO stories. However, the commander was glad that he had discharged his duty correctly by reporting the matter to the appropriate British authorities. If they chose to do nothing about it then that was up to them. He could not be so liberal. The USAF had to proceed with an investigation.

An A-10 flying overhead after dawn had recorded infra-red – a form of heat energy – being emitted from the site. A team from base security had begun to take proper measurements. As Penniston points out: 'The impressions were cylindrical – they were about one and a half to two inches (3.8 to 5.1 cm) deep – they were an equilateral triangle in pattern with sides measuring exactly three and a half feet (1.06 m).'

To almost everybody present, other than the British police, this proved one very important thing. Just as the witnesses had alleged, there *had* been a strange physical object – a craft of some sort – which had landed in the forest the night before.

8

THE HUNT IS ON

COLONEL CHARLES HALT (or Lieutenant Colonel Halt as he then officially was) had a vast amount of experience in the US Air Force. He was also academically well qualified, with a science degree (in chemistry) and a masters (in business administration). So it is not surprising that he did well in the military. He had tenacity and was a stickler for detail but also knew how to be discreet. Given his security clearance that was important.

Halt joined the USAF in 1964 and served in Vietnam and Japan, subsequently spent time debriefing prisoners returned by the Viet Cong and then moved to the Pentagon where he headed up the administration of the entire fleet of jet engines. His transfer and promotion to Bentwaters in 1980 was seen as a pleasant one because, although a challenging job, it was not in the front line.

In fact, Halt moved to the twin bases as the deputy commander. He was the highest-ranking officer to have any direct part in the events inside Rendlesham Forest, but his decision to speak out and stand by his men and to report his own personal sightings did not have any negative repercussions. In 1984 he was promoted to full colonel and made base commander of the entire Bentwaters/Woodbridge complex.

His career continued to rise even after that point – serving as base commander in both Korea and Belgium, masterminding the deployment of cruise missiles in part of Europe (and their subsequent decommissioning) and finally having a very influential administrative post in the US Department of Defence back in Washington before he finally retired from the USAF in 1992.

As can be seen, this is a distinguished track record and he was obviously well thought of by his superiors. Yet he stood at the centre point of one of the most bizarre set of UFO encounters in history and bravely put his whole reputation and future prospects on the line by endorsing their reality.

Halt's involvement with this case was hinted at to Brenda, Dot and me from the earliest days. While we knew of the three men who had witnessed the opening night's activity, had talked to one (Penniston) and were on the trail of another whose identity we knew and whom I eventually found 5,000 miles (8,000 km) from Suffolk (Burroughs), it was also soon apparent to us that this close encounter had been a prelude to the real drama that had unfolded later that weekend.

Because of this second major incident, which followed so swiftly after the sighting we have just discussed, it has been difficult sorting out dates and facts. Indeed, there were a lot more USAF witnesses to these subsequent events and much of what we were hearing in the period after that weekend understandably confused these two nights. However, we had spoken with one or two people who claimed to be directly involved with the later sightings and it was from this source that the association of the deputy base commander himself was suggested.

Although Charles Halt remained on base long after most of the junior-rank witnesses from both encounters had been shipped out of England, he remained very mindful of his rank and responsibility and did not talk openly to any investigator.

That position changed by a small degree in June 1983 when the official report on the case sent to the British MoD surfaced. This file was actually written by Halt and its release – to everyone's surprise (including his) – came as a result of a request made by a UFOlogist to the US Freedom of Information Act. In its wake, the colonel had several cautious discussions with UFOlogists (e.g. Dot Street and Manchester lawyer Harry Harris) but remained unwilling to breach his code of duty and give any proper interviews. Nor would he talk to the media. Some years later Halt confessed to me that he feared these public revelations about his report might wreck his career. 'I was initially quite angry at the UFO community for exposing what I had assumed to be confidential material', he explained. Yet he desperately wanted to talk, to clear up some of what he viewed as some outright nonsense being spoken in public by one or two people about the case. Unfortunately, as a good USAF man he felt obliged to remain silent until he was free to do so.

Indeed, Halt remained a career man until his retirement and only agreed to tell the full story after his departure from the air force in 1992. This detailed testimony from such a dedicated and obviously experienced officer has transformed our knowledge of what happened in the days after that first close encounter. It is also critical to our understanding of the second set of UFO sightings – on a night when all hell broke loose in the forest outside the twin NATO bases.

Halt told us that he first knew about the opening night's events when he arrived for duty at 5.30 am on Friday, 26 December 1980 – some three hours after they had happened. He was greeted by a chuckling desk sergeant who said, 'You'll never guess what happened last night.'

The sergeant told of Burroughs and Penniston chasing around the woods after a UFO and Halt asked why nothing was in the blotter (the base log book). The sergeant added that the night duty flight lieutenant had advised that the matter should not be reported officially. It seemed as if there was an air of embarrassment – as if nobody was really quite sure what to do.

The commander soon decided this had to change. 'It is very important that something be in the log,' he explained. He added that he knew the witnesses personally and they were credible. While not convinced that they had really seen a UFO, he believed that something must have happened.

As Halt points out, the incident could have involved an air crash, some natural phenomenon or just about anything. However, it was the responsibility of the base log to record proper details and correct times so that any future enquiry could have the facts. He suggested the language be muted and recommended the use of the rather tepid phrase 'unexplained lights' – a term which has dogged the case ever since.

Considering such a laudable decision, it is unfortunate that Halt's official report gives the date for the first sighting incorrectly as 27 December, confusing it with the second night (which it also wrongly dates as 29 December). This error has made life very difficult for the investigators, struggling to sift through a mass of conflicting testimony and second-hand evidence that referred to two complex and separate events, often without witnesses making the distinction clear. The error occurred because the report was not filled in until more than two weeks later. As Halt insisted to me, 'I was asked by the British officer on base – Squadron Leader Donald Moreland – to pen this report to London. But they already knew all about the case. In fact, my report to them was for the record only and submitted as a matter of principle. It was deliberately muted and left things out, such as the existence of several categories of hard evidence. I felt that they should contact me if they wanted more. But they never did.'

After chatting with the desk sergeant that Friday, Halt talked to Colonel Ted Conrad who told of the 'landing site' marks and the arrival of the British police. The men mutually agreed that neither believed in UFOs but that they needed to keep on top of the situation and maintain a record for possible official follow through. The radar trackings were especially important in this regard.

However, nothing much happened after that during the Friday and the holiday festivities were still affecting the normal run of things on base. On the Saturday a Christmas party for the officers was scheduled for Woody's Bar and minds were not on UFOs at all.

John Burroughs was not finding it quite so easy to forget. After being up all night thanks to his encounter, he slept soundly on the Friday night but awoke on Saturday with a curious foreboding.

'I got this funny feeling that something might have come back,' the airman recalls. 'I could not get it out of my mind.' It bugged him all day and he decided to go back out to the forest to try to shake the presentiment. Instead, just the opposite occurred. The feeling intensified that something was going to happen and Burroughs was not mistaken.

As another bitterly cold winters night progressed witnesses throughout East Anglia were observing strange triangles and lights as already recorded in Chapter 3. These headed for Rendlesham Forest where local people, such as Gerry Harris and Sarah Richardson, were about to experience several hours filled with spectacular observations.

The military also saw these things develop that Saturday evening. A four-man patrol by the east gate spotted the lights over the forest and radioed through to Sergeant Adrian Bustinza, then supervising the base police at Bentwaters. Bustinza was in the alert area on the base but was about to take a routine drive along the access road that would take him towards the Woodbridge gate and the forest. He contacted the duty flight commander for the security police – his immediate superior. This man, Lieutenant Bruce Englund, approved Bustinza's request that he should mount an investigation.

Meanwhile Charles Halt and the officers and their wives – a party of about 40 – were enjoying the convivial atmosphere in Woody's on the Woodbridge base as the pre-arranged Christmas party thrived. They were blissfully unaware of the new drama that was taking place by the east gate.

It was now about 10.30 pm on Saturday, 27 December. Suddenly, the security chief, Bruce Englund, burst in to Woody's and took Halt and Conrad aside, asking to speak to them alone. His face was ashen and he hit them with words that Halt had not expected to hear.

'It's back!'

'What's back?' Halt enquired quizzically.

'The UFO,' Englund told him as calmly as possible.

The three men looked stunned but Conrad responded swiftly. Halt was to head up an investigation and sort this problem out once and for all. Conrad could not go himself because he had a speech and presentations to make after the dinner was concluded in the bar.

Halt says that he was determined to resolve the situation and was convinced that there would be a logical explanation for what the men were seeing. He notes that he planned to: 'Go out there and put this to bed once and for all.'

This determination was put into effect as the Colonel left Woody's and set about getting a team together. He decided to take four others with him – a security police officer, another patrolman to operate the searchlights that he felt would be required, an officer from the disaster preparedness team who could operate a geiger counter, and a base photographer. One of these men was chosen because of his long tour on base and his familiarity with Rendlesham Forest. The geiger counter was felt advisable because the A-10 jet had picked up energy emissions from the first landing site the day before.

Halt was planning to make a thorough job of recording all that happened so that nobody could be in any doubt as to what they found. Because of the cold, he ordered utility jackets to be worn. It was also windy so he suspected that note taking would be difficult. For this reason, he stopped by his office to pick up a battery-powered dictaphone-type tape recorder to facilitate this process.

That tape recorder was to provide the 'holy grail' of this case – the infamous 'live tape' of the proceedings that was first reported to the radar staff at Watton in January 1981 and which UFOlogists spent the next three and a half years hearing about from numerous sources before eventually securing it. It is some of the most explosive evidence in the history of UFOs.

Of course, as Halt went back to his quarters that night to change clothes and his team began to assemble on the base, nobody knew that a major UFO event was underway. Halt expected to sort the situation out very quickly and end the stories and rumours that were flying about the base.

None the less, out on the rim of the forest the security patrol that had witnessed the UFO's return had now been joined by a gaggle of men – the news having rapidly filtered out across the base that the UFO was back. These included Master Sergeant Ball, one of Conrad's team who had studied the landing traces, Lieutenant Bruce Englund, of course, and – perhaps the most stunned of all the observers – John Burroughs who could not believe that his premonition was coming true. The UFO which had shattered his life less than two days ago *was* back, exactly as he feared. Only this time it seemed like half the US Air Force would see it.

'When I got out to the area there was already a lot of activity going on,' Burroughs explains. He went into the woods on foot along the logging road close to the site where he and Penniston had been two nights before. 'This time the lights were different. They were blue glows flying around in the air. And they were also beaming light rays down towards the ground.'

As this was happening Adrian Bustinza was coming face to face with his own personal nightmare. Bustinza has never made a big deal out of this story. He left the USAF soon afterwards and became a prison officer in the south-western USA. In 1984 he did grant an interview to prominent American UFOlogist Ray Boeche who is also a church minister and commanded the sort of respect that the former security sergeant apparently required to break his code of silence. He told of the astonishing things encountered in that forest and then chose to say no more about it – shunning the publicity that the case has subsequently generated.

According to Bustinza, as he and his team entered the forest he was confronted by an eerie scene – like mist or fog rolling in. However, there was an object amidst this – 'thicker at the centre than at the edge' but almost not quite solid in appearance.

'We came upon a yellow mist about two to three feet (60-90 cm) off the ground,' he explained. 'It was like dew, but yellow. The object was hovering low down and moving up and down. There was a red light on top and several blue lights on the bottom, but there was also an effect maybe like a prism – with rainbow lights scattered about. It was weird.'

Later, John Burroughs recognized this description. It was not unlike what he had seen on the Friday morning. However, by now Burroughs was elsewhere in the forest as little groups of airmen had split up and scattered – hunting evidence hither and thither. It was little short of pantomime.

Adrian Bustinza says that he was utterly terrified. 'My life literally passed before my eyes and I was frozen in place.'

He and his team tried to close in on the thing but it seemed to retreat back across the woods towards Capel Green. At the same time a curtain of static electricity swept through the forest just as it had two nights before. Instantly the local wildlife went into pandemonium – deer and rabbits fleeing for their lives. This sudden activity was a godsend to Bustinza. He says that it contrasted so sharply with the ghost-like object moving ahead of them through the trees that it jolted him into normality.

However, the tingling forcefield emitted by the object was having other side effects. Despite the fact that they were wearing regulation headgear, Bustinza could see the hair on one man's head standing on end like it was a wire brush.

This was the final straw. An order was given to the patrol for a tactical withdrawal, during which a wooden fence was damaged as the men hastily moved back. I saw this damaged fence myself on my first visit to the landing site. It instilled a heady sense of reality to that fateful night.

This retreat was a strategic move, the plan being to meet up with Halt and his investigation team – who were by now known to be heading for the woods to sort the matter out.

Of course, there was more to it than a decision to meet Halt. It was a very emotional moment. Indeed, as one of the men later put it bluntly to me: 'We decided to get the hell out of there!'

Under the circumstances I doubt that anyone can blame them.

9

IF YOU GO DOWN TO THE WOODS TODAY

HANKFULLY, we have a great deal of evidence to help us to piece together an accurate picture of what happened during that extraordinary Saturday night and Sunday morning.

There is the eye-witness testimony of several of those who were present. This includes, most importantly, senior figure Colonel Charles Halt, plus Sergeant Adrian Bustinza and the now 'veteran' UFO hunter Sergeant John Burroughs, as well as more restrained comments from several of the other some 20 to 40 airmen (according to various estimates).

Most controversial of these USAF personnel is Larry Warren – a 19 year old on his first tour of duty at Bentwaters. He came forward in early 1983 and was the first military witness publicly to do so. Initially, he spoke only with an American abductee called Betty Andreasson Luca. However, Barry Greenwood, an experienced investigator in New England, recognized what Warren was talking about because he had read several of my articles on the case, which had by now been published in the UFO literature. At that time these were the only written sources about the incident. The case had not yet been mentioned in any British or American newspaper.

Barry Greenwood immediately sent me a copy of Warren's story for my comments. The young witness requested anonymity, stating that he was terrified. He claimed that he had spoken on the telephone about the sighting a few days after it happened when he called his mother back in the USA from a base payphone. In response, a bogus charge was brought against him and Warren was forced to leave the USAF. He felt that he was being victimised.

The case became public knowledge in the UK soon after Warren surfaced, thanks to the Halt memorandum release which we took to the press. Larry behaved unlike the other military personnel, who chose to remain silent even with the backing of Halt's report. Of course, Warren was out of the services and had his own reasons not to feel kindly disposed to the USAF. He appeared in the press and on TV (suitably masked with his voice electronically altered – stating that if he did not hide his identity, he might face danger).The pseudonym Art Wallace was used at the time, although Warren soon began to speak more openly and was even lecturing at UFO conferences within a year or so.

Larry Warren was always forthcoming in those early days and I have met him several times, both in the USA and on his return visits to Britain to research his story. This was for a first-hand account in a book called *Left at East Gate* written together with New York UFOlogist Peter Robbins. Despite many years of apathy from publishers, it was finally scheduled for release in early 1997.

I must say that I have always found Larry Warren to be a friendly, likeable and helpful man. If he stood alone as a witness in this case, I would probably accept his testimony. However, not everyone seems to share that view. Several of the military witnesses whose stories make up the backbone to this case have told me that they feel that Warren may not even have been involved. Others suggest he might have been in the forest on the second night but they do not remember seeing him out there. Some witnesses have even (according to Warren) refused to take part in TV interviews if he was to be included as well, a claim that has, understandably, provoked this young man's deep concern. I take no sides in this issue but report these facts only as I understand them.

In Quest's news-stand magazine (UFO, January 1995), Colonel Charles Halt, who had just given his first public lecture on the case in England, is quoted saying of Warren: 'He was not there and did not participate.' This seems very blunt and flatly contradicts what Warren insists to me is the truth. Indeed, the colonel seemed annoyed about some of the extreme stories being spread about this case from a variety of media sources. I have heard similar sentiments expressed by other witnesses.

In June 1997 I had the opportunity to discuss Warren's recently published book with Halt. He was typically circumspect about it, noting that prior to reading it he had given the young airman the benefit of the doubt. He added, 'I thought that perhaps he was out there on a third night when I was not present, because I certainly knew he was not with my group. But this book seems to suggest he was there on the same night as myself. All I will say is that he was not out there officially. I have also checked with the records and he was not supposedly on duty either.' The Colonel understandably refrained from stating that Warren was not in the forest and so could not have experienced what he claims to have done. However, his reservations about the airman's story were evident. He noted, 'I did not see the fantastic things Warren claims. I did not see the wing commander out there communicating with aliens. Nor to my knowledge did anyone who was with me in the forest that night. What we did see was incredible enough and it bothers me that this could be compromised by some of the wild stories I have seen in the press.'

Warren is also nearly alone among the military in contending that aliens were present in the woods and engaged in some sort of open contact with a senior USAF officer – Wing Commander (later Brigadier General) Gordon Williams. Williams has adamantly denied that he was ever involved in the case. All of the other witnesses I have talked with also say that this particular element of the story is totally untrue. John Burroughs, for example, told me: 'This is non-sense. Williams was not there. If he had been it would have changed everything. Take my word for it.'

Of course, it was part of the case that I had written up before Warren came forward because it was 'fed out' to us from the start by sources that have not otherwise been confirmed. At that time it appeared a central feature of the case. Now – from speaking with numerous witnesses – I can only doubt that this 'alien contact' ever happened. So why was it given out to Brenda Butler and alleged to the radar staff at Watton who then passed it on to me? Either way, Larry Warren supported it in his early testimony, while Burroughs, Halt and others denied seeing any such incredible scene.

Resolving the problem of Larry Warren's role in this case is perhaps its greatest single difficulty and will be exacerbated by the publication of his book. Being the first of the military witnesses to go into print (although not, I suspect, the last) he is sure to gain notoriety. It is therefore necessary that I try to put his claims into some context. Despite the fact that I personally like Larry and greatly respect his co-operation in the past, I have no way of knowing if he was really present. I must take his word for that and yet also make my readers aware that others seem to dispute some (although by no means all) of what he has to say.

The truth about this case lies somewhere between these two versions and we can only try to pick our way through the debris of evidence and try to make a reasoned judgement.

There seem to be three options. One is that Warren may be telling the truth and the witnesses who dispute that simply never came across him on the night. There was chaos in the forest so this possibility cannot be dismissed. As to his testimony, a good deal of it matches what the other witnesses say and the stranger parts cannot be utterly rejected.

It is worth recalling that other witnesses do hint at reality distortion and a period of missing time during the close encounter. They infer that the object was under intelligent control – even if its controllers were never seen by them, so Warren's story cannot be regarded as inconceivable.

A second option might be that Warren was peripherally involved in the events of the Saturday night but has exaggerated some aspects of his story. Larry was certainly at Bentwaters at the time and did leave under curious circumstances, just as he contends. That has all been verified. Moreover, he is clearly aware of the case in detail and his testimony includes features that were not known to the investigators back in 1983 which have subsequently been verified by other military witnesses. Therefore, Warren must, at least, be reporting the story as heard from someone really involved or, of course, describing his personal association with the landings, however great that was. Warren also suggests he was subjected to intelligence agency interrogation techniques that involved mind altering substances – something he is partially supported in by at least one other witness. One or two of the USAF witnesses I spoke with have suggested that maybe this young man's distorted perception about what took place is the result of these methods rather than a clear recall of what actually took place.

The third possibility – that he is making it all up for personal reasons – seems less likely to fit the facts. Warren appears to me to have been genuinely associated with the case in some way. Yet his evidence is sufficiently different that, clearly, it has to be viewed with a degree of circumspection.

The military eye-witness testimony from all of the personnel (from Halt to Warren) is backed up by the statement in the official report that was signed by Halt and submitted to the British Government on 13 January 1981. While the UK Official Secrets Act ensured that this was never made public in the land where the events took place, the US Freedom of Information Act allowed a copy to be released two and a half years later. The Pentagon says this copy was given to them *by* the British MoD for purpose of that release – an event which would make folly out of famed British secrecy. The MoD have denied that they released the file to the Americans so this remains an impasse – but wherever the memo came from it is the most significant and well-documented UFO file ever to escape from the MoD archives.

Halt's report mentions no aliens, but then it also mentions no radar trackings, photographs or other features of the case, when we have strong proof that these *did* exist.

In addition to all of the above, and of perhaps the greatest value to unravelling this story, is the tape recording made by Charles Halt on the second night. Again, that is not mentioned in his report to the MoD but certainly does exist. I have a copy. This tape was not recorded continuously. The cassette spans several hours (from just after midnight to around 4 am into Sunday, 28 December). Across approximately 18 minutes' duration it records some of the most dramatic sightings 'live' as they actually happened.

All the conversation that follows in this chapter (printed in italics) and which provides an exciting flavour of 'being there' during this encounter is transcribed directly from that tape recording. No artistic licence is used to recreate these words. What you read is exactly what Halt and his investigative team said as they confronted something far stranger than any of them had expected.

The drama captured on this tape was to dispel the colonel's bold assurance in Woody's Bar that he would sort the matter out and end the silly UFO stories that were starting to affect the normal operation of the base. What he and his team of USAF investigators encountered in the forest that night was to shape their lives profoundly and leave them in no doubt as to the reality of UFOs

As Halt and his men approached the edge of the forest they left their vehicles and set off on foot. Once inside the woods, near the site where Burroughs and Penniston had met a landed UFO 48 hours before, there was no sign of any strange activity. However, the airmen were apparently struggling with the three light-alls – large gas-powered searchlights that were being set up to illuminate the cold darkness of this isolated spot.

The problem was intermittent. They were just not working properly. Colonel Halt recalled that he had brought his tape recorder, pressed the button and commenced his log of the night's events:

'Ah one hundred fifty feet (46 m) or more from the initial— er, I should say 'suspected' – impact point. Having a little difficulty. We can't get the light-alls to

work. Seems to be some kind of mechanical problem. Gonna send back and get another light-all.'

Halt reports that this effect was very unusual. Light-alls are extremely simple pieces of equipment and hardly ever fail unless they run out of gas. Even the replacements brought out to the site malfunctioned and during the next few hours only one out of half a dozen worked – and that failed occasionally as well. The soft whining hum of its generator can be heard incessantly throughout early parts of the Halt tape.

Larry Warren suggests that his involvement in the case began around this time. His story is of being asked to load up a light-all on Bentwaters and go out to the forest with it to aid what he took at first to be some kind of night exercise. It was now after midnight into the Sunday and there seemed to be a problem with the loading gauge, leading to a later dispute as to whether the light-alls were properly fuelled. Warren says that they were. Halt agrees that this possibility was assessed but the light-alls *were* found to be correctly set up.

On his way into the forest bringing the new light-all, Warren says that he saw many men, one of whom was on the ground being tended by medics (although, again, no independent corroboration of this story exists so far as I know). Warren's estimate of the numbers involved is much greater than the figures provided by Halt, Burroughs and Bustinza, although it is likely that uninvolved airmen from the base hovered around the edge of the forest, but were denied entry by a security cordon that Halt had now set up. Indeed, there is evidence on the tape that this took place.

This cordon prevented the public from entering the forestry track and a staging post served as a radio relay, mindful of the problems with reception described by Burroughs and Penniston two nights before. But Halt confirms that they still had trouble with their radios. An unusual amount of static was making them inoperable. Despite using three different frequencies they kept losing range. The trees may have been a factor, but the military are used to operating inside wooded environments and the effects were considered unusual. Alongside the baffling problems experienced by the light-alls, it did seem as if some sort of electrical interference was taking place.

Halt was glad of his decision to take the tape recorder with him as the events intensified. He says that: 'Without it I would have trouble believing what happened that night.'

As Halt put in his request for replacement equipment, he began to mount a responsible investigation, telling the tape: *'Meanwhile* we're gonna take some readings with the geiger counter and, ah, chase around the area a little bit waiting for another light-all to come out here.'

The study continued for some time. Halt reported, 'Okay we're now approaching the area to within about twenty-five to thirty feet (5-9 m). What kind of readings we getting – anything?'

'Just minor clicks,' advised the geiger counter operator.

Then Halt asked to be directed toward the landing impressions, which he had yet to see, expressing surprise at their relatively small size. 'Is that all the bigger they are?'

'There's one more well- defined over here,' a helpful voice pointed out.

The geiger counter operator now began to take measurements using the 'five tenths' scale – the results reaching up to half way. As this process continued, taking readings from the ground inside and outside the 'landing site' as well as within the 'pod marks' (as the holes supposedly left by the UFO legs were termed) there was no hint of any concern that radiation levels might be anomalous or worrying. Halt told us later that he *was* indeed rather worried for the safety of his men and local citizens who might be in danger from radiation. This was why they took geiger counters out there.

'This one's dead' and 'Just minor clicks' were expressions used to report what they recorded. Even when more serious readings were taken, nobody became unduly alarmed. Study has indicated that the figures detected were several times the expected background count, but no discussion is heard on tape as to whether this might prove a health hazard. The investigation of the site proceeded as a matter of routine.

In the background, radio chatter could be heard (with no obvious interference), seemingly the security patrol – Alpha One – and the east gate relay site discussing the arrival of the replacement light-alls.

By now the man using the geiger counter, distinctive on the tape because of his deep southern accent, was at the third 'pod mark' and here reported success: 'Yeah – now I'm getting some residual.'

Halt took this news on board and stated, 'Okay, let's go to the centre of the area next and see what kind of reading we get out there – Ah – are you reading the clicks? I can't hear them. Is that about the centre, Bruce?'

Lieutenant Bruce Englund responded to this and confirmed that it was the centre. It was here that the geiger counter really started to respond.

'That's about the best deflection needle I've seen yet!' Halt pointed out, rather startled. 'Can you give me an estimation – ah, we're on the point five scale and we're getting . . .?'

The discussion focused on these readings. One voice told of detecting seven clicks. Another interpreted this as being half a millirem (although no time base was given – e.g. half a millrem per second).

The investigation of the trace evidence continued in its systematic manner and then another strong reading was picked up in the 'level one indentation'.

As this occurred, a new voice interceded – in what sounds like a New Jersey drawl.

'*Looks like an area here possibly that could be a blast . . .*' His words trailed off as the geiger counter went crazy.

'*This thing's about to freak!*' cried the operator.

The panic was short lived – unless the tape was switched off at this point and many minutes passed by unrecorded – as they may have. However, the investigation team soon returned its attention to the 'blast mark'. Halt described it methodically into the recorder.

'*We've found a small blast – what looks like a blasted or scruffed-up area here. We're getting very positive readings.*' These were coming from the 'dead centre' of this mark on the ground within the landing zone. The geiger counters (at least two were in use) clicked away merrily in the background of the tape .

For the first time a hint of caution entered the proceedings as Halt announced, '*Okay, now we've got the gloves on. Let's make a sweep of the whole area about ten foot (3 m) out – make a perimeter run round it. I'm gonna depend on you to count the clicks,*' he told one of his men.

As they strode gingerly around the trace evidence in the glare of the occasionally working light-all, they now found what were called 'abrasion marks' on the trees surrounding the site. Halt is clearly unimpressed at this stage, saying that they '*look like they might be old*'. He was undoubtedly correct. These appear to be the score marks put on to the trees by the forestry workers to indicate that they would be scheduled for felling some time in the new year.

The airman with the New Jersey accent was more intrigued by this and continued to scan the trees, pointing out that each one had an abrasion facing in towards 'what we assume is the landing site'.

Halt perked up at his report: '*You're right about the abrasion. I've never seen an, ah, pine tree that's been damaged react that fast.*' By which he meant a '*strange crystalline sap*' that was apparently oozing out. He ordered sample bottles to be used to capture this evidence.

The colonel now entered into discussion with the disaster preparedness officer, a Sergeant Nevills. The two men discussed how to stake out the area and identify points on it for a detailed site map and the further extraction of soil samples and other data (including, Halt has since told us, plaster casts of the indentations on the landing site).

As this was going on the radio jumped into life.

'*Alpha One Security. We got two other personnel requesting the possibility that they can come out to the site.*'

The chief of security at the landing site barked in reply: '*Tell them* **negative** *at this time. We'll* **tell** *them when they can come out here. We* **don't** *want them out here right now.*'

Evidently the investigation at the landing site was not to be visited by anyone undesirable or not under the strict control of the USAF.

Ignoring this new turn of events, Halt and Nevills were still discussing the bottling of the trace evidence. Halt described into the tape recorder how the crystalline sap was coming from trees about 5 ft (1.5 m) from the site and on the trunks 3 ft (90 cm) off the ground. It is interesting that his caution about that phenomenon was still present. He was not carried away by what would prove to be the dubious view that this evidence was somehow mysterious. Halt still warned that the damage looked old to him.

In any case, he suggested a new strategy – the photographing of the trace marks.

'*Okay – why don't you take a picture of that?*' Halt advised. '*Remember your picture, Neil, and be writing it down . . . Oh, it's coming out on the tape,*' it suddenly occurred to the deputy commander.

The careful nature of the investigation up until now was impressive. Halt can be heard telling his men to keep in mind what they were seeing because they might be asked to sketch things later. Then he reported that he was switching off the tape recorder so that he could study the trace damage more closely.

An unknown period of time later (very few time checks are given in this first part of the tape) we pick up the continuing investigation as the team are still studying the physical damage to the forest floor.

A more detailed description of the traces followed: '*It looks like something twisted as it sat down on them. Looks as if someone got something and sat it down and twisted it from side to side. Very strange.*'

'*Interesting,*' Halt concurred, although these are the sort of marks which foresters such as Vince Thurkettle were later to insist were simply dug by a marauding rabbit.

A new tactic was now employed – the use of a star-lite scope. With this an infra-red beam looks for heat emissions – invaluable for seeking out people at night via their thermal emissions. When shone at the tree where the score marks were found, a definite heat impression was returned, causing the area to 'glow'.

'*Hey, you're right. There's a white streak on the tree!*' Halt exclaimed after trying it for himself.

'*That indicates a heat source . . .*' the star-lite scope operator pointed out.

But Halt was still engrossed in what he was seeing: '*Hey – this is eerie. This is strange.*'

Looking upwards, Halt now related into the tape the evidence he was seeing directly above the landing traces: '*Looking directly overhead one can see an opening in the trees plus some freshly broken pine branches on the ground underneath. Looks like some of them came off about fifteen to twenty feet (4.5–6 m) up – some small branches an inch (2.5 cm) or less in diameter.*'

The star-lite scope was now turned from the trees on to the ground traces. Again a 'residual' was picked up, although seemingly less noticeable than before. The men were all wary of using emotive words – preferring military jargon like 'pod', 'impact point' and 'residual' – but Halt was clearly becoming astonished by what their investigation was uncovering and had to stop himself short from using the 'R' word.

'*There's some type of abrasion on the ground where the pine needles are all pushed back and we get a high radioact . . . er, a high reading . . . You're sure there's a positive after-effect?*' He asked the man with the star-lite scope, the airman with the New Jersey accent.

'*Yes, there is definitely. There is an after-effect. It seems that when the lights are turned off and once we are focused in and allow time for the eyes to adjust we are getting an indication of a heat source coming out of that centre spot, which will show up on the scope.*'

'*Heat or some form of energy,*' Halt interrupted. '*It's hardly heat at this stage of the game!*'

A few hundred yards from where Halt and his team were debating the nature of this glowing 'energy', another group of airmen – including Adrian Bustinza and possibly Larry Warren – were suddenly confronted with the UFO again. A strange light had appeared out towards the east. As if in response to its reappearance, the local wildlife erupted into pandemonium.

They radioed through to Alpha One Security who relayed the message through to Halt. He had already switched on the tape to record the animal uproar when these incredible events interceded.

'*Zero one forty eight (1.48 am). We're hearing very strange sounds out of a farmer's barnyard animals – very, very active making an awful lot of noise.*'

Many voices started chattering at once seemingly looking for the UFO and Halt cut through them like a knife.

'You just saw a light – where? Slow down? Where?'

The operator of the star-lite scope spoke out: 'Right on this position – here. Straight ahead in between the trees. There it is again! Straight ahead of my flashlight beam. There it is!'

All the men in Halt's group followed the New Jersey airman's direction. Halt was first to react. 'I see it too. What is it?'

'We don't know, sir,' a voice admitted.

Various ideas were tossed back and forth and while the men were discussing the options Halt spoke into the recorder. 'It's a strange, small red light – looks to be maybe a quarter, half mile, (400-800 m) maybe further out. I'm gonna switch off now.'

Halt has since described to us what he saw in more detail. 'We saw this strange object in front of us – a glowing red sphere. It looked like the sun when it first comes up in the morning, although it had a black centre and it pulsated as though it were an eye winking at you. It appeared to have molten metal dripping off it. We watched it for several minutes as it moved from side to side horizontally. It appeared to come near to us and then receded a bit.'

The sceptics say their case is strengthened here. A bearing for the object is given on tape and this is a close approximation to the position of the lighthouse on Orford Ness. If you measure the gaps on the tape between the light appearing and disappearing, through phrases like, 'There it is again', there is another match with the pulse frequency of the lighthouse. Moreover, the image of an 'eye winking at you' is certainly reminiscent of a rotating lighthouse beacon.

One can see why critics of this case feel that they have a point.

Of course, there are major difficulties. The red coloration, the 'molten metal dripping off' and other features of the UFO sound unlike any lighthouse. Many of the men out there that night – including Halt and Burroughs – say they saw the lighthouse as well as the UFO. But, perhaps most important, the lighthouse is a permanent feature of the environment. Halt and his team had been in Rendlesham Forest for almost two hours when the UFO arrived just as the animals went crazy. If it was merely the lighthouse then why did the investigation team not see it much earlier in the night and why were local animals, who live in its presence and must have been completely familiar with it, so patently upset?

The colonel ordered his men to douse flashlights and they decided to pursue the object across the clearing over which the first night's object had finally disappeared. The tape records him advising them to head 'towards the edge of the clearing' and to 'try to get the star-lite scope' on the UFO.

As they did so, the animals all stopped their noisy cacophony. Halt reported: 'The light is still there and all the barnyard animals have gotten quiet now. I'm through to the clearing about 110 degrees from the site (i.e. east south east). Still getting a reading on the meter (i.e. geiger counter) about two to three clicks.'

More debate followed. One man thought the glow was a few feet off the ground. Halt said he thought it was 'something on the ground. I think it's something very large.'

Were they really being fooled in almost incredible fashion by the lighthouse shining through ground mist or were these trained USAF airmen encountering what they appear to describe – an astonishing UFO?

As they walked across the clearing towards the red object, Halt recorded more detail in a voice beginning to express the awe of the moment: 'We're about a hundred fifty to two hundred yards (137-183 m) from the site. Everything else is just deathly calm. There's no doubt about it, there's some type of strange flashing red light ahead.'

'Sir, it's yellow,' one of his team suggested.

'I saw a yellow tinge in it too,' Halt agreed. **'Weird!'**

Halt's voice now began to falter slightly as he pondered the motion of the object. 'It appears to be moving a little bit this way . . . It's brighter than it has been. It is definitely coming this way . . . Pieces of it are shooting off . . . There's no doubt about it – this is weird!'

Charles Halt has since described in more detail the events that occurred at this stage.

'There was what was like an explosion. Not with any loud noise. Just an explosion of light and it disintegrated and broke up into three to five different objects. Then it was gone. It disappeared.

He adds that until this point he had had a reasonable explanation for everything or could assume one. But now he was confronting a phenomenon which none of his training or logic could accommodate. Halt told me emphatically, 'I knew where the lighthouse was. This thing was not it. I saw the lighthouse as well but I never mentioned it. Why should I? Everybody present knew what that was.'

The deputy commander continued, noting that his usual job was to 'routinely deny this sort of thing and diligently work to debunk them'. But, as he said, 'I had a lot of things going through my mind. Was this something we could contact? Something we could actually touch? Something we could work with, perhaps? I had no idea.'

The US Air Force did not prepare its officers for what to do when face to face with a UFO. But that is what Colonel Charles Halt and his small team of men now confronted. They had gone out there to solve a mystery and, instead, found themselves in the thick of something stranger than they could possibly imagine.

10

THE LIGHT SHOW

ANOTHER TWO HOURS of UFO activity were to follow the close encounter during that Sunday morning, although, unfortunately, the tape recording condenses this into two or three minutes. Presumably Colonel Halt had more to think about than pressing his dictaphone button.

There is considerable debate among the UFO community as to the nature of what was being described during this latter phase of activity. Long-duration sightings of this type are almost always explained in conventional terms – often as some sort of astronomical phenomenon. At least that has been the way of it in all cases that I have researched during my 25 years as an investigator. Of course, what was happening in Rendlesham Forest that night was anything but a normal situation.

It should be recalled that Halt and the other airmen were not the only witnesses to these subsequent events. We have civilian eyewitness testimony from the likes of Gerry Harris and Sarah Richardson during the early hours of that Sunday. As they were both local residents and still felt that the events were very strange, this adds further suggestion to the idea that something truly bizarre was taking place.

Immediately prior to the near silent explosion during which the big UFO had vanished Halt had reported on tape that this object had *'a hollow centre – a dark centre – like the pupil of an eye looking at you, winking. The flashes are so bright through the star-lite scope that it almost burns your eye.'* However, with its disappearance we learn that *'the residual has been removed'* – as the geiger counter operator put it. Halt translated on to the tape that this meant they were now getting only normal background radiation – not the bursts recorded when the UFO was in front of them.

As a result, Halt decided to lead his team across the clearing and head off towards the coast. They were in pursuit of the spot where the UFO had seemed to be. That would, of course, have been in the direction of Orford Ness island – some 4 miles (6 km) away.

In the clearing, although not with Halt or his team, Larry Warren alleges that he saw something quite fantastic follow the silent explosion. He times this as being about 2.30 am.

'It looked like there was a mist or ground fog in the clearing. It glowed very brightly and had the shape of a circle. Suddenly someone called out: "Here it comes!" and a red light appeared in the sky and made a downward arc heading into this fog. The red ball exploded silently into a blinding flash of light, leaving me having to shield my eyes. When I could look at the field again a strange craft was sitting on the ground or just above it.'

Warren describes the object variously (in different interviews) as triangular, arrowhead-shaped or like an aspirin. He says that it had two stubby wings or flaps on the edge and was a strange opaque or pearly white colour that reflected light in a curious way, throwing up rainbow-coloured scintillations that constantly fluctuated. There was a bank of blue lights below it and tiles or boxes across the surface, making it not unlike a space shuttle in appearance.

The strangest feature of all was that the shadows of himself and the other men were cast on to the object in extraordinary fashion, moving out of sync with their actual body movements. It was as if the UFO's surface slowed down time and caused a delay in the registering of their shadows. Was the surrounding energy field that had been described by Burroughs and Penniston two nights before distorting time and space in a visual equivalent of the sound delay introduced during satellite transmissions and making long-range phone conversations so difficult? Perhaps the rainbow light effects occurred because of the energy shifts during this physical process?

Larry Warren reports that more weird things followed when he and several other men were ordered to surround the object. A green light started to move across the surface and had a near hypnotic effect on them. It was then that a shaft of white light poured from underneath and three small beings with large heads floated into view hovering within this. For some years Warren did not recall this missing time during which the men seemed to be in a hypnotic trance.

It was during that (hypnotically retrieved) phase of the experience that Warren claims Gordon Williams – one of several senior officers whom he says were already present – had come forward and seemed to communicate with these alien beings in some non-verbal manner. The young airman also commented that the senior officers appeared more prepared for what was happening than did the junior ranks. Indeed it was as if the younger airmen such as himself were being studied by those officers, keen to judge their reactions to the unfolding drama.

The truly fantastic story told by Warren continues. He adds that one officer tried to 'mount' the UFO like a horse and was carried along by it for several feet as it moved. On his way out of the forest Warren also says he met a startled truck driver who swore that one of the alien beings had passed straight through his cab – floating like a wraith. The driver lunged at this spectre with his foot in blind terror, but only succeeded in cracking the windscreen glass. Other airmen told of balls of light that flew straight through trees as if they were not really there.

These stories – if they are true – imply that the UFO and the aliens were both amazing forms of holographic image, rather than a structured craft or beings. There has been some speculation that Warren is describing some sort of an experiment conducted on the airmen to test their reactions. Was it a fantastic 'living' film show generated by some type of unknown military weapon? Needless to say, most of the witnesses scoff at that suggestion.

It seems difficult, if not impossible, to make this bizarre version of events fully compatible with the more modest accounts by Charles Halt, John Burroughs and the others. While Warren's amazing adventure certainly does share some of the details of their story, it also contains aspects which they have never referred to. It is hard to believe that if aliens really did communicate with a senior figure of the stature of a wing commander in a British forest or, if wraith-like ETs floated through trucks, then the other witnesses would not be aware of that fact. Indeed, the British Government could never have ignored any event that had involved a man as important as Gordon Williams.

However, there are features in Larry Warren's story that are reported by others – not in such graphic detail and not involving aliens – but recognizably similar. It is as if they saw more or less the same things but described them in more restrained terms. Or, as some suggest, but Warren emphatically denies, is his story a pastiche of the complex range of accounts given by various witnesses?

Either way, truly remarkable events took place in those woods that night. Indeed, as John Burroughs put it to me: 'It is impossible to find the words to adequately describe what I experienced . I doubt that the words even exist. I have no way of understanding what I witnessed and cannot to this day decide if it was some sort of intelligence with magical properties or some quite fantastic natural phenomenon. I only know that it was not the lighthouse. No way.'

Meanwhile, Halt and his team were on their way towards the coast, pausing to record occasional messages into the tape machine and still looking for the vanished UFO. From their new vantage point, the Orford Ness lighthouse was much more readily visible as there was less tree cover.

'We've passed the farmer's house and crossed into the next field and now we have multiple sightings of up to five lights with similar-shaped orbits. Seemingly steady now, rather than pulsating or glowing with red flashes.' They had at this point 'just crossed the creek' and were now well past the rim of the forest at a site known as Capel Green.

Of these newly observed lights Halt has since offered a better description. To me they sound rather like stars and the sceptics have predictably argued that this is precisely what they were. On the other hand, they do match what Sarah Richardson says she saw that night from her mother's house.

'We were right in the farmer's field looking about and somebody noticed these objects in the sky. When we looked to the north about ten degrees off the horizon there were two large objects – looked almost like the moon, only not as large. They were round and as we watched they changed shape from round to elliptical. They did it simultaneously which was quite puzzling. It was almost like an eclipse.'

About the same time, another of the men saw an object in the south. This was moving about as were the ones to the north. Indeed, Halt describes the lights as being engaged in a 'grid search – sharp angular movements, pulling very high Gs'.

Again, as a UFO investigator, I have heard this often before when a witness is describing a star. The movement is not, in fact, exhibited by the star, although it appears to be. It results from a phenomenon known as autokinesis. The jerking motion of the eyeballs when straining to see lights against a dark sky moves the image on the retina. The brain assumes that it is the object – not the eye – that is moving as this is how it is used to decoding data – and a convincing optical illusion follows. It has nothing to do with intelligence or expertise. All human beings experience the autokinetic effect.

I am not stating with assurance that this is what happened here. The fact is that many witnesses reported the effects that night and things did become stranger as time progressed. There is also the independent testimony of the civilians to take into account. However, I do not think we can afford to ignore the possible effects of autokinesis. This is especially true of the objects to the north, which simply behaved like stars throughout the encounter in my estimation.

Halt reports that twice he called the relay site by radio and asked them to contact Eastern Radar at RAF Watton to see if they had these objects on screen. On both occasions Watton said they had nothing anomalous in view – which they would not have done if the objects were stars. The timing of these calls (from Halt's description and time checks on the tape) fits well with Watton's written statement that they were contacted by Bentwaters to report a UFO at 3.25 am on 28 December 1980.

These two star-like lights stayed in the north for at least another hour. When Halt and his men went back to the base they were still there. All of this reinforces my opinion that these were simply stars being distorted by ice crystals in the sky and the involvement of autokinesis. Vega was very bright in the north at the time and there were other candidates for the second star. Nothing in Halt's testimony about these two particular objects contradicts what I have seen from other sightings that did reliably turn out to be stars. The credibility of the witness in no way affects human capacity for false interpretation. It happens all of the time, even with highly trained observers.

The object seen by these airmen to the south is a different matter, however. This now began to project streamers towards the ground. As Halt phrased it : 'These were beams of light – like lasers.'

On the tape Halt tells of these various experiences as follows. 'Three oh five (3.05 am) we see strange strobe-like flashes – very sporadic, but there's definitely something out there – some kind of phenomenon . . . At about ten degrees horizon directly north we've got two strange objects. Half-moon-shaped, dancing about with coloured lights on them. Appears to be about five or ten miles out (8 or 16 km) – maybe less. The half moons have now turned into full circles – as if there was an ellipse, er, an eclipse, there for a minute or two.'

Then came the sighting to the south: 'Zero three fifteen (3.15 am) – now we've got an object about ten degrees directly south . . . but the ones to the north are moving away from us.'

Suddenly the geiger counter operator yelled in his southern tones: 'It's moving out fast!'

He was joined by another airman adding, 'This one on the right's heading away too.'

Halt was concurring with their remarks when fate intervened and his voice and those of his men clearly began to register the tension of the moment.

'Mmm – they're both heading north . . . Hey! . . . Here he comes from the south. He's coming towards us now . . . Now we observe what appears to be a beam coming down towards the ground – **this is unreal!'**

The stunned shock in that last sentence is unmistakable. It is not difficult to imagine how it must have been for those men, some way from civilization, alone in a coastal field, seeing things all around them which they believed to be UFOs. How would you react?

Halt tells us that he was truly concerned at this point. 'I wondered if this was a friendly probe or a weapon? Were they searching for something? At this stage my scepticism had definitely disappeared. I was really in awe.'

The colonel explained that the object from the south came really close and the beam of light struck the ground at the feet of his party some 5 yd (4.5 m) away. It was about 12 in (30 cm) in diameter and lasted for about five seconds. When it hit the ground it did so instantly and then it vanished instantly as well. All the colonel's scepticism drained away at this point.

Halt recalls hearing radio chatter as the beam struck the ground nearby. Nobody knew what these 'lasers' were but they were apparently falling all over the forest and being widely observed. Some were coming down on to the base itself. Many people saw this happen, Halt insists.

'I didn't know what was coming next,' he points out sombrely. 'I expected the worst.'

But the light just went out like a switch being thrown.

John Burroughs was one of the many who saw these beams from his position in the forest. He describes what occurred in terms that are interestingly similar to parts of Larry Warren's story.

'All of a sudden a blue light streaked out of the sky and went past us. It shot through the open window of our truck – going off into the distance. Then the light-alls went out. There was no noise. It just went by us in a blur.'

John told me that these lights were darting about the forest and passing straight through trees and metal as if they were transparent. Yet a blast of cold air struck as the light shot past their truck, indicating that it had physical substance and that air was rushing in to plug the gap.

Adrian Bustinza's account of this episode is noteworthy and perhaps the closest to that offered by Larry Warren. The security police sergeant tells of 'a carpet of yellow mist on the ground or just off it'. He saw this replaced by an object 'dark silver but with rainbow-coloured lights on it. I could not tell if it was breaking light up like a prism or these were the actual colours of the light.'

We know that Warren and Bustinza talked to one another after the encounters. So it may not be surprising that their stories are the most well matched. This is not to infer that they colluded. UFOlogists quickly learn that witnesses who discuss their sightings with one another afterwards tend to reinforce each other's stories subconsciously. Precisely the same thing occurs with witnesses to traffic accidents or crimes.

Bustinza also supports another aspects of Warren's story – the strange moving balls of light that defied physics; that photographic evidence was being captured by base personnel; and that British military were out there in the forest as well that night (possibly from RAF Bawdsey) – something the MoD vehemently deny.

Warren even says that a USAF film crew was recording everything that happened – as if they had been expecting it to take place. This is one reason why some people suggest that the whole scenario was a 'set up' by some secret service operation; that the UFO encounters were 'created' by some kind of weapon (e.g. a holographic or laser projection system) and the cameras were used to record the reaction of the men who were confronted with this unexpected terror.

Was such a thing possible? The technology seems remarkably advanced for 1980 given that (so far as is known) we are not capable of doing anything like it even today. If it was true, however, then one can well understand why these USAF men might have been used as guinea pigs. Unleashed upon unsuspecting soldiers in a jungle warfare situation, such a weapon would be very powerful. You might be able to get the enemy to flee without firing a single shot.

It has been said that no such test would ever happen on 'foreign soil', as Britain was to the Americans, of course. Just as the USA did with its own troops in the 1950s when testing exposure to atom bomb radiation, you would surely test dirty tricks in your own backyard.

However, to make an effective evaluation of a projection weapon such as is being suggested here, you could not operate miles from anywhere. You would have to simulate conditions where it might be used in warfare by duping your own troops as part of the evaluation exercise. It might even be safer in a country such as Britain where UFOs are treated with official and media scepticism (indeed, this was even more true in 1980). The odds must have been good that the light show would not have been taken seriously even if news of it leaked out. That might not have been so easy had the forest been in Pennsylvania.

Woodbridge and Watergate might both start with the letter 'W' but there would be less chance of a political scandal erupting if a secret test went wrong and it was staged 3,000 miles (4,800 km) away from US soil. Such a test would have to be kept secret, even from the more senior officers who were innocently brought into play. Their responses might well have been part of the whole test procedure.

There is much about this case that actually makes sense in the light of this sort of theory. The spreading of 'alien contact' stories – to the radar staff at Watton and to UFO investigators who would be sure to garner maximum attention – seems absurd *unless* some secret organization (such as the NSA) wanted that wild idea to get promoted to 'account' for the experiences which they might expect would leak out. The scale of the events that night meant they could not be covered up but such an absurdity as base commanders chatting with little aliens would ensure that nobody who might be a budding Woodward or Bernstein would dig too deep. The whole thing would be written off as the ravings of a few deluded squaddies.

Besides which, an 'alien contact' may have been precisely what the weapon was designed to project in front of these men. The idea could have been to simulate its effects.

Needless to say there are problems. All on base – even Halt – would have had to be duped. As trained, experienced officers, could they be so successfully fooled?

The Halt tape contains only two brief comments after the light beams are seen to be fired towards the ground. These describe how the team headed back towards the base leaving the lights in the north still visible. The time check is given as *'zero four hundred'* (4 am).

Halt explains why the mission was then aborted. 'Most of us had been up since five or six the previous day and were quite tired. We had managed to fall in the water on the way out across the field and got wet. It was very cold – about thirty-eight degrees – and the wind was blowing hard. These objects (in the north) seemed to persist and they would not go away. We decided it was time to go back to the base.'

Back at the base, the first traces of dawn were appearing on the eastern horizon and Colonel Halt notes that 'the objects were still in the sky – however, it was getting light and they were getting faint.'

I suspect that this is the final clue that demonstrates that these star-like lights to the north were, indeed, just stars. As daylight paints the sky they become more difficult, and finally impossible, to see.

It is unlikely that this opinion will be well received by the witnesses. I offer it as my judgement of this phase of the evidence, based on years of experience in other UFO cases. I think it is probably correct, but I could not prove it to be so.

Of course, even if the men did misperceive some stars that night, much of their other testimony is a lot more difficult to explain away.

Something truly strange clearly did occur earlier in the night (as well as on the night of 25/26 December) and the mistaken evaluation of a few bright stars is perfectly understandable under the torturous conditions that they faced in that forest.

Unfortunately, such an easy diagnosis cannot account for the majority of this case. It remains truly baffling and one of the most intriguing close encounters of all time.

11

CLAMP DOWN

I T IS NOT DIFFICULT to imagine the problems faced by the senior staff at Bentwaters and Woodbridge after the events of that startling weekend.

Many military witnesses had seen something flying about. It was the talk of the base. There was little hope of containment, but there must have been some concern as to what might happen if the story made it into the press.

'USAF officers chase UFOs through woods.' 'NATO base attacked by alien lightbeams.' 'Spaceships irradiate Ipswich.' The headline writers could have a field day and the potential for a PR disaster was huge, especially at a time when the USAF were struggling with peace campaign demonstrators desperate to prevent nuclear cruise missiles being brought into East Anglia.

As the senior officer involved in the case, Colonel Charles Halt took the responsibility to follow through the investigation. He had to balance his desire to report the matter and get to the bottom of what had happened with the need to follow procedure, clamp down and ensure that the story did not appear in all the tabloids on Monday morning.

Of course, the case was already out of Halt's hands as Sunday, 28 December, dawned. His base commander, Conrad, knew all about it. Chances are that other high-ranking officers in the USAF throughout Europe did so as well. The reports to Eastern Radar had probably alerted the British MoD. All sorts of wheels would be in motion, not necessarily any of them known to Charles Halt.

According to a Bentwaters officer who was not an eye-witness but who did attend the Monday meeting with senior base staff, some confusion followed as to what should happen next. Gordon Williams ordered that no report be made to the base public relations office. It was decided that the story could get out of hand and it was wisest to say nothing at all in public.

It is hard not to sympathize with that decision. The USAF had no real idea how to cope with this sort of situation. Halt himself says that he had no written guidelines to follow. Officially the USAF Project Blue Book had been shut down in 1969 and there was now no policy for dealing with UFO sightings at all. Everyone also knew that UFO witnesses were frequently ridiculed, particularly by the British tabloid press. Silence may well have seemed the only sane option.

Halt was properly concerned about his future career prospects and was thankful when he was taken seriously by his immediate superiors. As he points out, he soon got promotion and his security clearance remained intact – things that would never have happened if there had been doubts about his mental state or capability.

Even so, if it became publicly known that half the staff at this NATO base had chased UFOs, it could have had a serious effect on public attitudes towards the presence of the USAF. Plans to bring Cruise missiles on to UK soil were afoot and were set to create much controversy. UFOs were an extra headache nobody wanted. One can imagine the questions that would have been asked by politicians if it were suspected that the men who had the ability to detonate atom bombs above Britain believed in little green men and spent nights chasing starships.

In addition, there was the problem of jurisdiction. Although Conrad had made an aborted attempt to get the British police involved (and their scepticism must have shown further danger signs) the sightings had, none the less, occurred on land outside the province of the USAF.

Indeed, on the second night, Halt and his men had wandered a mile or two from base property across Forestry Commission land, several farmers' fields and more. They were very likely trespassing in the process. Without the permission of the MoD (which they presumably did not have) there were some doubts as to the ethics, or even the legality, of what Bentwaters had got up to in pursuit of these UFOs, although few would probably challenge the right of these men to investigate what was happening.

Even so, the official line, that Halt and his team were 'off duty', was to be expressed by the USAF to try to cover that dilemma. It was hardly true, but even the MoD later reiterated that same point like a litany. Halt's and the others mens' stories insist they were out there under orders to solve the UFO mystery with expensive equipment that must have been requisitioned from the USAF and could not just be taken out on a pleasure trip. They were, at least tacitly, 'on duty' as well as being clearly on British soil when these events took place. This must have been a serious complication.

Indeed, I have been told by sources within both British and American Government agencies that there was a degree of conflict between the two countries as to who should take on the task of damage limitation. Perhaps each side left it to the other, which might explain why, officially, very little seems to have taken place. One MoD source told me that the British Government felt that the Americans had overstepped their responsibility by acting without MoD involvement. As this person told me, in confidence: 'What I don't think the Americans had figured was that they were just pursuing this thing in the dark, without any recognition of what it might be. They might have been chasing a terrorist attack or an attempt by some foreign power at espionage. By taking the matter into their own hands they circumvented the NATO rules. Rules mean a great deal to the MoD, even when UFOs are involved!'

Charles Halt paints a rather different picture. He says, 'When I got back to the base I reported to my superiors who were puzzled as to what to do. Nobody really knew for sure. They took it under advisement for a few days. A decision was finally reached that we should turn this over to the MoD since it was really their territory.'

This seems fair enough, in so far as it goes.

Halt approached Squadron Leader Donald Moreland, who served as the base liaison officer with the MoD. Technically, he was a sort of caretaker, in charge of the base for Whitehall, who had leased it to the Americans as part of their NATO defensive duties. He was there to act as a go-between on policy matters but there were no other British staff on Bentwaters or Woodbridge. The entire complement and make-up of the twin bases was American. Moreland – especially in a situation such as this – was responsible for any negotiations that the USAF might require with their 'landlords'. However, he was also rather isolated – miles from London and all on his own. As reported, Moreland had already been in touch with his bosses in London about the affair – who in any event were aware of the alleged radar trackings via other sources.

Of course, reports also went from Halt to higher levels of the USAF – at first in the UK (via the headquarters in Mildenhall) and then to Europe (via the offices at Ramstein Air Force base in Germany). However, nothing filtered back from anyone above him. Halt expected to be called in for interviews to answer awkward questions, to be grilled and debriefed. Mentally, he psyched himself up to defend his own credibility and to present the hard evidence (tape, samples, plaster casts and films). What he did not expect was to be totally ignored. Nobody came back to him at all.

In fact, it was years later, after the case became public knowledge, that Halt was first asked to tell his story to a high-ranking USAF official in Washington. Even then no follow up to that meeting occurred. This official disinterest was almost as mysterious to the colonel as the UFO sightings themselves, although a similar dilemma has been widely noted by senior USAF and RAF witnesses in other cases. As long ago as September 1947, a US Army Air Force memo puzzles over this lack of 'topside' enquiries and speculates whether it means that the US Government was behind the sightings in the first place. In other words, were UFOs secret USAF devices or military activity?

Why else would such apathy occur? Is it because the powers-that-be are too embarrassed to study UFO reports made by their own officers? Is it tactically more simple to sweep them under the rug and accept the minor irritation of UFOlogists crying cover-up? Naturally, UFO buffs perceive this lack of action as being absurd and, understandably, assume that some steps *must* have been taken and the official denial is thus a lie. They assume some secret investigation had to be mounted.

But then who takes UFOlogists seriously except themselves? Such cries of 'cover-up' appear like paranoia. Or do the authorities know the truth without needing to investigate cases? If there was a secret experiment and Halt and his team were guinea pigs, then nobody would tell them about it, would they? You and I stand even less chance of being told the truth.

While the powers-that-be prevaricated, the news clamp down was facing more than a few difficulties. On Monday, 29 December the USAF intelligence staff, presumably responding to Halt's report, visited Watton to take away the radar film, giving them the most fantastic version of events in explanation. This was, as you will now see, like a combination of the credible parts from the stories of Halt, Burroughs and the rest (including the officers going out there from a base party), plus the more extreme claims that have only ever been supported in open public debate by Larry Warren (such as the supposed communication with aliens involving the wing commander).

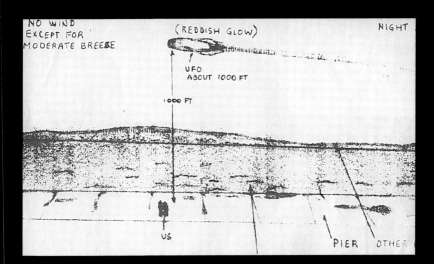

Sketch of the 'Cosmos' sighting at
Paco de Arcos, 25 December 1980.

Jenny Randles plans a 'Strange
But True?' television programme
on UFOs at the window area site
in the Pennine Hills, where the
Walsden close encounter took

Document 1: (*above*)
Document released under US Freedom of Information Act, showing existence of Project Moon Dust, an operation which exists to respond to any crash of space debris. According to Clifford Stone this indicates the link with UFOs.

Document 2: (*above*) One of the 'UFO files' released by the MoD in early 1983 as a 'token of faith', instead of the requested file on Rendlesham Forest, describing a sighting on 19 January 1983. The poor nature of data is indicative of the generally limited investigations carried out by the MoD's publicly admitted UFO team 'Air Staff 2A'.

Document 3: (*left*) Extract from Hansard, October 1983, showing questions asked about Rendlesham in the House of Commons by Major Sir Patrick Wall MP, and the reply from the armed forces minister John Stanley.

Document 4: (*right*) Letter from the MoD to Jenny Randles in April 1983, in which the reality of the sightings in Rendlesham Forest is admitted for the first time. The letter also confirms that the sightings remained unexplained.

MINISTRY OF DEFENCE
Main Building Whitehall London SW1A 2HB   Defence Secretariat Division 8
Telephone 01-218
01-218 9000   (Direct Dialing)
(Switchboard)

Miss J Randles

Somerville
Wallasey
Wirral

Your reference

Our reference
D/DS8/10/209
Date
13 April 1983

Dear Miss Randles,

Thank you for your recent correspondence on the subject of UFOs.

As regards your offer to summarise the reports held by this Department there really is very little to summarise. I attach a copy of a blank report form showing the type of information we require together with a couple of examples of completed reports (with the name and address of the informant deleted for reasons of confidentiality). I am sure you will agree that, although we hold a large number of reports, each one is indeed very brief.

Turning now to your interest in the sighting at RAF Woodbridge in December 1980 I can confirm that USAF personnel did see unusual lights outside the boundary fence early in the morning of 27 December 1980 but no explanation for the occurrence was ever forthcoming. There is however, no question of the account being a cover-up for a crashed aircraft or testing of secret devices as you suggest, nor was there any contact with "alien beings".

I understand that an article on the Woodbridge sighting has been published in the magazine "OMNI" (Vol 5 No.6) in which you may be interested.

Yours sincerely

P J Titchmarsh

P J TITCHMARSH (Mrs)

DEPARTMENT OF THE AIR FORCE
HEADQUARTERS 81ST COMBAT SUPPORT GROUP (USAFE)
APO NEW YORK 09755

13 Jan 81

TO   CD

SUBJECT: Unexplained Lights

TO: RAF/CC

1. Early in the morning of 27 Dec 80 (approximately 0300L), two USAF security police patrolmen saw unusual lights outside the back gate at RAF Woodbridge. Thinking an aircraft might have crashed or been forced down, they called for permission to go outside the gate to investigate. The on-duty flight chief responded and allowed three patrolmen to proceed on foot. The individuals reported seeing a strange glowing object in the forest. The object was described as being metallic in appearance and triangular in shape, approximately two to three meters across the base and approximately two meters high. It illuminated the entire forest with a white light. The object itself had a pulsing red light on top and a bank(s) of blue lights underneath. The object was hovering or on legs. As the patrolmen approached the object, it maneuvered through the trees and disappeared. At this time the animals on a nearby farm went into a frenzy. The object was briefly sighted approximately an hour later near the back gate.

2. The next day, three depressions 1 1/2" deep and 7" in diameter were found where the object had been sighted on the ground. The following night (29 Dec 80) the area was checked for radiation. Beta/gamma readings of 0.1 milliroentgens were recorded with peak readings in the three depressions and near the center of the triangle formed by the depressions. A nearby tree had moderate (.05-.07) readings on the side of the tree toward the depressions.

3. Later in the night a red sun-like light was seen through the trees. It moved about and pulsed. At one point it appeared to throw off glowing particles and then broke into five separate white objects and then disappeared. Immediately thereafter, three star-like objects were noticed in the sky, two objects to the north and one to the south, all of which were about 10° off the horizon. The objects moved rapidly in sharp angular movements and displayed red, green and blue lights. The objects to the north appeared to be elliptical through an 8-12 power lens. They then turned to full circles. The objects to the north remained in the sky for an hour or more. The object to the south was visible for two or three hours and beamed down a stream of light from time to time. Numerous individuals, including the undersigned, witnessed the activities in paragraphs 2 and 3.

CHARLES I. HALT, Lt Col, USAF
Deputy Base Commander

Document 5: (*left*) The infamous 'Halt Memo' submitted to the British Government in January 1981. This remained confidential for two and a half years, and was finally released in June 1983 under the US Freedom of Information Act. It was published four months later, despite risks of breaching the Official Secrets Act, after Jenny Randles had taken the document to the MoD.

FOR TRANSCRIPTIONS
SEE PAGES 210-14

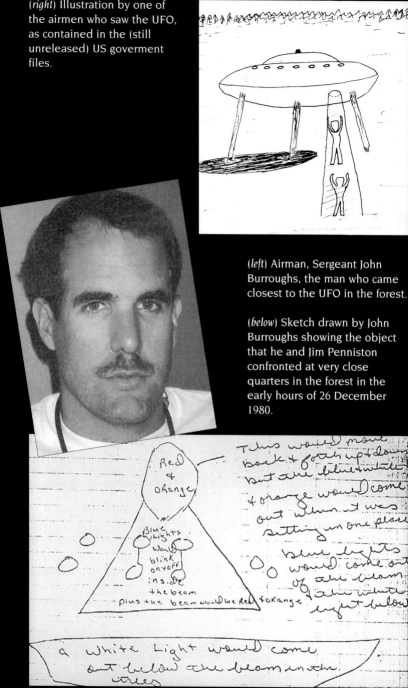

(*right*) Illustration by one of the airmen who saw the UFO, as contained in the (still unreleased) US goverment files.

(*left*) Airman, Sergeant John Burroughs, the man who came closest to the UFO in the forest.

(*below*) Sketch drawn by John Burroughs showing the object that he and Jim Penniston confronted at very close quarters in the forest in the early hours of 26 December 1980.

(*above*) Gordon Levett's house at Sudbourne. The UFO hovered over the house before crashing into Rendlesham Forest immediately behind the house. Gordon and his dog were standing in the garden when the radiation struck.

(*right*) Witness, Gordon Levett.

FOR TRANSCRIPTIONS
SEE PAGES 215-7

Document 6: (*left*) Sketch map by Steve Roberts describing the directions to the landing site. This was given to Brenda Butler in January 1981. The confusing directions do not lead from the gate itself, but from the forestry commission access road that passes by the gate and the runway's end.

Document 7: (*right*) File from the Public Record Office at Kew, showing the starting point of the British government's study into UFOs. WSC stands for Winston Churchill, the then Prime Minister.

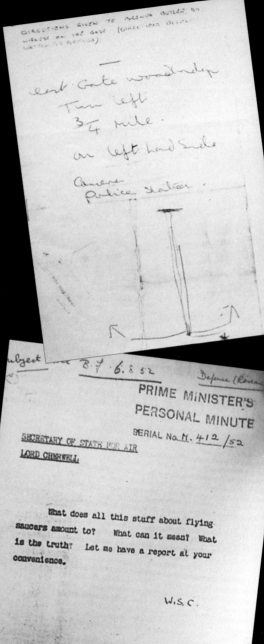

PRIME MINISTER'S
PERSONAL MINUTE

SERIAL No. M. 412 /52

SECRETARY OF STATE FOR AIR
LORD CHERWELL

What does all this stuff about flying saucers amount to? What can it mean? What is the truth? Let me have a report at your convenience.

W. S. C.

28 July 1952

Document 8: (*right*)
One of the replies received by Liberal Democrat MP, David Alton, from the Under Secretary for the Armed Forces, Lord Trefgarre, acting as deputy for Minister of Defence, Michael Heseltine. Alton was acting on data supplied by Jenny Randles.

MINISTRY OF DEFENCE
MAIN BUILDING WHITEHALL LONDON SW1A 2HB
Telephone 01-218 (Direct Dialling)
01-218 9000 (Switchboard)

PARLIAMENTARY UNDER SECRETARY OF STATE
FOR THE ARMED FORCES

D/US of S(AF)/DGT 5173

19 March 1985

Dear Mr Alton,

Thank you for your letter of 21 February with the enclosed from Ms Jenny Randles of Birchwood, Warrington.

I should first of all point out that the sole interest of the Ministry of Defence in reported sightings of Unidentified Flying Objects (UFOs) is to establish whether they have any bearing on the defence of the country.

There is no organisation in the Ministry of Defence appointed solely for the purpose of studying UFOs, and no staff are employed on the subject full time. The reports we receive are referred to the staff in the Department who are responsible for the air defence of the United Kingdom, and they examine the reports as part of their normal duties. Unless there are defence implications we do not attempt to identify sightings and we cannot inform observers of the probable identity of the object seen. The Department could not justify the expenditure of public funds on investigations which go beyond the pure defence interests.

The only information we have on the alleged "UFO sighting" at Rendlesham Forest in December 1980 is the report by Colonel Charles Halt, of the United States Air Force, which Ms Randles mentions in her letter. We are satisfied that the events described are of no defence significance. I can assure you that there is no question of attempting to cover up any incident or mishap, nor are we attempting in any way to obscure the truth.

I am also enclosing with this copies of 2 Parliamentary Questions, one of which is that put down by Sir Patrick Wall and which Ms Randles also mentions.

Yours sincerely,

Lord Trefgarne

From: N G Pope, Secretariat(Air Staff)2a, Room 8245

MINISTRY OF DEFENCE
Main Building Whitehall London SW1A 2HB
Telephone (Direct Dialling) 071-218-2140
(Switchboard) 071-218-9000
(Fax) 071-218-

Ms J Randles
7 Heathbank Road
Cheadle Heath
Stockport
Cheshire
SK3 0UP

Your reference

Our reference
D/Sec(AS)12/3
Date
1 November 1993

Dear Jenny,

Thank you for your letter dated 28 October, and for sending a copy of "Northern UFO News", which I found very interesting.

I agree that many of the UFO sightings on 30/31 March were probably generated by people having witnessed the re-entry of Cosmos 2238, although there would appear to be some reports that might not be explained in this way.

I agree that most of the recent sightings in the Bristol area seem to have been generated by Venus. I believe that there was also a display of lasers or searchlights that might explain other sightings.

You mentioned two other specific sightings, and asked whether we have any reports that might tie-in; we have no such reports, although I seem to recall that a researcher mentioned a case to me recently which involved a UFO being seen on a security camera.

I have seen the video of the Lockerbie sighting, but it is difficult to come to any firm conclusions. While lights can clearly be seen, it was dark at the time, and there were no other visible features that might have given an indication of the size, speed and distance of the objects filmed.

Finally, I was delighted to hear that "Tony B" is recovering. I think that the handling of this case shows the sort of positive result that can come from cooperation between ourselves and serious UFO researchers.

Yours sincerely,

Nick Pope

Document 9: (*left*)
Correspondence between Jenny Randles and Nick Pope in 1993, during Pope's tenure at Air Staff 2A. Pope voluntarily worked with UFOlogists, and here it is evident that Pope (an MoD representative) willingly cooperated with Randles (then BUFORA Director of Investigations). Of particular interest are the views expressed by Pope on the Cosmos 2238 sightings. (See pages 32–3)

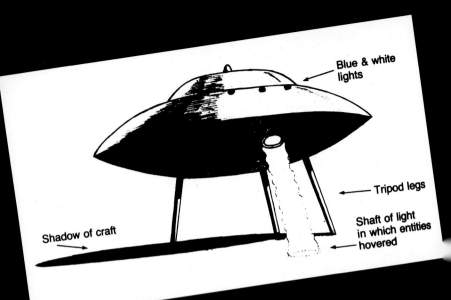

Blue & white lights

Tripod legs

Shaft of light in which entities hovered

Shadow of craft

Sketch of the UFO seen in the forest by original witness Steve Roberts

The UFO as drawn by airman Larry Warren.

On that Monday, Bentwaters also had to contend with the first report from the mysterious farmer who claimed his cattle had been disturbed by an exploding white light and sent scurrying into the road where they were then hit by a taxi. At first, the base wisely sent him packing with the truth; that none of their aircraft were flying that night. However, he soon came to hear the UFO stories from local villagers. So he was back pestering the USAF and demanding compensation.

Although there has never been official verification by the USAF that any money was paid, we were told by local farmers that he was compensated and had used the sum to pack up and ship out. Our search for this farmer – whose name was Higgins – took us three years. We eventually traced him several hundred miles from Suffolk.

Yes, he advised, he *was* finally paid something after he told the USAF that if one of their aircraft did not spook his cows then it must have been the UFO that people were talking about. That was still the responsibility of the USAF as they were supposed to be defending local citizens. Higgins refused to tell us how much he was paid, wryly adding, 'Whatever it were, it weren't enough.'

We can never know if, as some suspect, this man's silence was bought by the US Government, especially as he genuinely believes he was due money because the USAF were there to protect his cows from big white lights. Even so, his disappearance from the area at the crucial time must have made life a lot easier and ensured that the story never made it into the local press.

Undoubtedly, many rumours were flying around the base as the new week began, no doubt becoming ever more fantastic each time they were reported to another airman and he decided to tell someone else over a few drinks. It is fascinating to look at the various anonymous sources who contacted Brenda Butler and Dot Street during the first two or three months, and see which of them gave an accurate version of the case. There were major discrepancies.

Looking back now at the testimony of James Archer (aka Jim Penniston?) as told in *Sky Crash*, it is clear that he *was* a witness. His testimony has very little in it that is not now an accepted part of the storyline, distilled from the accounts of all those who have gone public.

Much more of a problem is the man to whom Brenda gave the pseudonym 'Steve Roberts' – her long-time friend from the base whom she had come to know via the local country and western scene. He was the first USAF witness ever to talk to a UFOlogist – approaching Brenda as early as Friday, 2 January 1981, just a week after the sighting and 11 days before Moreland had even come back to Halt with advice about how to report the matter to the MoD.

Roberts claimed to be a security police officer and told his story as if he were one of the three men involved in the first night's events. However, he was definitely not John Burroughs or Jim Penniston and I very much doubt he was the third man, Kavanasac. I know Roberts's real name (or the real name he gave to us) and it has never been recognised by any of the witnesses who were indisputably a part of this case. Roberts would never talk to me, even though he stayed on base for some years after the sighting – itself an unusual fact as most of the witnesses were soon split up and packed off to bases all over the world. So I cannot personally judge his evidence, but have to say that I perceive serious problems with his testimony.

The story that Steve Roberts told Brenda Butler, and which first alerted us to the existence of the case, was accurate in some details but features the more dramatic version – of the aliens floating under a disc-shaped craft, suspended in a light beam and communicating with Gordon Williams via sign language – very similar to many aspects of what Larry Warren later had to tell us. Roberts also alleged that the UFO was under guard by the USAF while aliens repaired their craft, and even inferred that the US Government had been expecting this extraterrestrial arrival.

The way in which Steve Roberts's story was casually fed out to Brenda has always worried me. Indeed, there was an interesting call from another anonymous airman who somehow knew that Roberts had talked to us. He insisted that this man was not involved and that the more fantastic elements of his story – e.g. the aliens and the contact with Gordon Williams – were deliberate inventions to make us look foolish. Other parts were real, he said, but the absurdities were constructed to make the case seem too ridiculous for the cautious UFO community in Britain to make any proper investigation. The more sober truth would then get lost in the mess and nobody would follow through. Halt told me that he believes he knows the identity of Steve Roberts. If correct in his assumption, he argues, this man worked for the public affairs office on base. Halt suggests that his story of involvement in the case was untrue.

Whether this was information, disinformation or a downright lie, that caller was correct in his assessment. Until the release of the Halt memo in June 1983 nobody in the British UFO community believed a word that Brenda, Dot or I told them about the case. They all thought we were wasting our time chasing a fantasy. The arrival of that memo brought them in line very fast.

This mysterious phone call from the base went on to provide this particular airman's own version of the story and it was virtually identical to the consistent accounts from people like Burroughs, Penniston and Halt, so there are grounds for suspecting that he might have been telling the truth.

Of course, back in 1981, without a single USAF witness yet going on the record, sorting out this confusion was well nigh impossible, so his story was just one further tall tale. Who was really providing genuine eye-witness testimony without breaching USAF security? Who was relaying stories they had heard on base and claiming some personal association when they had none at all? Who was making up wild tales to see if they could string along a bunch of gullible UFO nuts?

The book *Sky Crash* shows this confusion all too well, although, now that we have a larger set of stories from reliable witnesses, it is easier to spot the rogue testimony and make a fair guess as to who was misleading us within its pages. Indeed, John Burroughs had never read it when we first met in 1989. He told me others had led him to assume it was nonsense. That night in Phoenix he read it through and told me: 'It's all in there. Parts of it are way out. Parts of it are remarkably accurate. You just have to know which right bits to pull together.'

Into which category does the evidence of Steve Roberts fit? It would be simple to conclude that he was making things up – and I certainly have very serious doubts that he was a witness. However, there was something he did do which gives me cause to ponder.

Roberts knew the case well from long before any version of it was published for him to copy. Despite the elements in his story which do not fit, he reported much that we now know was a reality. Moreover, he drew a sketch map directing us to the site before anybody else and that map was accurate. At least it led us to the site which everyone now accepts as the first night's 'landing point'. On the other hand, we should remember that false traces were reputedly laid in the woods. Can we be sure we were directed to the right place?

Possibly the most significant thing that Steve Roberts did was to 'prove himself' when I think he suspected that doubts might be growing in our minds about his status. To this end, he gave Brenda a drawing of the UFO in the forest. It was on the back of a photocopy of a document that he told us he had sneaked from the intelligence files on base to prove he really had access to security data. Halt told me, 'I'd love to know how he got that file out to you'. (See document on page 215).

That photocopied document was a letter that had not been made public, even under the US Freedom of Information Act. It was dated 1 September 1977 and was sent by Colonel Charles Senn of the USAF community relations division of the Office of Information in Washington. It was addressed to a retired USAF officer working for NASA, one Lieutenant General Duward Crow.

At the time President Carter was attempting to get NASA to take on a public investigation into UFOs, for which he was offering the space administration major funds. He was doing so partly to fulfil a brave election pledge made in 1976, that he would take action on UFOs if he became president. Carter had made such a daring promise because he had once made a UFO sighting. Frankly, Carter's UFO was almost certainly explicable as a bright planet seen through unusual atmospheric haze but it had obviously been influential in regards to his interest in the subject.

In the explosive letter that Steve Roberts sent to us, Colonel Senn tells General Crow: 'I sincerely hope you are successful in preventing a reopening of UFO investigations.'

This begs many questions. Why would a senior USAF officer want to interfere in NASA's decision whether or not to make an independent study of UFOs – as requested of them by no less a man than the president? None the less, soon after the Senn letter was written, NASA risked Carter's wrath by turning down his plea. The plan for an official UFO programme at NASA has never been revived. And Carter's promise to do something about the UFO matter died with that decision.

Regardless of the real truth about Steve Roberts, this leaked document helped to establish his good faith with Brenda, Dot and me and we did not seriously challenge his testimony for a good while. Indeed, it was to be some years later – when the more sedate and consistent reports came to light from the other military witnesses – that his story appeared at significant odds with what others were insisting was the truth.

Was Steve Roberts acting on behalf of an intelligence agency trying to spread disinformation through UFO contacts? Had he simply heard what others claimed had happened and pretended that he was involved? Or was he, like Larry Warren, witness to these more fantastic events which really did occur but were not experienced by Halt, Burroughs, Penniston and the others?

Certainly, the similarities between Roberts's story and the one fed out to the radar staff at Watton are fascinating. Of course, the more fantastic features are the very ones that have tended to be associated with this case by the media. But are they the truth or a distraction? And if the latter, who fed them out and why? It would be a huge risk to draw such attention to the case if what they really wanted to do was to stop people taking it seriously.

Ralph Noyes, a former senior figure in the British MoD, who has studied this case, told me assuredly that this ploy would never be attempted by any intelligence service. You do not hide a truth by telling people an exaggerated version of reality. He is supported by Nick Pope, the man who ran the MoD's UFO section between 1991 and 1994 and created a massive public image for himself when he went public in 1996. Pope told me that these stories about contact cannot have been disinformation, but he could not say why the other witnesses so strongly deny them.

So, are we to believe that the Steve Roberts and Larry Warren claims are real? Are the other witnesses hiding the fact that the wing commander *did* contact extraterrestrials in a Suffolk forest?

The problems in sorting out this evidence are considerable. However, regardless of the status of the Steve Roberts story, we have solid evidence that the intelligence services were involved in this case immediately after it happened, but outside of the knowledge of its witnesses – Colonel Halt included.

John Burroughs told me that on the first few days after that weekend, strange military activity was underway at Bentwaters. 'Odd things were happening, in the woods as well as on the base flight line. An airplane came in late at night which was far from routine – especially at that time of year. Helicopters were flying out into the woods, hovering over the suspected landing site. The transporter aircraft made me suspicious because it was parked in an area on base not normally used for such purposes and there was strange activity going on there. Things were being loaded and unloaded from the plane.'

He was not alone in his concern. Jim Penniston also noticed peculiar activity, lasting from the Sunday after the encounter for a few days into that week. 'There were several unscheduled flights that were coming in. They were C 141 types. We were briefed that we were supposed to ignore the activity on the Woodbridge side of the base.'

Penniston says that the flights puzzled him and he began to suspect that they were connected with the UFO landings. He approached a superior officer and was told to keep the matter quiet and not to discuss it any further.

Halt is reluctant to discuss any thought about a cover-up, saying that he was party to none on the base. Halt did confirm to me that a plane landed on base, was secreted in a corner and despite his own status even he was not allowed to know why it was there. This, Halt came to suspect, was part of a covert investigation into the case which by-passed all the witnesses from himself downwards. He tried hard to report the matter correctly and was astonished at the lack of feedback from higher authority. On Wednesday, 31 December, while awaiting instructions from the British squadron leader as to what to do next, he began to take witness statements from Burroughs, Penniston and others. He also had the taped recording to consult.

There were also the photographs taken at the site by Nevills, and numerous stories about photographs of the UFO being filmed by one or other of the airmen in the woods that night. These have always been a source of huge controversy and the witnesses prefer not to discuss them, but I have it on good authority that such pictures *were* taken. Two separate witnesses have confirmed this to me. I believe they will be published one day. Indeed, I sense a pact between the witnesses to await the day when they have all left the USAF. Then, together, they will show the world what they have.

Some doubts exist as to whether these photographs show anything very much. Halt told me that they all came out mysteriously fogged. However, he does say that the evidence exists. Indeed, church minister and UFO investigator Ray Boeche set up a discussion between a Nebraska senator called Exon and Halt in 1985. The colonel was asked if he could confirm the existence of photographs, to which he replied, 'I can verify that for the senator. I could substantiate that for him.'

John Burroughs told me that photographs were taken by himself and one other officer whom he knew about. However, he refused to be drawn into further discussion about what they show, if anything, and where they are today.

One witness said something to me in an off-guard moment that makes me wonder. He seemed to imply that there was something odd on the photographs and that those involved were awaiting the right moment to make this known. He then back-tracked quickly, as if aware he had spoken out of turn.

However, one of the main witnesses (who asked not to be named but whom I do consider credible) told me this: 'We took several pictures on the second night. But most of them came out all black. You could see the sky, or maybe the film was fogged. I don't know. But two did show little lights in the sky. That's all. No spaceships were on them. In fact, they were so useless nobody was interested in taking them away.'

These photographs – fogged or otherwise – would be important evidence (see page 210).

As the Halt tape reveals, samples were also taken at the site and plaster casts made of the indentations. These are in the possession of the witnesses but they have, so far, chosen not to make them public. One day I believe this physical evidence will emerge and revive interest in this case. Halt brought the plaster cast with him when we met in June 1997.

With regards to the 'special flights' that are alleged after the sightings, Halt says he was not informed of any such landings, as he normally would have been. As a result, the flights witnessed by Burroughs and Penniston 'must have had special significance' he concludes.

Indeed, the special nature of one flight was suggested in 1985 by an anonymous airman from the base who agreed to talk on camera to CNN's Chuck de Caro. He claimed that on the Monday after the encounter he was ordered to drive a senior officer from the base out to a plane. The officer got out of the jeep and handed a canister to the pilot who took it on board and immediately jetted off for Ramstein, the USAF HQ in Germany. On the return trip the jeep driver asked the officer what this special package was, to which he was reputedly told: 'We actually have pictures of the UFO in there.'

Possibly the most remarkable evidence we have about the days after the encounter comes from Clifford Stone, who came forward in 1994 to state that he was an intelligence operative for the US Government in 1980. While not directly involved in the aftermath of the Bentwaters affair, he became aware of the way it was handled by Washington.

The reason he was consulted about the affair was because he had already expressed views on UFOs, penning security papers and assessments as part of his work on USAF special projects at the time. The Pentagon were getting 'very interesting information from Bentwaters' , Stone claims.

He adds that 'the documentation and evidence picked up in England was flown to Germany – initially to Ramstein air force base. But it was routed from there to Lanzi air force base where the US Air Force Special Activities Command (AFSAC) out of Fort Belvoire in Virginia had a detachment.' Data released via Freedom of Information indicate that the special responsibility of AFSAC was 'getting witnesses to talk' and 'access to human intelligence by covert means'. In researching my book MIB: *Investigating the Truth behind the Men in Black*, I established the origin of AFSAC. It is a defence intelligence unit rather like its British equivalent DI 55. In the UK this small team is responsible for sending agents to interrogate and silence witnesses to UFO Activity. They seem to act in a very covert manner and are the real source of the so-called 'Men in Black' legends that inspired the 1996 Hollywood movie of that title. AFSAC, based at Fort Belvoire in West Virginia, have even been known to recruit confidence tricksters to aid in their task of fooling witnesses; although their association with UFOs is publicly denied!

Stone alleges that this group, known in 1980 as Detachment 24, was responsible for two coded projects – Moon Dust and Blue Flight. Moon Dust, as is partially known from Freedom of Information documents, exists to respond to any crash of space debris – e.g. from a Soviet satellite – and co-ordinate a retrieval operation under strict intelligence.

Given all of the references to Soviet military satellites in Chapter 1, the role adopted by AFSAC is most intriguing.

Blue Flight was there to control the collation and assessment of hard evidence from military encounters with UFOs – or indeed any technology garnered from an unknown source.

According to Stone, the special flights out of Bentwaters in the days after the sighting took not only the film evidence but other data, notably about the irradiation of the 'alleged landing area', as Stone phrased it. This even involved a defence attaché at the US Embassy in London, presumably because of the tricky diplomatic situation caused by the events occurring on British soil.

What were the findings of this investigation? Stone says that Blue Flight considered the UFO to be real, but that it had characteristics 'much more suggestive of a multi-dimensional phenomenon as opposed to an interplanetary one'.

He added that possible tests of a new weapon, in which 'RF radiation' was used to trigger hallucinations, were known to intelligence units, but the physical evidence led the team to conclude otherwise in this case. The illusions triggered by RF radiation tests would not show up on radar telemetry and there was film of radar footage in this case (presumably thanks to Eastern Radar at RAF Watton) which proved to Blue Flight that the object in the forest was no illusion.

Stone goes even further than this. He claims that Blue Flight liaised with the NSA and accessed high-altitude spy satellite images which provided further evidence that a real intrusion took place in the forest. He even claims that Blue Flight were somehow expecting the landing – 'within a window from October 1980 to August 1981' – but would not elaborate on *how* they knew it was coming.

He says that people like Burroughs, and even Halt, were way below the need to know and so got cut out of the loop. Congress was not even aware of the solid evidence of UFOs on the records of Blue Flight and the secrecy clauses built into the Freedom of Information Act ensured that their data were never made public. The reason was simple. The evidence was proving that 'someone on the block had a new gun and we had to get one too, bigger and better. Until we did the information had to be top secret.'

In other words, the cover-up was of the military need to use UFO data to build new technology. It had less to do with what UFOs actually were.

I have been told precisely this by a very senior figure in the British MoD. When I was invited to Westminster to brief politicians, I was advised that the MoD studied UFOs to gain access to technology – regardless of whether we were dealing with alien spaceships or natural phenomena. 'Don't forget,' he told me, 'the Ministry of Defence is primarily here to defend the country.' In other words, we need to harness any technology that we can glean from UFOs, whatever their origin. And we need to do so in order to build defensive and offensive weapons before any other nation.

Clifford Stone says that the process by which the Rendlesham Forest landings were followed up was masterful. Nobody on base was allowed to get involved with the investigation. Teams were sent in from various locations – hence the special planes that landed. Each one had only one specific task to perform (e.g. to take control soil samples). In this way they each had only a small part of the puzzle in their hands. The big picture was then assembled in Washington and the final report on the case – classified as very secret – was co-ordinated by the NSA.

Only a small handful of people have clearance to see this incredible dossier. Stone is not professing to be one of them but he understands that amongst its conclusions is the opinion that this case is one of the most persuasive on record that we are not alone.

Meanwhile, back with the witnesses on base, no inkling of this alleged truth was filtering through. However, Jim Penniston does recall that he was put under surveillance when he moved to another base. This was after being called for an interview (as was Halt in Washington). Penniston was reminded that being in the USAF meant he had an obligation not to talk in public. Then he noticed that his mail was showing evidence of being opened and re-sealed. When an investigation was mounted, a listening device or bug – was found planted in his quarters. Halt also told me that during some witness interrogations there were British defence intelligence staff present. This gives further lie to the MoD claim that there is no record of an investigation.

Colonel Halt – fed up with the lack of any interest from above in the USAF – was finally contacted by Squadron Leader Donald Moreland on 13 January 1981, nearly three weeks after the event. He was advised to write a straightforward account of the two nights to send to the British MoD. Halt did so, and made changes as suggested by Moreland. Then the squadron leader sent the one page, with a cover note, to London with the expectation of a quick response from Whitehall.

Halt and I discussed why he submitted such a limited version of the events to the MoD. This was seemingly what was required of him by the authorities. My conclusion, which he did not dispute, was that the British had their own investigation ongoing and wanted Halt's belated written account for a purpose. If they ever had to admit to possessing some data on the case then this could be released through the only publicly acknowledged UFO channel – Air Staff 2A. They knew this was a possibility should witnesses talk or a Freedom of Information Act be imposed by parliament. These files would contain none of the real data on the case but Halt's report would be a sop to appease the country into thinking the MoD had the incident covered. It was, if you like, Plan B if Plan A should fail – and plan A, of course, was to cover up the encounter if at all practically possible. In this the MoD succeeded between 1980 and 1983. Ultimately they failed to keep the lid on this case, as I suspect they feared they might, because there were just too many witnesses involved. I see Halt's written report as having its place in the MoD contingency plan just as did the efforts to make the story seem ridiculous by allowing tales of crashed spaceships and alien contact with base commanders to filter out to the UFO community. It was a well orchestrated strategy in my view.

That cover note made by Squadron Leader Moreland has never been released by the British Government. Several times the MoD have denied in writing that it even exists. They are lying. In October 1996 Nick Pope told me that during his three years in charge of the files at Air Staff 2A he accessed the records on Rendlesham Forest and Moreland's cover note was there – a simple affair that made no contentious statements. It is all the more puzzling then that, despite Moreland telling me about its existence face to face when I met him at Bentwaters in January 1985 (the day he retired!), and despite making this point to the MoD, (proving it was pointless to keep the letter secret), even such a small part of this case has been covered up by the British Government. One wonders just what else they do not want us to see. No doubt those extensive records are carefully secured well out of reach of the Public Record Office.

Neither Halt nor Moreland ever did get a reply from London. Nick Pope tells me he thinks the MoD just did not have a clue what to do about the case. Had he been in charge at the time: 'I would have been on the first train to Woodbridge,' he told me assuredly. I believe him, too. If, of course, the several layers of the intelligence stratum above his head that probably *were* involved in detailed investigations would have let a man with such a limited 'need to know' get in the way!

However, when Brenda Butler and Dot Street turned up at Moreland's office asking about the UFO landing, the British officer did momentarily think these two UFOlogists had been sent by Whitehall and began to open up about the then still secret case. It was only seven weeks after the sightings. How else could they have known about the incident, he judged. Moreland soon realized his error and asked them to follow proper procedure by writing to the MoD. The only reasonable conclusion we can draw is that the MoD were already studying the case and Moreland was not considered to have a 'need to know' what that was.

His frustration is easy to see. Despite the extraordinary nature of this case and the careful way in which he and Halt had set out their report to the government, the only people interested in talking to the two most senior military officers making statements were UFO buffs!

12

OPERATION WHITEWASH

J UST WHAT is the nature of American Government interest in UFOs? This question is crucial if we are to understand why they reacted as they did to the events in Rendlesham Forest.

We have many ways of judging the truth. Most important are the thousands of documents released through the Freedom of Information (FoI) Act which became law in 1976 and has meant that any request to see government files must be met – *unless it contravenes national security*. As a result, the USAF intelligence services, the FBI and CIA, and (as we saw in Chapter 1) the NSA, have demonstrated an ongoing interest in UFO data via countless released files.

Given that we have such a wealth of data apparently *not* contravening national security, one can only speculate about data that have never been released because of their high sensitivity.

We can certainly prove that there are some such data. The continued denial of access to hundreds of files from the NSA is an example. In response to FoI requests, they have admitted that such evidence exists but not even a top security-cleared judge could get access to see it.

More specifically, with regards to the Rendlesham Forest case, the existence of the live tape recording was denied under an FoI request in 1983, although we know for certain it was in the possession of the USAF when that request was filed. A year later it was covertly released, proving that it was real and confirming that the US Government is willing to lie in reply to FoI requests for data on UFOs – something that is illegal under US law.

In 1986 they also released a few teletype messages to American minister and MUFON UFOlogist Ray Boeche after further FoI requests about the case. In essence, these were internal memos between Washington and the USAF, trying to decide how to handle public relations headaches from the CNN broadcast by Chuck de Caro and the book *Sky Crash* that Brenda, Dot and I had published in 1984.

However, several other documents were denied. On appeal, just one of these was released – a teletype message in which the operator printed computer-generated pictures of little UFOs! The other documents on the case were still kept secret and we have no idea what is in them or why they were deemed to be unreleasable.

Aside from such hard evidence, we have comments from a number of people who have worked on the US Government study of UFOs across the years. I am not including any controversial figures making wild and unsupported statements. This is not necessary. We have enough solid data from very trustworthy people.

There is Dr J. Allen Hynek, an astronomer who became Professor Emeritus at Northwestern University in Chicago. He was scientific consultant on UFOs to the USAF between 1948 and 1969 and, before his death in 1986, both published data about, and told me personally, of his many experiences during that period.

There are also former intelligence officers, such as Kevin Randle, a USAF captain who became persuaded of UFO reality and now investigates such matters in a private capacity. Others include Captain Edward Ruppelt who was head of the USAF investigation into UFOs during the early/mid 1950s and who wrote a very positive book on the subject which gives many insights into his time while chasing UFOs for the government.

Then we have the statements of Dr Thornton Page, a leading physicist who was chosen by the CIA in 1953, as a security-cleared scientist, to take part in their top secret analysis of UFOs. Page has since regretted the CIA actions and come to accept the need for serious research. In 1972 he published the findings of a major scientific symposium as part of the American Association for the Advancement of Science. He co-authored this positive report with an up-and-coming cosmologist called Carl Sagan. These two men and several other top scientists also signed a declaration to the US Government, urging them to release their UFO records into the hands of the academic community.

I trust you will agree that sources of this calibre are sufficient to allow us to paint an accurate portrait of US Government interest in UFOs. It is a picture free of sensationalism and lack of credibility.

US Government UFO study began in late 1944 when bomber crews over Europe reported glowing lights that followed their aircraft during raids. The name 'Foo Fighters' was coined for them and they were assumed to be a new Nazi weapon. However, this identification was never proved, the war ended and the objects disappeared. Indeed, after the war it was learnt that Axis air crews saw 'Foo Fighters' too but had presumed them to be an American secret weapon! Intelligence studies of these never-resolved sightings had at least alerted the Pentagon to a problem.

In 1946 numerous rocket-like UFOs were seen over Scandinavia. The surmise at the time was that the Soviet Union had, like the Americans, 'adopted' some Nazi scientists and were developing their secret weaponry under the tutelage of their new masters – perhaps creating a modified version of the V rockets that had terrorised London in the final months of the war. Again this idea was largely ruled out and history suggests that, as with the 'Foo Fighters', these so-called 'Ghost Rockets' were probably not what they seemed. However, the US intelligence operation was already in motion come 1947.

On 24 June that year, pilot Kenneth Arnold saw a formation of crescent-shaped objects over the Cascade Mountains. The press coined the term 'flying saucers' for these (although, in fact, Arnold had never suggested that they were shaped like saucers – only that they had *flown* like one bouncing over a flat pond). As a result, the modern era of UFOs began with millions searching the skies looking for such objects. The media reported each new story and speculation about 'alien visitors' soon took hold.

From the viewpoint of the US Government things were different. Foo Fighter and Ghost Rocket waves were still in mind (although the public were largely ignorant of them both). To the Pentagon the real fear was that flying saucers might be novel aircraft designed by the USSR. As soon as it became evident that military pilots were seeing these things as well – not just people talking to the tabloid press – it was clear that action had to be taken. Several early assessments around September 1947 show, as one senior USAF officer told Washington: 'Something is really flying around.'

As a consequence, a government project to collate UFO data was created at Wright Patterson air force base in Dayton, Ohio, home of the 'Foreign Technology Division', or FTD. The FTD is where any wreckage of an enemy craft was taken so that scientific and technical intelligence staff could analyse its make up and try to unravel whatever new information might be gleaned.

The project was officially code named 'Sign' and, from the start, in January 1948, they took on board Allen Hynek as chief consultant. The public knew that a project was underway, but its detailed operations were secret. It was popularly known by the media as 'Project Saucer'.

Within the year Sign had impressive evidence of UFO reality and penned what is known as an 'Estimate of Situation' report. This apparently concluded that real craft were being seen, picked up on radar and chased by military jets who could not catch up with them. Intelligence had revealed that they could not be manufactured by any nation on Earth – which left the possibility of alien visitors to be taken very seriously. A 1949 paper by a leading government astronomer (Professor Valley) argued that any such civilization may have seen our discovery of atomic weapons and our quest to reach space and decided that we were now a threat to their welfare and had to be monitored.

This 'Estimate of Situation' report has long been sought by the UFO community. Officially, all copies were destroyed when USAF Chief of Staff, Hoyt Vandenburg, rejected it, demanding physical evidence – not speculation – from his team of UFO investigators. Some suspect it was simply regarded as too politically sensitive to be made available via the FoI.

In any case, there was a major reshuffle in Project Sign. The staff who wrote the report were reassigned and a new, more sceptical, team was brought in. Another code name, Project Grudge, was applied and ordered to co-operate with journalists who would write stories downplaying UFOs and to ignore reporters who thought something really was going on. Grudge was also told to concentrate on making public any cases they could explain as, even then, it was becoming recognized that most sightings were misperceptions of mundane phenomena such as weather balloons and aircraft lights. The unsolved cases – of which there were about 20 per cent each year – were not to be discussed in public.

This period (*circa* 1949) is critical as the government reaction to the 'Estimate of Situation' report is very hard to comprehend in the way it is portrayed. At the least, one might have expected more resources and more rigorous standards in the wake of its potential; not a whitewash. Allen Hynek, as science advisor, kept telling the Pentagon precisely this. But he – like all the Project Grudge team – were unaware of things happening way above his head.

As discussed in a previous chapter, between 1949 and 1951 the top secret research laboratories in New Mexico – where rockets, atom bombs and other revolutionary technology were being developed – literally came under siege from UFOs. High-level conferences at Los Alamos involved scientists with security clearances far above Hynek. Intelligence staff superior to the fairly minor figures working for Grudge were in charge. From the data being assessed here, as part of Project Twinkle, it was worryingly evident that some intelligence was spying on the one place on Earth where technology was at its zenith. It seemed to fulfil precisely Valley's warning about the anticipated behaviour of an alien civilization sensing our progress and having come to Earth to monitor our defences.

We can only make reasoned inferences at this point, but it seems as if a two-tier structure was created. A high-level intelligence team was set up to monitor the major UFO data and made so secret that few were privy to its very existence. It was probably working on the premise that we *might* have alien visitors spying on US technology – possibly as a prelude to an invasion. That prospect alone (however remote it was viewed to be) probably guaranteed maximum security.

Unfortunately, there was a problem. Flying saucers were too public a phenomenon to ignore. The existence of Project Saucer was well known. To shut it down might have required awkward explanations. One way around the problem was to use the team at Wright Patterson as a scapegoat. They would distract the public into thinking that they were the only place where UFO activity was being studied (indeed, the team at Grudge would believe this to be so because they were not security-cleared high enough to be aware of the truth).

At the same time, Grudge could steer public interest away from UFOs by trying to defuse attention, and by sending signals to the rest of the world that suggested the Americans were not much interested. This was necessary in case the originators of the phenomenon did prove to be Earthly (e.g. the Russians). All good intelligence dictates that you do not alert your enemy to the fact that you know they have better weapons than you do. That would force them to strike quickly while they still had the edge and before you were able to match their advanced technology. This was the era of the Cold War and that factor probably dictated most decisions taken about the UFO phenomenon.

All of this fits the otherwise baffling changes forced on the UFO project at the FTD. Given their findings via the Estimate of Situation report, coupled with the frightening (and very secret) events over New Mexico, what Grudge was ordered to do is inexplicable *unless* real responsibility for UFO study was transferred elsewhere and went several rungs up the ladder of 'need to know' secrecy.

Unhappily, a new problem reared its head in 1950. Some awkward civilians started to perceive the possibility of a 'cover up' because they could not imagine the US Government virtually ignoring the worrying UFO evidence that was piling up in quantity and calibre. Most influential was Major Donald Keyhoe, a retired Marine officer, whose contacts in the military were leaking him cases that Grudge could not explain and so were not allowed to discuss! His book, *Flying Saucers are Real*, was a huge bestseller and led to the formation of today's UFO movement with its strong belief in a cosmic conspiracy.

Although Keyhoe – and four decades of UFOlogists after him – were contending that the US Government *knew* that aliens had landed and were hiding *proof* of that, all indications are that the truth was far less substantive. Very likely the US Government *suspected* possible alien visitation, but had no proof of anything other than that UFOs existed. The cover up was mostly of ignorance, not knowledge, and protected the need to find out more, not the need to prevent the world from discovering what was already known.

None the less, Keyhoe and the UFO movement posed a big threat to Washington. It is hard to imagine why they would do so if the truth was as it was publicly portrayed – i.e. that UFOs were unimportant misidentifications. If that were so, surely Keyhoe and the UFO groups could be ignored as cranks.

They were not ignored.

In January 1953 the CIA convened a UFO panel in Washington which dissected the best evidence accrued by Project Saucer. Their team was not cleared to attend all sessions – Hynek, for instance, being dismissed from several of them. The findings were also kept secret from the team at Wright Patterson. The panel comprised several government scientists with high security clearances, headed by relativity physicist Dr H. P. Robertson. Given that the government stance on UFOs was that these were misperceptions, it is intriguing that not one psychologist or psychiatrist was included. The Robertson panel had rocket scientists and atom physicists at its helm.

Years later we were finally to discover (through the FoI data and statements by Dr Page, one of the Robertson panel who became disenchanted with its actions), what the CIA *forced* the US Government to do. This was to try to debunk UFOs out of public consciousness.

Sightings were to be explained at all costs. Cartoonists were to be employed to make 'flying saucer' films that belittled the subject. The 'dangerous' people like Keyhoe and the UFO groups, were to be monitored as if they were Communist spies and attempts made to control their public influence by making them seem foolish. If that included feeding them bogus wild tales, it may have been a lesson applied in early 1981, when the wild accounts about Rendlesham were easily allowed to reach the ears of UFOlogists like Brenda Butler.

Indeed, quite remarkably, in August 1997 the CIA issued a statement on UFOs which made global headlines in responsible media sources such as *The Guardian* and BBC national news. They claimed that they had often spread disinformation about UFOs as part of a government plot to hide their own secret technology. In effect, they claimed, UFOs were American stealth aircraft! Regardless of whether this is a reasonable solution to most of the sightings (and it was surely to blame for some – and no doubt still is today!) the statement has a more stunning effect. The fact is that the American government has openly admitted not only to involving intelligence agencies in the UFO mystery but also to deliberately misleading the public about the facts. Bear those comments in mind when you contemplate some of the extraordinary claims within this book. What may have seemed to you to be rather improbable manipulations of the truth have now been confirmed as part of the game plan by Washington.

By 1953 the USAF had adapted Project Grudge into its final guise – as Project Blue Book. They had also brought in a first rate investigator to head the team – Captain Ed Ruppelt. The thinking was that as most UFO sightings could be explained, he would prove that fact with his tenacious research and help rid the idea of alien spaceships from public perception.

This thinking backfired. Ruppelt quickly dispensed with the misperceptions and cut to the heart of the mystery – the unsolved cases. From these he rapidly concluded that something very serious was going on and you could not rule out that alien spacecraft were observing us.

Recognizing the monster in their midst, the US Government went to extraordinary lengths to force Ruppelt out. The obstacles placed in his way during investigations are well described in his 1956 book, *The Report on Unidentified Flying Objects* (Ruppelt had created the term 'UFO' to replace the misleading phrase 'flying saucer'). Again and again he found the government one step ahead in any major case, as if another body were doing the work that he was supposed to be doing. If he got too close to a big story, he was ordered home to shuffle papers. If a witness needed interviewing he was told to take the bus, making it impossible to get there in time. He was even threatened with court martial for doing his job too thoroughly. In the end, even the rational and far from credulous USAF captain was forced to speculate, 'Maybe I am just the front man for a big cover up.'

I suspect he was right in that assessment.

Ruppelt finally quit to write his devastating book when he was not told the outcome of the Robertson panel and actively misled about its findings. There had been an office bet at Blue Book and everyone was sure that the reality of UFOs would finally be proven by their data. In fact, they did not even know the panel was being masterminded by the CIA, with a very different agenda afoot.

Ruppelt and Hynek knew nothing of the cartoons and spying missions on civilian UFOlogists that Robertson had ordered; nor the fact that the real UFO project was probably located elsewhere. Instead, Ruppelt was told that Blue Book would now be required to fiddle the statistics to make it look as if virtually all of the unsolved cases had vanished. He was ordered to try to convince the world that UFOs did not exist – something he knew was a lie. He could not be a party to the scam.

We have plenty of evidence from 1953 onwards that the monitoring tactics were employed to try to frighten the UFO community. My book, Men in Black, discusses this period in some detail. There is also reason to believe that some of the wild UFO tales that appeared during the mid-fifties were engineered by the intelligence agencies. Witnesses professed trips to the moon, requests to join the interplanetary parliament and other, utterly dotty, 'contactee' stories appeared. These were completely unlike the UFO reality that came before 1953 or has followed in the period after the mid-fifties. I suspect a number of these barely credible stories were planted as a response to the Robertson proposals to find ways to discredit the UFO subject and make it look ridiculous.

Indeed, the contactee stories won their biggest victory in 1959 when Ed Ruppelt was convinced by them that UFOs were, after all, just nonsense. He rewrote his book and disavowed his previous opinions. Sadly, he died soon afterwards at a tragically young age, and did not live to see that the contactee fad proved very short lasting and was quickly overtaken by a sea of persuasive evidence which just got more and more comprehensive.

Unfortunately, by the time this happened the damage had been done. Whether they were an intelligence agency undercover masterplan, or just a bunch of crackpots using UFOs to promote their mystic ideals, the contactee movement set serious UFO research back many years and proved a godsend to the secret underworld of US Government investigation.

Indeed, a 1954 memo says as much, stating how well the Robertson masterplan had worked (without specifying details), and crooning at the value to them of the highly publicised claims by the like of hot-dog-stand manager come space-traveller extraordinaire, George Adamski.

For many years Blue Book continued to act as a smokescreen for whatever was going on beneath the surface. We have no way of knowing what that was as the files are immune to public release. The USAF were so fed up with being a public whipping boy that they tried to pass on the problem but failed. Finally, a team of scientists was created on a government grant at the University of Colorado, to spend two years researching UFOs and deciding what to do.

Yet again the team was put in the hands of a government-cleared atomic scientist, Dr Edward Condon – a man who had been part of the ultra-secret Manhattan Project to build the bomb. He was a perfect government patsy. From day one of the study in 1967 he was publicly stating it would disprove UFO reality. His brief was to select the best cases from Blue Book files and follow up newly reported sightings. Instead, he preferred kooky tales such as a man who was in contact with a universe populated by giant bears. These, of course, made a fine after-dinner anecdote – seemingly an important criterion to Condon – but had no chance of expanding scientific data on UFOs, as many unselected cases did.

I spoke with some of the scientists who worked on the project when I visited the university in Boulder in the company of Dr J. Allen Hynek. Most intriguingly, during the two-year project the paper-thin cover that masked the top secret UFO project was nearly breached by the university team.

Although Colorado University were supposedly given *all* the government UFO data to work with (i.e. the Blue Book archives), a case came to them which was not in those files. It was offered by a serving military officer who was a witness and had heard of the taxpayer-funded project which would study all the UFO files. Naturally, he assumed his case was one of them. He was not to know that, as a significant military incident, it had apparently been siphoned off and not given to Blue Book at all!

The case, by intriguing coincidence, involved the air base at Bentwaters. It also included air crew at USAF Lakenheath as well as RAF personnel who chased the UFO in two Venom aircraft. The incident had occurred in mid-August 1956 and included a remarkable set of evidence. Several independent radar systems had tracked the target; ground staff at Bentwaters had seen it pass above and alerted Lakenheath – towards which the UFO was headed – where staff saw it as well. The crew of a USAF transport plane, flying at 5,000 ft (1,500 m) saw the yellow oval pass *beneath* them in the vicinity of Rendlesham Forest. Finally, the Venoms were sent in pursuit by the RAF and they obtained airborne radar lock-on of the target but were unable to close in on the phenomenon.

It is of fundamental importance that a case of this magnitude was routed past Blue Book and must have ended up at the other secret UFO centre in the USA. It was kept from the public between 1956 and 1967 and, but for pure chance, would no doubt never have been revealed. Almost on its own it proves the lie that Blue Book was the only place where UFO data was being located in the USA. It also makes you wonder how many other cases of this extraordinary nature were conveniently shunted out of sight of Blue Book and buried so that they were never heard of?

The final Condon report was published in January 1969. It reached the predictable conclusion that UFOs were of no scientific value. The scientist went further, making extraordinary suggestions that children be docked marks for writing about the subject at school or that action be taken against those who promoted UFO nonsense, e.g. by writing books such as this one.

Sadly for Condon there was a big problem. His short conclusion was utterly out of phase with the thousand pages of text that followed it. Of the 60 cases studied in depth *one third* were rated as unexplained by the battery of university scientists after two years and several million dollars expenditure. Often the conclusions reached were that real UFOs were involved, or unknown craft, or a phenomenon so rare it has never been seen before or since – exactly the sort of statements that proved UFOs *were* of scientific interest. The 1956 Bentwaters case was one of the unsolved mysteries.

In the final months of the project a major rift had developed when it became clear that Condon's conclusions were going to misrepresent the findings. The scientists knew that most journalists would only report what the team leader said about the project. So it was decided to leak a memo in university files that established how the project was won from the government. This spoke of using a 'trick' to make it look as if they were taking UFOs seriously while knowing all along that they had zero chance of finding anything. In other words, the project was rigged and was never going to be objective.

The scientists who leaked the memo were fired. Others walked out in sympathy. Half the Condon team then wrote their own report – 'UFOs? Yes!' – which reviewed the same cases, of course, but established very different conclusions from them. The government ploy degenerated into farce.

In any event, the Colorado report convinced many scientists who read it in its entirety that there was a real UFO problem. A year after its publication it led to the AAAS (American Association for the Advancement of Science) debate in Boston – the one where Thornton Page finally threw off his Robertson panel shackles. It also led to Allen Hynek founding the world's first scientific UFO group, the Center for UFO Studies (CUFOS), which attracted several ex-Condon supporters.

Condon's conclusions were seized upon by the US Government as the chance to end public interest in UFOs. It was decided to terminate Blue Book. Staff like Hynek were told early in 1969, but the news was not announced. Meanwhile the AAAS debate was being co-ordinated and Condon was blowing a gasket trying to stop it. He even attempted to get a friend, vice-president Spiro Agnew, to intervene. Agnew refused. Even so, it cannot have been coincidence that, after waiting nine months, the US Government announced the end of Blue Book just a couple of days before the AAAS debate began. It was clearly timed to try to discredit that prestigious meeting.

Years later, under FoI, we got to see the close-down orders for Blue Book. Although the public were to be told – and still *are* told that all US Government interest in UFOs ended with its cessation, those orders carry the interesting words that 'UFO cases which affect national security' should continue to be handled by the other structures set up for that purpose.

What structures? There were not supposed to be any other agencies dealing with UFOs! Yet again, the existence of this phantom top secret department shines through to those who take the trouble to probe behind the smoke and lights the US Government put in their way.

Officially the position today is exactly as it was when Blue Book closed down. Yet FoI releases show that UFO data continue to attract the attention of various government departments.

There are tantalizing glimpses in released documents which refer to the data retrieval at AFSAC at Fort Belvoire (the location to which Clifford Stone says UFO data from the Rendlesham case was sent). There are notes in CIA documents about scientific and technical intelligence staff reviewing UFO data and trying to assess the options for novel propulsion systems. But the big cases, like Rendlesham Forest, which must be happening with some frequency – based on the fact that we know they were happening in the past – hardly ever filter out into the public domain any more.

Why? We hear from time to time from ex-military witnesses that they were ordered into silence. Someone is collating data on these cases, but it is not being made a part of the public record.

Blue Book became redundant in 1969 when the likes of you and I were deemed an unnecessary complication in the government battle for truth about UFOs. It is a battle which still goes on almost undetected by the vast majority of the population. Sightings by civilians are no longer needed. The real UFO agency has far better access to evidence from satellite surveillance, radar, film taken by pursuing jets and high-level military witnesses to cases like those in a Suffolk wood in December 1980. Sadly, it seems that most of these can be successfully hidden from public view.

13

DEFENSIVE TACTICS

S UCH IS THE WAY of things in the USA, but what about the United Kingdom? It seems that to quite some degree this country can be likened to Uncle Sam's pet poodle. Certainly, we have followed the American lead – or, rather, been dragged along by a leash held by the Pentagon for almost 50 years.

One immediate huge difficulty is that Britain has no such thing as Freedom of Information. Instead it has the Official Secrets Act. What this means is that far from having to release any files unless they are deemed to contravene national security, pretty much everything is assumed to do so and thus kept secret as a matter of routine. Given that one cannot, for example, even access one's own medical records without great effort, getting data on UFOs is not the easiest task in the world!

However, there is a large modern building, known as the PRO (Public Record Office), at Kew in South London. Here – under some tight security – it is possible to scour the archives to seek out data on many items once part of government files. This *does* include UFOs – if one knows where to look. Unfortunately, because of the so-called '30-year rule', no data more recent than three decades ago are available. Every January a new year's batch of data is opened up to scrutiny. This is like jumping in a time machine and travelling back to the swinging sixties, but it does make checking out the data rather difficult as witnesses have often moved or are dead when you try to find them.

Thankfully, this dimly illuminated picture of government defensive tactics over UFOs is aided by some support from friendly employees, such as Ralph Noyes who, for 30 years, until the early 1980s, worked at a high level in the Air Ministry (and the Ministry of Defence as it later became). He spent some time working in areas that dealt with UFOs and is convinced of their reality.

More recently, Nick Pope has come forward. He still works for the MoD as I write (late 1997) and between 1991 and 1994 operated their UFO files, and – rather like Ed Ruppelt – became excited by what he was discovering; although, unlike Ruppelt, Pope had no jets at his disposal to fly off chasing witnesses. All he could do was sit at a desk and talk on the phone to people. Pope's rank was much lower than that of Noyes but his day-to-day dealing with UFOs was perhaps more marked.

I have spoken at length to both of these people and spent some days at Kew accessing the files. I was also fortunate to be invited into the Houses of Parliament to brief politicians at their request. In the process I have been able to talk to a number of fascinating figures, such as Lord Hill-Norton, admiral of the fleet and former chief of staff at the entire MoD. Now he is a member of the House of Lords. Various others have included Major Sir Patrick Wall, an MP who asked questions in the House about UFOs across four decades and who was a member of the NATO defence committee.

All of these sources have allowed me to try to grasp the situation.

Although there were some intriguing UFO sightings before that time, the first real evidence of any action was in July 1952, when Prime Minister Winston Churchill wrote to his Air Minister asking for comments on what 'this flying saucer business' meant.

He was referring to a wave of sightings over Washington DC that month – during which radar had tracked objects – and civil and military aircraft had observed them breaching secured air space over the White House and the Pentagon. It had caused quite a furore in the USA and was one of the triggers for the CIA convening the Robertson panel (see page 215).

Churchill was told that the Americans had investigated UFOs and found them to be mostly mistaken identity and no big deal. He was given the Project Blue Book party line. Ralph Noyes tells me that during high level MoD discussions the argument went rather like: 'But I thought the Americans had sorted all this out? Wasn't that what they told us? So why are these things still happening?'

Within days the problem was given a massive new spin when, for four consecutive dates during September 1952, UFOs got involved with a NATO exercise called Operation Mainbrace, held over Britain. RAF jets chased UFOs across Yorkshire. The world's only nuclear weapon-carrying aircraft carrier (a US ship) was off the east coast and was overflown by a UFO that was photographed in broad daylight. It was now very evident that the Americans did *not* have it sorted out after all.

Piecing together what happened next is difficult as major documents hinted at or even referred to in the PRO files are not on the public record. However, from what we do have, from comments by Noyes and others and interviews I have carried out with a number of military personnel – including Wing Commander Cyril George Townsend-Withers (who had a major mid-air encounter at this time while on a secret mission aboard a Canberra from RAF Boscombe Down) – we can form some impression.

By early 1953 a government investigation was underway. Townsend-Withers told me it was based at Farnborough which is a reasonable location as it shares some characteristics with Wright Patterson air force base in the USA.

In January that year (the same week the Robertson panel reached their conclusions) an official order was given to all RAF crews. If they had a UFO sighting this had to be reported officially but they also must not discuss it in public. The rationale – sounding as if it was dictated by the CIA – was that the public trusted pilots and so their sightings would be taken too seriously if they got out. The existence of this memo is referred to in the PRO but the memo itself has disappeared.

Even so, it would seem as if Operation Whitewash crossed the Atlantic faster than Concorde.

Interestingly, from the archives of the Royal Australian Air Force (where, unlike Britain, there *is* a Freedom of Information Act) we see a major case from this same time period in which a top civil aviation official took film of a UFO over New Guinea and filed a report. The film was taken from him by the Australian Defence authorities who promptly sent it to the USA where it reached the hands of the CIA. By the time the witness got it back, all the frames depicting the UFO had disappeared – allegedly consumed during the investigation process.

It would seem that Australia, like Britain, was under the thumb of the USA.

This position appears to have continued until the Lakenheath/Bentwaters case in August 1956. According to Ralph Noyes, that really disturbed the Air Ministry as it was so clearly inexplicable and represented a defence threat to the British mainland. However, this episode was far from unique. Several other radar visual cases occurred – including one a week later over the Solent, when three RAF jets on a practice combat mission were vectored on to a target picked up by a secret radar site near Bournemouth and closed in on the silver oval craft – which promptly flipped on edge, shot skyward, leaving the jets behind like paper toys.

Neither of these cases is to be found within the PRO files, but both are very real. Not only was the Lakenheath/Bentwaters case leaked to the Condon team in 1967, but in 1996 – with help from the BBC – I managed to find and talk with three of the four air crew that were aboard the two RAF Venoms. They had never spoken in public since their debriefing 40 years earlier. I filmed two of them at Lakenheath, describing their mission. They even still had their log books recording the intercept.

Wilbur Wright had his log too. He was one of the RAF pilots in the Solent intercept case. His testimony about the stunning aerial encounter and the way his Javelin was useless in the face of this incredible unexplained object makes chilling reading.

Of course, if neither of these cases has found its way on to the PRO, it raises the question of how many other impressive cases like these also did not do so; and, just as with the situation in the USA, whether there is another location which does not need to release its data to public scrutiny, to which such major cases are being siphoned off and stored.

A further dramatic case in 1957, at RAF West Freugh on the Galloway peninsula in Scotland, was tracked by several radars and – Noyes tells me – established with absolute certainty in the minds of the MoD that UFOs simply could not be ignored. For once we do have data on this case at the PRO, although it was an incident which the cover-up failed to hide at the time. Indeed, it made some press stories and so could not be so easily spirited from the archives. Intriguingly, the media in 1957 were told that the object was probably a balloon. The PRO records show conclusively that this was *not* the case and that the RAF eliminated the option very quickly. In other words, they lied to the public to ensure that the sighting was not considered to be as important as it truly was.

During the early to mid-1960s – in the period for which we *do* have PRO files to study – a department was created at the Ministry to receive reports from the public. Its function was very much like that of Blue Book, taking reports from the public and eventually setting up a chain of contacts whereby airports, coast guards and weather centres were asked to forward sightings made to them by the public. This is still in place today.

A report form was created, although this was never sent to a witness. In fact, there never was *any* direct contact between the Ministry and that witness; unlike the operation of Blue Book in the USA, where this often took place. The form was held at the reporting site – e.g. the airfield – which asked its questions of the reporting witness over the phone, then filled it out for the witness and forwarded it to Whitehall. Often the reporter had no idea they were now 'on file' at the MoD.

This department went through several names but was eventually known as DS (Defence Secretariat) 8. This was altered in the late 1980s to its present appellation – Air Staff 2(A). (See page 211.)

Air Staff 2A (as I will call it for simplicity) has never done much in the way of investigation. I have spoken to and exchanged letters with several of the people who held the post before Nick Pope took the job in 1991. They were relatively low-grade clerical officers who had no interest in UFOs. (Pope was interested which is why his approach to the job was so different.) These people spent only 2-5 per cent of their working day on responding to UFO matters – which ranged from sightings (usually between 200 and 300 received per year) and letters from UFOlogists, often expecting the recipients to have some massive database or to be far more aware of UFO reality than it is certain that they were.

These people were like glorified filing clerks. There was a standard party line that has barely changed since the 1960s – in which they responded to letters from the public by explaining that the MoD investigated UFOs to see whether they had any defence significance. No UFO ever did. So they did not proceed to investigate the matter to a point where an actual identification was attempted. As one phrased it to me: 'We are the Ministry of Defence. Our job is not to investigate UFOs. Once satisfied the object is no threat – and they never have been – then that is the end of our jurisdiction.'

Of course, I asked the obvious question. 'If there has never been any defence interest in 40-odd years of investigation, and thousands of reports, then why do you still maintain a department to investigate?'

I was told that: 'We can never presume that there will be no defence interest.' This begs the interesting question as to why there is no department collecting reports of the Loch Ness Monster. On the logic of this MoD justification for the continued funding of Air Staff 2A then there surely ought to be such a unit. It has as much likelihood of providing data of defence interest, for example to nuclear submarines, as the alleged forty-year failure of the UFO team. Surely Air Staff 2A would not exist under these terms of reference being suggested by Whitehall, meaning that it must have an ulterior motive to have survived through cost conscious days when quangos were rigorously scrapped if they can save money for more important budgets. In my estimation Air Staff 2A is a scapegoat. It reassures the public that UFOs are not being ignored whilst the real work goes on out of sight in a much more secretive location. It is a ruse to distract attention away from what is really going on.

The hundreds of cases already visible on Air Staff 2A files at the PRO are largely worthless. By no stretch of the imagination was an adequate investigation conducted. A few questions (such as date, time, size ,shape, etc.) were asked, but I have looked into a number where it has been possible to trace the witnesses. Almost without exception, significant data are missing from the PRO record simply because nobody ever interviewed the witness. The scrap of paper on the MoD file may say, 'Witness A saw a light in the sky.' In truth, witness A was a doctor responding to an emergency call and the light in the sky was a huge triangular craft drifting silently overhead. It was also seen by another witness not mentioned in the file. He was an RAF engineer standing on the perimeter of a nearby base above which the giant object also drifted. When these two witnesses – who have never even talked to one another – are asked to draw what they saw that night, their 'light in the sky' takes on the proportions of a chillingly identical structured craft. (This is a real case from the Air Staff 2A files reported in Cardiff.)

Indeed, while for much of its life Project Blue Book was a less than impressive investigative unit, its files make those of Air Staff 2A look like a pathetic waste of space. 2A did not even have a scientific consultant like Hynek; as demonstrated by one amusing period in 1966 when Blue Book wanted Hynek to visit his UK equivalent to swap data when he happened to be in Britain at a conference. The MoD engaged in Monty Pythonesque dialogue trying to come up with someone who had the faintest clue what to say to the American astronomer.

However, one other factor does emerge during the mid-sixties. The PRO files contain several references to consultation with an agency called the DSTI. No coherent pattern emerges and no findings of this body— let alone DSTI files – are available. However, the fact is that Air Staff 2A were aware of, and liaised with, this body on UFO cases.

In the early 1970s Ralph Noyes became the head of the department which included what is now Air Staff 2A. Upon taking on the job, he received a briefing about UFOs. This included sight of gun camera film taken by RAF planes chasing UFOs. The time period was the late 1950s/early 1960s – i.e. the era for which, supposedly, all government data on UFOs are openly available.

Noyes was advised that the MoD knew that UFOs were real, but were not sure what they were. An ongoing monitor was in place in order to try to find out. Noyes has always believed that UFOs are not alien, but some sort of strange atmospheric phenomenon. He says that nothing on the film was a structured craft of alien origin. The visual evidence was simply blobs of light.

All of my findings with the MoD confirm that they are *not* hiding knowledge about UFOs. They are still struggling to find out and are covering up their *lack* of understanding.

Interestingly, when Nick Pope took the job at Air Staff 2A in 1991, he tells me he was not given much of a briefing and was left to fend for himself by reading books and calling UFO investigators. Nor was he shown any gun camera film. This is not in the PRO, nor is there any reference to the events during which it was taken. So where is that evidence and why is it still secret?

Bear in mind that Noyes was several ranks senior to Pope and his security clearance was probably higher. Noyes says that UFO data were on a floor at the MoD to which access was highly restricted. The fact that he got to see visual evidence that Pope was not even told about establishes fairly clearly that Air Staff 2A mirrors Blue Book as a public relations interface. It is not – and never has been – the real home of UFO research and its workers are evidently not considered to have sufficient need to know even to be aware that something beyond them is in existence.

When I questioned him, Nick Pope adamantly insisted that there could not be any other department handling UFO data. To exist it would need regular contact with him because he was getting all of the incoming data. Certainly he was getting the lights in the sky reported by the public. He was clearly not getting the high-level military cases such as Boscombe Down (1953), Bentwaters (1956), Solent (1956) and various others I am aware of from later years, which I am sure will never find their way into the fine building at Kew via the records of Air Staff 2A.

This is indicated by the Rendlesham Forest case. Being a good UFOlogist, as he is, Pope quickly saw the significance of this case, even though it happened years before he took the job at Air Staff 2A. He requested the now-stored files and was amazed to discover how little is in there. While he thinks that the record simply contains

Halt's memo, the cover note from Squadron Leader Moreland and little else, because nobody at the MoD knew how to tackle this case, I profoundly disagree.

For a start, the letters I sent to the MoD about the case are missing (as is the reply I got in April 1983 in which the MoD admit the unsolved nature of the case two months *before* Halt's memo was released in the USA thanks to their FoI Act).

This letter is real. I still have my copy, signed by Pam Titchmarsh, who was Nick Pope's equivalent in 1983. So, if this letter has gone from the Air Staff 2A file, it can only have done so to be relocated elsewhere.

Equally, there have to be data on record to cover the checks made to ascertain whether Watton or another radar site had detected the object. We know such checks were made. Even if they proved negative, the enquiries had to establish that fact. Moreover, someone sent those two British 'ministry' men to interrogate farmers and foresters. This was 12 days before the Halt memo arrived at Air Staff 2A. It is also beyond belief that over a case of this magnitude there was no communication between the MoD and USAF to ask why they were trampling all over forestry land and wrecking a farmer's fence.

No – very clearly – a file *does* exist somewhere and it is apparently not in the archives of Air Staff 2A. All they have are a few scraps that refer to items already in the public domain. They are on the 2A records as a sop which can be released whenever that is necessary. That will be either after 30 years in 2011 or earlier (if an FoI Act is imposed upon Parliament by gathering public pressure).

I suspect we can view the entire Air Staff 2A operation in this way. It is a big red herring meant to convince the public that this is the sum total of government UFO study. We must not be taken in. Those who work at creating this Whitehall facade are pawns in a chess game far beyond their reach.

So where are the files if not in Air Staff 2A?

DSTI is the key. This is the Directorate of Scientific and Technical Intelligence which, in Australia (where secrecy is less obsessive), comprises defence intelligence specialists and security cleared science staff who assess gathered secret data regarding foreign technology. I dare say the same sort of definition applies in the UK – and UFOs certainly fit the definition of foreign technology .

There is also another department known as Defence Intelligence 55. Both this and DSTI between them get *three times* as many copies of UFO files as Air Staff 2A. We can prove this because, for a brief period during the late 1980s, the MoD released selected 'modern' cases to UFOlogists such as myself. They were not important cases – just lights in the sky – and the move was probably meant to appease momentum then gathering force for freedom of information in Britain.

However, the MoD made an error. They quickly corrected the mistake but, before it was spotted, they left the distribution list on the rear of several released files. This established that DSTI and DI 55 were key recipients of UFO data at the MoD and not, as claimed, simply Air Staff 2A.

In a 1997 release to the PRO we have the first proven admission that this MoD defence intelligence unit (then called DI 61) have attempted to silence witnesses – a claim that has been frequently made by concerned citizens but always denied outright by the British government. These records show how agents visited a police officer in Wilmslow, Cheshire, after his January 1966 close encounter. Physical evidence was even taken away for analysis in London. The sighting was hushed up for three months and only the personal intervention of the police officer's deputy chief constable seems to have prevented a Rendlesham style cover up from ensuring that we never learned the truth. Even so, despite this very belated revelation about a covert MoD investigation no copies of the files of the defence intelligence unit involved have been released onto the public record. There is no analysis data on the glassy substance taken from the site. These things remain protected from public view and one must ask why. If there is nothing to hide, as the MoD constantly insist, why are they hiding the records that prove this!

So, just as we found in the USA, the UK Government tried to dupe us into thinking that it has a very low-key operation to receive UFO sightings and that this does very little with the data. In fact, somewhere out there all the important evidence is being channelled away from our view, rendering the '30-year rule' a nonsense.

We will only get to see the real truth about British Government research into UFOs when someone at a very high level decides that we deserve to find out.

Unfortunately, on past performance that day might well be sometime never. As we have seen in the USA, even a Freedom of Information Act will have limited effect. Much data remains secret, protected by the claim that it would contravene national security were it to be released. But if UFOs contravene national security in any way then clearly they are much more important than the powers-that-be in either the UK or America are letting on.

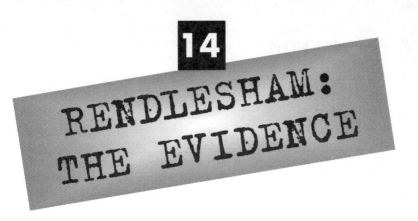

14

RENDLESHAM: THE EVIDENCE

W E SHOULD NOW summarise the key evidence to support the events in Rendlesham Forest. We have considered the eye-witness testimony from civilian and military witnesses as well as the somewhat contentious debate over the radar trackings. Let us assess the situation regarding the more solid evidence.

DOCUMENTS

The first documentation about the case was obtained by Brenda Butler in January 1981, around the time that Halt and Moreland were covertly sending their report on the case to the MoD (13 January 1981). This memo itself, of course, would not surface for more than two years.

After being satisfied (via Steve Roberts and his map and sketch of the UFO) that an incident had occurred in the forest, Brenda Butler and Dot Street visited Squadron Leader Donald Moreland's office on Bentwaters on 18 February 1981. The MoD representative clammed up and would not help.

So Brenda wrote to what is now Air Staff 2A in Whitehall. The MoD replied with its usual spiel on 25 March. Simon Weeden, then the clerk in charge, stated the party line about the MoD only being interested in cases with 'defence implications'. Intriguingly, the direct questions Brenda had posed about Rendlesham were flatly ignored with the simple words: 'We are unable to help you in your quest.' By irony, the code used on this letter by the MoD was ET-1!

The British Government have always denied any cover-up regarding this case but I find it hard to explain this blank refusal in any other way. Clearly, the MoD *knew* about the sightings. Air Staff 2A had held the Halt memo for two months when this reply was penned. They deliberately chose to say nothing and, in my view, that clearly constitutes a cover-up.

Brenda gave up on her frontal assault and focused on gathering witness stories, but during 1981 and 1982 I was alerted to the case by the radar operator's story and so fired off several further letters to the MoD, trying to reason with Department DS 8 (as it was still called). I even engaged the support of Bill Chalker, who was my equivalent as national director of UFO investigations in Australia and who had been successful in getting to see the Royal Australian Air Force files in Canberra. He backed my call to the MoD that if – as they claimed – they had nothing to hide on the UFO subject, opening up their data was a logical and helpful step to take.

This initiative took time to bear fruit but it did eventually succeed. In October 1982 the MoD wrote to me to advise that they had decided there was nothing wrong in principle with making the UFO files available earlier than the usual '30-year rule' allowed. Indeed, I was informed: 'We are currently discussing the best means by which this might be achieved.'

I feared that it might not help to make this news public and chose not to do so, but gently requested the co-operation of the MoD by asking for the release of the Rendlesham file. They ignored my request but replied with a surprising letter dated 20 January 1983 in which I was given permission to make public their new policy.

Pam Titchmarsh, now secretary at the department, told me that they were 'currently discussing the mechanics of printing and distributing the reports and once agreement is reached on those aspects it will, of course, take a little while before we can assemble all the material in a form suitable for printing. However, once we are in a position to start releasing these reports you will be informed.'

Clearly a decision *had* been taken. Indeed, in a cover note, it was implied that the Minister of Defence himself had sanctioned the move. It was just a question of time. Naturally, I again asked for the Rendlesham file to be one of the first, but was put off by being sent several very recent MoD files instead. These were just copies of the UFO report form used by coast guards and airports to submit cases to the ministry. All witness identification was removed, but they were very fresh. For example, I got a case dated 19 January 1983, from South Wales, within a fortnight of its occurrence! (See page 211.)

The way these (near worthless) bits of paper were fed to me instead of a reply to my direct questions about Rendlesham is worrying. Are these the actions of anyone not trying to cover something up?

I chased up some of the files the MoD sent to me with the help of both BBC Wales (for whom I made a TV documentary that summer) and *The Observer* newspaper. With the help of these resources we found impressive cases, utterly uninvestigated by the ministry, involving high-level witnesses who usually had no idea that their report to the local police or airport meant they were now on file in Whitehall. None had received any comeback from the MoD regarding their sighting.

Even so, the real prize – the Rendlesham file – was conspicuous by its absence.

By this point – February 1983 – the only public writing about the case had come from me. I had published two articles in the UFO magazine *Flying Saucer Review* and had written a series for the Orbis partwork encylopedia *The Unexplained*, which was available in shops throughout the UK, Australia and other countries. These had set out the case in some detail and emphasized my growing concern about the way the case had reached the UFO community and the speculation that a military accident might be masked behind the UFO stories.

It was against this background that Larry Warren surfaced in the USA, telling his story (very similar to the testimony given to Brenda by Steve Roberts and to me via the Watton radar officer). Barry Greenwood sent me a copy of Warren's testimony, saying a Freedom of Information Act request was to be filed to secure any US Government data on the case. This news reached me in March 1983.

Another surprising twist concerned the popular science journal OMNI. This was printed in New York but copies were widely sold in the UK. It had a one-page UFO column in each issue. In late 1982 the editorial team had called both Brenda and me to say they were doing a piece on the case. This was not because of Larry Warren (who did not feature) nor, it seems, directly because of my articles; but because journalist Eric Mischera had been approached by a USAF colonel who offered to tell the whole story.

This man was Ted Conrad, a name that has not reappeared in connection with the case. Conrad was indeed at Bentwaters at the time but he has never been named by any witness that I have spoken with, nor has he agreed to talk since that single interview with

OMNI 15 years ago. Mischera told me that the deal was that Conrad would go on record once and never speak out again. Despite attempts by the OMNI reporter and myself, Conrad remained true to his word, making his dramatic appearance in this fashion one of the many riddles still posed by this case.

The OMNI interview appeared in the February 1983 issue – thus almost side by side with Larry Warren's dramatic arrival on the scene. After more than two years of stony silence and MoD denials, these two events in the USA left Brenda, Dot and me baffled.

Conrad's story in OMNI is a muted version of the first night. It is fundamentally accurate but leaves quite a bit out, including the events on the Halt tape. Conrad adamantly refutes the 'aliens chatting to the base commander' storyline, saying he was the man who would have had the contact had there been one, but there was not. Of course, these claims (dubious as they are) had always referred to Wing Commander Gordon Williams and not Conrad, so this shouldering of the burden was curious.

Even more fascinating was that MoD man Donald Moreland agreed to speak with OMNI as well. He confirmed that Brenda and Dot had visited him on base in February 1981 and said, 'I told them I didn't know anything and they went away.' But this – he confirmed – was not true. He *did* know something. A 'minor incident' had occurred which involved 'a few lights flipping amongst the trees' . However, Moreland also stressed that 'any talk of humanoids is just absolutely ridiculous'.

I was also quoted as expressing the possibility that an accident with a nuclear weapon might have leaked radiation into the forest and the clear up of this incident had provoked the secrecy and the UFO stories as a smokescreen. Having now spoken with so many eye-witnesses, I do not think that theory is valid but it seemed an option after two years of government obfuscation.

All of this is intriguing. Leaving aside whether you regard Moreland's choice of words as appropriate for the story as Burroughs and Penniston describe it, why were he and Conrad willing to talk about a case at a time when the MoD was continuing to deny its very existence?

Were they scared by the appearance of Larry Warren with his renewal of the 'alien contact' scenario? Had my expression of doubt that the case was even a UFO encounter at all provided the need to reinforce the UFO angle? Cruise missiles were being shipped into Britain in 1983. This was a heavyweight political issue at most USAF bases.

In any case, the OMNI article – isolated and puzzling as it is in the overall context of the long history of this case – had a monumental effect on public awareness. It achieved what my letters to the MoD had not. To my utter amazement, Pam Titchmarsh replied to my latest 'tell me about Rendlesham' plea with a letter, dated 13 April 1983, that was a landmark in MoD coverage of UFOs.

'I can confirm that USAF personnel did see unusual lights outside the boundary fence on 27 December 1980, but no explanation for the occurrence was ever forthcoming. There is, however, no question of the event being a cover-up for a crashed aircraft or the testing of secret devices . . . nor was there any contact with "alien beings".' (See page 213.)

This is a stunning letter for many reasons. It was the first time that the MoD had ever admitted in writing to having an unexplained UFO case on file in which military witnesses were involved. Of course, it was also their first ever admission that this case even existed. One can only assume that they now had little choice, given the very public quote from the RAF squadron leader who looked after Bentwaters and Woodbridge for the MoD!

It is interesting that the dating is wrong (although that stems from the errors on the Halt memo). The tepid wording yet again underemphasizes reality by quite some margin as a great deal more than a few 'unusual lights' form the cornerstone of this case.

Personally, I was even more intrigued by the categorical denial of the main 'identification' theories – i.e. the aircrash and secret test options. By flatly rejecting them, the MoD were painting themselves into a corner and effectively supporting the unexplained nature of the encounter.

Even as I wrote back to Pam Titchmarsh yet again to request the file (now with rather good cause!) I could see how lights in the sky over Cardiff were being given to me to try to distract my attention. However, across the Atlantic events were swiftly overtaking me.

On 28 April – two weeks after my MoD letter – the present base commander at Bentwaters (Colonel Cochran), in consultation with his deputy (still Charles Halt), replied to Barry Greenwood and Larry Fawcett with the news that: 'There was allegedly some strange activity near RAF Bentwaters at the approximate time in question (but) . . . not on land under United States Air Force jurisdiction.'

As such, the letter claimed, no 'official' investigation was mounted by the USAF and therefore there are no records in existence about the case. Yet we know that such records *did* exist. Halt was a few doors from Cochran on base and could presumably have supplied any data on the incident (including his memo) and we know that Cochran had, on base, a copy of the 'live' tape recording because in June he and Halt invited a Manchester lawyer to Bentwaters, the tape was played, sketches of the UFO were shown and witness statements were allegedly taken from a base case file!

Undeterred, Bob Todd of the legal action group CAUS (Citizens Against UFO Secrecy) used the Cochran letter, my MoD letter and Larry Warren's anonymous statement, to prove effectively that there was a case. On 7 May 1983 they appealed for any data under the Freedom of Information Act.

On 14 June, unusually fast, Colonel Peter Bent on behalf of USAF forces in Europe, responded and confirmed the incident. He released the famous Halt memo sent to the MoD in January 1981.

Yet Bent also insisted that the USAF file had already been 'properly disposed of' and only after 'diligent enquiry' had they finally found a copy of the data thanks to the 'British Ministry of Defence'. Despite the fact that copies were at Bentwaters in May 1983 and no such 'diligent enquiry' ought to have been necessary, it is still incredible to suppose that the USAF would destroy their only report on this matter within little more than two years of the incident. This surely implies that the USAF copy of the Halt memo was in a low-level area and was superfluous because the real data on the case were under lock and key in America's real UFO repository.

Total destruction of the memo makes no sense, for the sightings could have been proved by later events to have been a terrorist surveillance on a nuclear base, or even a peace campaign, or many things, so that the instant disposal of all the evidence seems impossible to take seriously.

As can be seen (See page 213), the Halt memo is one of the most dramatic UFO case files ever released from any government archive, let alone the ultra-cautious MoD. Despite the many things it leaves out, it refers to ground traces, radiation, a landed craft and so on. It is political dynamite.

Armed with the Halt memo and risking prosecution under the Official Secrets Act, I took this document to Whitehall on 18 August and demanded to see someone. That I was breaching the Official Secrets Act is clear. The MoD had repeatedly refused to release this file to me despite several requests, the most recent of which was still unanswered, despite Pam Titchmarsh confirming that she had got this request more than three months earlier. She had not replied 'because of the Falklands War' which had ended 14 months before I sat in Whitehall that day with armed guards nearby.

The truth of the Halt memo was confirmed to Brenda, Dot and me that day. A shocked MoD official agreed it was on their files but that it comprised the only thing in writing on the case. Titchmarsh confirmed that she could not stop us publishing (which we did, on the front page of the *News of the World* six weeks later) and added that the MoD definitely did not supply it to the US Government, a statement seemingly at odds with what the US Government had claimed under Freedom of Information.

These events seemingly stung the MoD, for their decision to release the files was quickly reneged upon. When, after a year of unfulfilled promises, I grew tired, Martin Bailey of *The Observer* backed me with an article on 7 March 1984: *'It's official – there are* UFOs' in which he followed up one of the files released to me in early 1983, and got the MoD to admit they would now only 'consider' releasing a report provided a specific request for a named date and event was filed. I told him to file for all data on Rendlesham and he got nothing – not even the Halt memo which had just been seen by four million readers of a national newspaper! So much for the MoD and their promises.

Within days, on 24 April 1984, Andrew Mathewson at the MoD told Dot Street that: 'Your suggestion that the MoD has documents relating to the alleged UFO sighting at RAF Woodbridge in December 1980, other than Colonel Halt's report, is quite mistaken.' As Nick Pope told me in 1995, he personally accessed the file while he was in Mathewson's post. There *are* other data. Moreland's cover letter *was* there. While saying nothing contentious, to this day that has still not been released.

The saga of the quest for further documentation could fill the rest of this book but I will not get side-tracked into such matters. What often happens is that statements are made as if they reflect official MoD policy but which simply could not be made if it is true that the Halt memo is the only thing on record. For example, Mathewson wrote that there was: 'no question . . . of anything having intruded into our airspace or having landed near RAF Woodbridge'. Yet Halt's memo (reflecting the witness testimony) very clearly *does* say that something landed and this fact cannot be denied without any investigation (which the MoD insist did not occur) or documentation (which the MoD say they do not have).

The same is true of the referenced intrusions into airspace and the alleged radar trackings. Either there *were* intrusions, which the MoD deny, or there were not and documentation exists on file to prove that, upon investigation, the radar tapes failed to establish any such intrusion. Yet the MoD also say that no documentation exists.

They cannot have it both ways. Either they did not investigate and so cannot make such assured statements about the status of the events, or they did investigate, in which case where are the records?

Frankly, it would be deeply disturbing to think that our national defences do not even bother to check out reports from high-level military officers at one of our frontline bases which clearly provides physical evidence that something unidentified has landed near the base perimeter.

I am very sure that this would be music to the ears of the IRA or Middle East terrorists and also utterly certain that this is not the case.

If so, why are the MoD continuing to lie on this matter – and to lie so badly?

PHYSICAL TRACES

As we have seen, the ground traces consist of three important aspects.

First, there were the indentations in the ground. All the eye-witnesses insist that these were in the form of a well-measured equilateral triangle and were dug into hard frozen earth as if by legs on a heavy object. According to forester Vince Thurkettle and the police officer called to the site these marks were probably made by rabbits. If so, they had to have been there *before* the night of the landing.

There are rabbit marks in the forest. I have seen them. It is not impossible that this is the cause of the 'pod' marks at the site. However, all of the witnesses that I have spoken with dispute that theory and this includes some who have spent quite a bit of time in the country. They also point out that it would be some coincidence that, as the landed UFO had three legs, the rabbit holes at the site would so readily mimic this landing configuration.

It is difficult to decide the truth here. However, as the Halt tape clearly states, photographs were taken on site and these have never been released. Presumably the close-up shots of the pod marks would emphatically demonstrate one way or the other whether these marks are important or not.

The second set of trace evidence is the score marks on the trees. I am virtually certain from talking with foresters and from seeing similar marks that these are cuts made in areas of woodland to demark suitability for felling. It is crucial in this regard to note that Halt was very noncommittal on the tape as to whether he considered these to be important. He kept saying that they looked 'old'.

The 'heat energy' radiated via the starlite scope may be a natural consequence of the scoring. Without hard data about the readings taken it is difficult to know how seriously to take this evidence from the operators of this equipment as heard mentioned often on the live tape.

Finally, and I think by far the most significant factor, was the huge hole in the top of the pine-tree canopy. This is well described on the tape and was seen by a forester before the area was felled. Given that even *he* found it unusual, I am quite certain in my own mind that it was.

This seems to suggest that a heavy object descended through the trees towards the ground. The absence of any reference to this in comments about the site that Vince Thurkettle visited may imply that he was not at the real landing spot as, by all accounts, the hole in the trees was very obvious.

RADIATION

Was there any significant radiation in the forest after the encounter? This is not as easy a question to answer as it seems. The data in the Halt report are incomplete and this makes it difficult to judge the measurement scale being used.

Certainly, there would be increased background counts in a pine forest due to the accumulation of pine needles. Even so, the suggestion is that figures several times the normal background level were recorded in the landing traces but (significantly) nothing major anywhere else.

It is important to note that these readings were taken 48 hours after any potential radiating source was on the ground. In that case a much higher exposure must have been felt by Burroughs and Penniston at the time of the incident. Radiation decays to a greater or lesser extent depending on the type of energy emitted.

The fact that none of the witnesses seem to have suffered any obvious radiation sickness afterwards means that low levels were surely involved. Although Halt was obviously concerned enough to take geiger counters into the forest, there is no sign during the live tape of any fear being expressed or of clear precautions being taken to avoid exposure.

After discussing the matter with Dr Michele Clare, a plant bio-logist who was interested in possible effects on vegetation, my surmise is that, at most, we were talking of figures about three or four times normal background count. These would be interesting and hard to explain by any normal means, but not dangerous. Indeed, one sceptical physicist told me that he saw nothing remarkable in the radiation levels. They were only a little above what would be expected in a pine wood and he considers them to be irrelevant to any interpretation of the case.

That said, physicist Dr Alan Bond discussed the matter with Burroughs, Penniston and Halt when they came to Britain in 1994 to film *Strange but True?* From this he says that the figures were probably a little higher and in excess of any radiation left in the UK after the Chernobyl nuclear reactor accident in the USSR in 1986. This led to serious concerns about damage to the food chain and various health warnings throughout Europe.

Nick Pope goes even further. He says he took the data to the MoD sources used to assess radiation exposure while he accessed the Rendlesham file during the three years he worked at Air Staff 2A. They came back to him and asked, 'Where on earth did you get these readings?' They alleged a count of *ten times* normal and said that this was certainly enough to worry about.

If true, it is even more scandalous that the MoD played so recklessly with the health of the people of Suffolk. They deserve an explanation for such cavalier disregard.

DURING THE 17 YEARS since this case took place, a remarkable array of people have been involved in making comment about the matter. It is well worth looking at what some of them have concluded regarding what may be the most important close encounter on record.

I will give these soundbites in chronological order to give you some flavour of who said what during the period. I concentrate only on comments made since the case became public knowledge thanks to the personal intervention of editor Derek Jameson and the *News of the World* front page. This was on 2 October 1983.

On that day the *Sunday Express* asked the former British Minister of Defence, Sir Ian Gilmour, what he thought. He concluded unequivocally: 'I should think this is absolute rubbish.'

A few days later the US military journal *Stars and Stripes* were just as forthright, stating in their report: 'We have been answering queries for three years . . . no documentation has been withheld.' This is intriguing as the first public report on the case had only appeared in the summer of 1982 – so who was asking them about a case two years before any knowledge of it entered the public domain?. Also, the *Stars and Stripes* piece was written a year before the Halt tape was finally released, proving that documentation was certainly being withheld when the story was written.

Science reporter Adrian Berry is an outspoken sceptic of the UFO subject and on 17 October 1983 he reported in *The Daily Telegraph*: 'All that had happened was that a USAF colonel at RAF Woodbridge had seen an unexplained light in the surrounding woods. That was all

. . . (it) could only have been the rotating beam of the Orford Ness lighthouse five miles (8 km) away.'

NATO defence committee member and Conservative MP Major Sir Patrick Wall was less sceptical. He asked numerous questions in the House during 1983 and 1984 (see page 212) and on 27 October 1983 was cited as saying, 'There is evidence that something is going on and the government is remarkably hesitant to make any response.'

One man who did make a response was Minister of Defence Michael Heseltine. It was his only public comment on the case – he later declined several attempts by MPs to coerce him into elaboration. It came on 3 November 1983 when Heseltine replied to a letter from Labour MP and former Home Secretary Merlyn Rees – the man who, in 1967, had actually been responsible for ensuring that the MoD retained their UFO files for eventual release to the Public Record Office.

In a remarkable statement, full of points that may come back to haunt his political career, Heseltine told Rees: 'I can assure you that there is not a grain of truth in the allegation that there has been a "cover-up" about alleged UFO sightings . . . In the News of the World incident there was, in fact, no question of any contact with "alien beings" nor was any unidentified object seen on radar.'

The wave of criticism that tended to write this case off as unimportant reached its zenith in November 1984 with the book Lies, Damned Lies by Times journalist Henry Porter who claimed that the case was a story 'commissioned in the belief that it would amuse the (News of the World) readership . . .fiction from the Bouverie Street dream factory'.

However, as I was present during the commissioning sessions, and was briefing the newspaper on the case, I know that this claim is nonsense. The suggestion that the story is fiction is also insulting and says more about this Times reporter and his apparent inability to distinguish hard data and serious investigation from polemics.

More qualified to judge the truth was Ralph Noyes who had worked for the MoD for over 30 years and had reached the equivalent rank of air commodore. He was convinced by the News of the World reports and entered the UFO community as a result. On 31 December 1984 he told me of the MoD: 'I think they are baffled. Just as I am.' He added later: 'We now have evidence – I blush to say of my own Ministry of Defence – that they have lied about this case. They have covered it up.'

During 1985, with the help of Liberal Democrat MP David Alton,

I joined forces with Ralph and we pressurised the ministry. Michael Heseltine chose to get his deputy, Defence Minister Lord Trefgarne, to answer the letters that Alton sent, armed with the data Noyes and I had supplied. Trefgarne said on 19 March: 'We are satisfied that the events described are of no defence significance. I can assure you that there is no question of attempting to cover up any incident or mishap, nor are we attempting in any way to obscure the truth.' (See page 216.)

Meanwhile, Noyes pushed his then equivalent at the head of what is now Air Staff 2A – Brian Webster. It took three months for him to get a reply – and that was from Webster's employee, Peter Hucker. This, Noyes tells me, was a very significant move and demonstrated that they were concerned as to what to say to such a distinguished former employee who could read between the lines of their letter. However, on 15 May Hucker insisted to Noyes that: 'We treat all these reports seriously in case they show anything of defence significance . . . I can assure you that no unidentified object was seen on any radar recordings during the period in question and that the MoD has no knowledge of the tape recording . . .'.

This was nine months after the Halt tape had been released by the US Air Force.

That same month church minister and UFOlogist Ray Boeche had persuaded Nebraska senator and former state governor James Exon to look into the case. Even Halt, then refusing to talk in public to anyone, had agreed to assist Exon and discuss the physical evidence.

Interestingly, the senator became less and less communicative as the five-month investigation went on. His office staff informed Boeche that Exon had, most unusually, taken on all the work himself rather than delegate research. This seemed not to gel with the senator's initial scepticism about the case and his apparent uncertainty that anything worth studying had appeared in later statements.

On 14 August Exon gave the UFOlogist his final word: 'We have put in more time on this matter than any other case since I have been a United States senator.' It seems hard to imagine that any politician of his distinction would have been so dedicated to a subject that was leading nowhere.

In October 1986 two remarkable developments occurred. Firstly, former chief of staff at the entire MoD – Lord Peter Hill-Norton – spoke out about the case. He added that after studying the case (I had sent him long accounts of the evidence), he found it 'very difficult indeed to discount the almost certainty that something landed'. As to what this was, he added: 'I have no idea. I only wish I did.'

Central Television also persuaded Armed Forces Minister Roger Freeman to appear on camera for a local news programme and to answer questions about the case. He said, 'Clearly there was no threat to the American unit based at RAF Woodbridge or indeed RAF Bentwaters. If there had been then both ourselves and the American forces would have responded instantly. But there was no threat. There is, perhaps, doubt in the mind, certainly of the officer who reported the incident, what the occurrence was. But there are things which happen every day where you cannot necessarily explain what has happened or why it has happened . . . Our job at the MoD is in a rational – and I hope painstaking and calm – way to investigate all UFO sightings and reports. We are reactive. We investigate them thoroughly and satisfy ourselves that there was no threat to national security. If there had been at the time of the (Bentwaters) sightings then our reaction would be immediate.'

This idealized picture of the MoD study of UFOs in general, and this case in particular, is fascinating. If it could be justified by events on record then it would be very reasonable. In fact, it is at massive odds with what we know.

According to both the USAF and MoD there was *no* investigation at all and any glance at what they have done on older cases, via the files of the Public Record Office, show that Freeman's 'thorough' and 'painstaking' study of UFO cases is a joke – at least according to the data released.

Either Freeman's claim is nonsense or else this investigation does happen – and *did* happen in the Rendlesham Forest case – but was conducted by a covert department beyond Air Staff 2A whose data has never been released to the public. Yet government sources repeatedly tell us that such a place simply does not exist.

So Freeman cannot have it both ways; for the claim that there is only one piece of paper on the MoD file about this case – Halt's report – with no trace whatsoever of any investigation (thorough or otherwise) – is irreconcilable with this assertion by a government minister. If there was a 'painstaking' investigation into these sightings then where are the records, as they do not exist in any of the publicly admitted channels.

We shall end with two comments by more recent occupants of the chair at Air Staff 2A.

On 12 January 1990, in reply to a UFOlogist, Owen Hartop, of Air

Staff 2A put a new spin on the question by stating that: 'The MoD was content that the Rendlesham incident was of no defence significance because whatever was witnessed was not apparently hostile.'

Then, in October 1996, Nick Pope (who reopened the files when he was at Air Staff 2A between 1991 and 1994) told me: 'I think this is potentially one of the most important cases on record anywhere. Something significant happened and the MoD were just not up to finding out what that something was.'

But perhaps the truly final word is best left to a witness. After all he was there and none of these other commentators were. In June 1997 Colonel Charles Halt told me, 'I have no idea what we saw that night, but I do know what it was not. I am not surprised if the authorities were baffled because those of us out there surely were.'

16

SCENES FROM A DARK FOREST

RENDLESHAM SCENARIOS

AS YOU HAVE SEEN, the evidence for this case is impressive. We have no shortage of eye-witnesses – from both the US military and local British village folk. Nor is there any absence of hard evidence – from the highly unusual 'live tape' to the physical damage, animal interference, electrical effects on radio and USAF equipment and the anomalous radiation readings.

In addition there are the rather more controversial elements. Was there any radar coverage? Certainly we must accept that film was taken from bases such as Watton. Someone was *looking* for radar evidence with the expectation of finding some. That fact by itself is important, given that the party line from both the British and American Governments seems to be that nobody did very much investigation into this case and none at all until *three weeks* after these radar searches were made.

If that is true then who made those checks with Watton and Neatishead – and why?

However, if the MoD are claiming that no radar film was uncovered which depicted any unidentified object, why not release the proof that vindicates these statements? Clearly, for a man with as high a profile as Michael Heseltine to state with assurance that no such radar trackings occurred, then solid proof *must* exist to support that claim. He would not risk his political career (which, in 1983, was on track to challenge Margaret Thatcher for the premiership) unless he was certain of what he was stating. That has to mean evidence to back his story; not some vague assurance from an MoD department that claims it has nothing on the case in writing and did no real investigation anyhow .

The MoD denial of any records leaves us to balance the flat contradictions.

On the one hand sit Heseltine and Lord Trefgarne with their sharp words of no cover-up and no radar trackings (or, rather, no *'unidentified'* radar trackings as they were careful to insist – which might give one cause to wonder whether a UFO is sufficiently *identified* not to qualify for that description in MoD language!) On the other hand, we have the story told by the Watton radar staff, which cannot simply have been invented, because it is too similar to the truth about a sighting that was deeply hidden when Watton were approached to commandeer their visual records.

The key to all of this is the missing documentation on the case. There simply *has* to be more than the Halt memo in existence somewhere. If it can be prised out of the clutches of the Official Secrets Act we might start to make progress towards understanding what took place in this case. Unfortunately, it is being covered up for reasons that the MoD must consider valid.

Which leaves us assured of probably one thing. There are no easy answers. If Rendlesham was a simple case of mistaken identity then what is preventing the government from revealing the basis of that mistake? Surely it is preferable to speculation and uncertainty? Then we could all move on to more important matters.

There is also the huge problem posed by the alleged 'alien contact'. The witnesses who are highly credible must include Halt, Burroughs and Penniston. They are all insistent that while the UFO might have responded as if it were under intelligent control, there was no alien encounter of the much publicised kind that has turned this case into a living legend. Do we believe them or do we not?

Ranged against these more sober accounts of what took place is the 'alien version' – the image of a leading USAF officer exchanging sign language with floating extraterrestrials which was a key part of all the early stories.

It was what Steve Roberts claimed when he spoke to Brenda Butler just days after the landing – but this man has never gone on open record and we have no proof that he was ever really a witness, although he *was* a base officer and must have known about the incident. Was he being truthful when he approached Brenda Butler or did he have a hidden agenda?

A very similar tale was fed to the radar staff at Watton by USAF intelligence officers only days after the sighting. Again, this is unverified.

Such matters need to be judged when we try to work out the answers. In this concluding chapter I want to examine five possible options for what might have taken place in those woods back in December 1980. I suspect that the solution is in one of these scenarios. But which one?

FLYING LIGHTHOUSES
AND RADIOACTIVE RABBITS

Surprisingly, the sceptical theory to dismiss this case holds much sway in Britain despite the almost unprecedented level of evidence that supports it. Many people think the Rendlesham story is a nonsense that was debunked out of existence. One might even be tempted to argue that if a UFO case like Rendlesham falls, then none is safe. The whole mystery may collapse into misperception and witness exaggeration. Yet the sceptical argument has merit and deserves attention.

It has been compiled by a number of sources. The Woodbridge police claim they found its key components on the night of the first sighting, although they did not tell us this for almost three years. Forester Vince Thurkettle independently reached similar conclusions and advised *The Times* in October 1983, after the 'alien version' was hyped by the tabloid press. Similarly, astronomy writer and UFO debunker Ian Ridpath made a short film for the BBC that same week to develop the theory – without interviewing any of the witnesses. Since then new data have been added to boost – or in some cases alter – the argument, such as the extraordinary Channel 4 debunking exercise that was referred to on page 93. To me that farce is about as wide of the mark as I can imagine any theory to be.

However, what do these sceptics contest and where is their evidence?

We start with the initial sighting made from the Woodbridge east gate. The object that fell into the woods was, Ridpath suggests, the bright fireball meteor seen at 2.50 am on 26 December 1980. Alerted by this, Burroughs and Penniston entered the woods, became disorientated and saw the Orford Ness lighthouse shining through trees – mistaking it for a landed UFO. The subsequent ground traces were, as the police said right from the start, just rabbit holes. The score marks on the trees were ordinary woodcutters' notches. No significant radiation was found – just geiger counter readings that reflected normal background counts. Nor were there any unexplained effects on the light-alls or radio sets that might not have occurred inside a forest. As for the second night's adventure, this was Halt and his merry men chasing the lighthouse all over the woods and also mistaking stars for beaming spaceships in their now heightened state of what we might call 'UFOria'.

Could this startling case really boil down to a combination of such ordinary circumstances? The option is not as ludicrous as it appears for there are quite a few pieces of linking evidence.

For a start there was indeed a bright fireball meteor at the time stated. So confident was Ridpath that this was the initial source of the UFO events that he even insisted that Halt's report (which dated the first night as 27 December) must be wrong and the real date was earlier. Of course, there seemed no reason to dispute Halt's judgement in an official USAF memo penned from witness statements within days of the incident, but I have since established that Ridpath was right.

The police record supports the date as 26 December. This was also the first date cited by Steve Roberts to Brenda Butler (according to a note I found of her first mention of the matter in early January 1981, although Roberts changed the date to the 27th in all of his future statements and this was also the date that the Watton radar staff were told only 48 hours after the encounters).

The mix up occurred because of the second night about which, for several years, we knew nothing. That *had* occurred on 27/28 December and far more witnesses were present than 48 hours before. It was inevitable that these two incidents subsequently got confused. However, John Burroughs – the only man who was involved in both sightings – confirmed to me in interview that the dates for the two encounters were 25/26 and 27/28 December. I am now almost certain that this is correct.

So Ridpath was right about the dating. Might he not also have been correct to claim that the initial UFO was a fireball meteor blazing across the skies on that night?

Of course, the 2.50 am fireball is part of a train of 'comets in the sky' which turn that Christmas Day/Boxing Day period into something very weird. The brilliant meteor which Ridpath refers to could itself form a part of the problem – rather than the solution – and be just as strange as the Cosmos re-entry apparently was some six hours earlier.

More important is that the timings as offered by Burroughs and others indicate that the first encounter *preceded* 2.50 am by almost an hour. They saw the object land – not flash across the sky as a meteor does. And after it came down something was seen at the 'landing' spot for many minutes, flashing colours like a chemical fire. Unless the meteor hit the forest, for which there is no evidence, then this could not be what was seen. An impacting meteorite would have made a huge explosion and been discussed by astronomers as a scientific curiosity, not the source of a 17-year long UFO debate.

In addition, the sighting of the light from the control tower at Woodbridge coincides closely with the time when the meteor appeared. Witnesses have presumed this light to be the UFO departing and it provoked the woodland search for the now missing Burroughs and Penniston. However, it is certainly an option that this was just the meteor, as the control tower report calls it simply a 'bright light'. If so then it occurred well after the contact in the woods, and was *not* the genesis for the sighting, as this was already well underway.

Even had the two airmen been fooled by a meteor (and they believe that what they saw was no such phenomenon), what about the object seen by the four airmen at the east gate for several minutes before Burroughs and Penniston were ordered into the forest? The duration of this episode was too long for any meteor. Nor was it the lighthouse. I have stood by the east gate several times and have *never* seen the lighthouse through the trees. The dense tree coverage and the angle of view make it impossible. However, you can see the beam sweeping the sky well above the tree tops. Indeed, it is so obvious that I find it hard to believe that most people on the base who have been stationed there more than a week or two would not either know what they were seeing or be intrigued enough to ask.

Once the men entered the woods on foot and headed towards the clearing, the option that they saw the lighthouse certainly increases in strength. I have stood and watched it several times at night. If you did not realize what you were looking at (as some airmen newly arrived from the USA might not) it would seem peculiar. Being inside a forest several miles inland a lighthouse beacon would not be the first thought to explain a low-level pulsing glow. Because of the way the land slopes, the lighthouse sits on the horizon and appears almost on the ground – just as described on the Halt tape.

Of course, I have not seen the same scene as the men did on that first night because the tree cover was felled so soon after the sighting. However, the fact that there would then be many *more* trees would have made the lighthouse *less* visible. In addition, two other objects are just as easily seen at the site which the witness stories do *not* incorporate into the close encounter. One is the Shipwash lightship flashing further to the south. The other is a row of lights on a building on Orford Ness island. If the lighthouse was being mistaken for a UFO, these other lights should have seemed just as strange.

At the site the lighthouse does pulse like a winking eye, just as Halt describes on the tape. The pulses can even be timed as the beacon rotates (taking about five seconds) and there is a comparison with part of the tape where the men notice that the light briefly disappears and then shout, 'There it is again', as it reappears. This match is quite striking if you judge film of the lighthouse alongside the audio of the tape. Finally, the bearing given by the men for the location of the UFO as they walk toward the coast closely mirrors that of the Orford lighthouse as seen from the landing site.

Frankly, the first time I saw the lighthouse at night I was 80 per cent convinced that this was the explanation. When I first heard the Halt tape this conviction rose to 90 per cent. It only plummeted after talking to eye-witnesses like John Burroughs who were actually out there, although I did have some concern because the lighthouse appears as nothing more than a tiny pulsing light, not a massive red object throwing down beams towards the ground.

How could experienced airmen exaggerate such an innocent light so considerably?

However, the night of the second sighting was *misty*. Could this have magnified and reddened the lighthouse beam to create an optical illusion? Did it also distort stars, creating the later sightings? Was there a temperature inversion in the atmosphere – a fairly rare weather effect that creates a sort of mirage and bends ground lights and stars into a blurred and flattened shape?

All of this is certainly possible. I have seen many such things provoke strange UFO encounters and know that nine out of ten cases do get explained. This could be one of them. Halt told me that he considered this possibility himself, but rejected it because there was too much wind for any mist to settle nor meteorological evidence of an inversion layer. He and his men also both saw the lighthouse and the lightship and so can be certain these were not the UFO.

Indeed all of the witnesses – from Halt to Burroughs – openly ridicule the theory and say they *knew* the woods and had seen the lighthouse many times but the UFO was *not* it. Burroughs (who had lived locally for 18 months and was familiar with the woods) said he saw the lighthouse *as well as* the UFO that night but never mentioned it because it was 'just sitting there as always'. Of the structured craft seen at close quarters, which had moved through the forest, he added, 'I have never once seen a lighthouse that flew.'

If these witnesses are being honest – and I have no reason to think otherwise – then there are real problems in accepting the lighthouse as the basis for this case. Sceptics suggest that the witnesses *think* they are being honest but subconsciously misremember the facts so as to avoid embarrassment in looking like fools, given the apparent demonstration that their UFO has such a simple answer.

I personally have huge difficulties accepting that the lighthouse was the object that Burroughs and Penniston confronted in the woods on 26 December. Enormous witness misperception would be needed to introduce the shape, the symbols on the side, the flying motion and the electrostatic field reported around the landed craft, not to mention the Oz Factor influence which distorted time and space. In addition, without the mist that night, the lighthouse was plainly visible *as* a lighthouse. Less than two hours later the Woodbridge police saw it on the site, easily recognized it, and not a single airman out there with them tried to suggest this light was anything other than a lighthouse. In fact, they just ignored it – as you would if you knew it was part of the surroundings.

None of this supports the contention that the first night's UFO was a lighthouse. Nor does the opinion of the Orford Ness lighthouse keeper himself. He told me assuredly when we met in 1997, 'For some time the sceptics have been pestering me in an attempt to get me to support their theory. I cannot do it. I know what my lighthouse looked like from the forest. I have seen it in all weathers. It just could not do what these airmen and local people describe the UFO as doing.'

Nevertheless, it is far less difficult to conceive of the lighthouse being the culprit for the winking-eye object on 27 December. Perhaps it was seriously distorted by sea mist and looked unrecognizable to the witnesses. One can easily listen to the tape and reach the conclusion that this was what was taking place, although Halt and the others out there are adamant that this is nonsense and one cannot just reject their opinion. They were in that forest. We were not.

Moreover, would not the various trips into the woods at night – which we know many men from the base made in the weeks after the encounter – have speedily revealed the truth to someone? If it were just the lighthouse, the UFO would have been seen every night during this skywatching and someone would have worked out the all-too-sober truth before this case was officially reported.

As for the ground traces, it is possible that the holes in the ground resulted from rabbits burrowing but the coincidence with the landing legs on the UFO should be noted and the frozen nature of the ground taken into account as well.

The tree marks, I am satisfied, were *not* strange. They were just forestry score marks.

However, the vital clues are the huge hole in the pine-tree canopy far above the ground and the radiation. These were both recorded where the 'pod' marks were located. There seems good reason to think the radiation was sufficiently above normal background levels to intrigue the MoD experts consulted by Nick Pope (although it was not excessively dangerous). Also, clearly, something *fell* from the sky and smashed the hole at rooftop height.

So far as I know, the rabbits of Rendlesham Forest are not irradiated. Nor are they training to enter the pole vault competition at the next Olympics. This evidence has never been successfully tackled by any of the sceptics.

The theory to resolve this case works far better than we might expect – too well to be ignored, in my view. Unfortunately, it leaves a number of serious problems outstanding, particularly in regard to the first night (which in my opinion is crucial to unravelling what really went on). We must take this idea seriously. It may have answers to contribute towards the truth, particularly for the events of 27/28 December. I do suspect that some of the lights seen that night could well have been stars distorted in some way by weather patterns. But these are only side issues.

I doubt that it explains everything and, conceivably, it explains nothing. Like most aspects of this case, you have to weigh the evidence and form an opinion.

NATIONAL STEALTH

In late 1983 we received one of many anonymous calls from the base. This caller told us that he was an intelligence officer who wanted us to know the 'truth'. The UFO stories were deliberately allowed to develop, he claimed. We had been used by the US Government in order to spread such disinformation. But an object *had* indeed come down in the forest on 26 December. It was *unidentified* by all who saw it but its origins were very terrestrial. It was, in fact, a secret US test device which was triangular and about the size of a Mini car. On this occasion it was under remote control and had gone astray after an electrical problem. The home base had tried to land it safely at Woodbridge but it crashed just before it reached the end of the runway. The secret intelligence services had taken over the clear-up operation from base staff who were without 'need to know' and the witnesses were allowed to think that they had actually seen a UFO. This was perfect cover because military intelligence realized that news of the event was likely to filter out as there were too many potential witnesses. Steve Roberts had deliberately exaggerated the 'alien' story for our ears. The Watton radar staff were told an equally silly yarn by the intelligence operatives who were clearing all possible evidence by taking away radar tapes (regardless of whether they showed anything or not).

The grand plan was to hide the truth, if possible, but to allow this absurd alien spaceship story to reach the UFO community and even the media, so as to deflect serious consideration should news of the incident escape. The eyewitnesses who saw the object were shipped out of Britain as fast as possible so that none were left together to tell a consistent story and pose a threat to the tight security. As for the second night's events, these were not connected with the secret aircraft. Someone just got 'carried away', we were told.

This call seemed about as credible as many others coming in at the time – which meant we had no way to establish its authenticity or otherwise and just let it sit in the growing file of 'possible answers'. Fourteen years later the view that this might point the way towards the truth is just as valid.

There is no doubt that secret aircraft are being built and tested all of the time. Usually these are developed in locations well away from prying eyes – such as the notorious 'Area 51' in the Nevada desert where several generations of stealth aircraft have been designed and test flown and where – UFO legend has it – captured alien spacecraft also reside under top secret cover.

In my view, this 'alien spaceship' tale is an example of disinformation. From my conversations with aircraft designers who worked on stealth projects in the USA, there are craft under various design stages at Area 51, which are more than a decade from being revealed to the world. Some have stunning experimental designs that incorporate, for example, nuclear-powered motors. To stop too much snooping the 'alien' rumours have been happily allowed to spread. These may attract 'UFOlogists and assorted kooks' (as was said to me by one technician) who go to look for ET from neighbouring mountain tops, but who are not considered a threat to the research. The air of ridicule that most aviation competitors attach to UFOs ensures that they leave these wild legends alone and defuses any real attention that might otherwise be paid to the projects.

Building and testing aircraft in the middle of a desert is one thing but there comes a time when the bird has to fly the coop and spread its wings in an environment more like the one it would face during operational conditions. At such a point several are located at strategic bases with good security cover and are flown on exercises in the middle of the night to minimize potential witnesses. Certain 'enhancements' simulate the UFO-like appearance of the object in test flight conditions so that if it is by chance seen during its travels then it will be reported in overly exotic terms. In this way the truth about what is really flying around is effectively obscured. This has worked many times, I was assured.

Looking at the UFO records it is very easy to see how this is possible. In October 1978 reports began to appear of a small triangular craft which developed the nickname 'the silent Vulcan' in UFO circles. It was frequently witnessed in Leicestershire and surrounding counties. The name was given because it resembled a Vulcan bomber but was whisper quiet, which Vulcans most definitely are not!

The reports were so consistent that a few UFOlogists suspected these to be secret aircraft and plotted them as coming from Alconbury (the joint RAF/USAF base where Jim Penniston was first transferred on his arrival in the UK). Years later the existence of a so-called 'Stealth' jet became suspected and, despite further years of outright denials by the Pentagon, the existence of this aircraft was finally admitted. Although it is still covered by top security, the first generation US Stealth has now been on display and is, indeed, a small triangular aircraft which is remarkably quiet and designed so as to minimize its radar detection profile. It was used effectively during the Gulf War and seems remarkably like the 'silent Vulcan' of UFO lore.

Stealth was first designed and tested at Area 51, but from 1975 (a decade before it was widely recognized as even being 'on the drawing board') several prototypes were flown according to Jane's, the aviation historians. There were a number of accidents which were very quickly covered up by the secret services to prevent news about this sophisticated technology from getting out. The first Stealth to fly in Britain were allegedly flown from Alconbury, probably in the late 1970s/early 1980s. This seems too much of a coincidence and it is surely likely that this was the real origin of the 'silent vulcan' sightings.

Of course, technology does not stand still. It is certain that in 1980 things were under test that are only now coming 'on line' as acknowledged aircraft and that fascinating devices are being flown today which we shall probably not see at air shows until well into the twenty-first century.

Britain is also a world leader in the field of what are called *drones* or RPV (remotely piloted vehicles). In effect, these are like super-sophisticated multi-million pound model aircraft. Usually only a few feet in diameter, they are under electronic control – perhaps from many miles away – and can be flown into areas where it would be too dangerous to risk a pilot on a spying mission.

Often the design of a truly revolutionary aircraft does not progress straight from a little model being tested in a wind tunnel to a full-sized craft that is flown just like the real thing. An inter-mediary stage tests the technology by building a mid-sized remote-controlled drone.

This appears to be what is happening at the British Aerospace plant at Warton on the Lancashire coast. There were countless reports of triangular UFOs between 1995 and 1997 in an area that ranges from Derbyshire to Cumbria. It is now widely believed by UFOlogists that these are small RPV testing a new generation stealth technology known as HALO (high agility, low observability). According to Tim Matthews, a Lancashire UFOlogist, who has gone to considerable lengths to investigate the matter, contacts have told him that this includes research into two new extensions of the orig-inal stealth technology: first, VTOL (vertical take off and landing capability) and, second, a new microwave propulsion system that generates incredible manoeuvring power but which still has poten-tial side effects (such as electrical interference on the ground below). They are being flown at night, usually over the ocean, but are seen – and reported – as UFOs when over land.

These Mini-car-sized triangles are probably just the latest phase in an ongoing research project. They will not be the last. Almost cer-tainly other covert military aviation projects have produced waves of UFO activity in the past and lurk undetected in the files of UFO asso-ciations.

What does this tell us about the events in Rendlesham Forest? It is very possible that some project was being tested. Christmas night would be an ideal choice as there would be very limited media avail-able to pay attention to any possible witnesses, who would probably be disregarded as in the party spirit anyhow! If it was under control from Mildenhall or Alconbury and something went wrong, attempting to land at Woodbridge makes sense. In 1980 this was where the Aerospace Rescue and Recovery Squadron was located. Tied to the intelligence units of AFSAC and Project Moon Dust (the very people who, Clifford Stone tells us, were brought to Woodbridge after the close encounters) this was originally set up to recover military space hardware that the USA might bring down in the waters of northern Europe. Of course, it would also be the perfect choice to recover speedily and clear up signs of another kind of secret technology. Its staff were used to dealing with top secret missions.

The Aerospace Rescue and Recovery squadron still exists – one of the few USAF units left in Britain after the pull out of troops. With the closure of Woodbridge in 1993, it transferred to Alconbury.

Intriguingly, the triangular object allegedly involved in the 1980 crash landing returned to the vicinity of Rendlesham Forest several times afterwards, supporting the prospect that some kind of secret aircraft might indeed have been under test .

One event occurred on 7 October 1983 when a number of villagers at Hollesley near Orford Ness observed a small dark triangular object with red lights that hovered above the marshes and then accelerated towards Woodbridge. It emitted only a faint humming noise, like an electrical motor.

If this was a remotely piloted drone it might explain tragic circumstances three weeks later on 28 October when two RAF jets were lost in East Anglia on the same day. A Harrier flying east from Cambridge towards the coast suddenly fell out of the sky for no apparent reason. The pilot was killed and the mystery never solved as the aircraft seemed to be in good mechanical order.

In the other incident a Tornado over Norfolk had a two-man crew. While both ejected, the pilot's body was never found and the navigator could only compound the mystery. He said that the jet was behaving perfectly when they just lost all electrical control. He could not talk to the pilot by radio and the navigation jammed, causing the Tornado to plunge at a steep angle towards the North Sea.

Were both of these aircraft affected by some mysterious electrical interference? That possibility was apparently taken seriously by the RAF at the time. They sought a natural phenomenon and found none. But what if it was an artificial by-product of a top secret experiment by the US Government?

At just before 1 am on 24 August 1984 another major incident involved a Kondair Trislander freight aircraft. While flying from

Stanstead, it was struck in mid-flight when passing over Rendlesham Forest. It lost an engine but managed to land safely at Amsterdam. Inspection found a hole in the fuselage and metal debris that suggested some kind of small craft had hit it side on. Unfortunately, there were no scheduled flights – either civil or military – that might have been responsible. The national defence services were consulted in an attempt to discover what might have collided with this plane but the answer was never discovered – or at least never admitted if it was. This craft was undoubtedly a terrestrial object. I corresponded with Kondair and saw some of the fragments pulled from the damaged aircraft. These were not exotic but very down to Earth. Was it a drone on another nocturnal mission over the forest?

Certainly it is possible to imagine this being the cause of the events on the first night of the Rendlesham landings? It also explains the nagging problem of why UFOlogists seem to have been spun a line about aliens chatting to the base commander as a deliberate distraction. Perhaps we might even get an explanation for the lack of any follow up to Halt's report and the MoD's apparent knowledge of what happened and their assurance that this case had no 'defence significance'. If it was a rogue drone that was 'identified' as non hostile then no UFO investigation would have been necessary.

However, you must remember that people like Michael Hesletine and Lord Trefgarne *insisted* in writing that there had been no 'testing of secret devices'. Would they really risk putting such a lie in writing? Did they even *know* the truth if it was a USAF project?

Former French Minister of Defence Robert Galley, said in a recent interview granted to UFO *Presence* magazine that he had received reports of a 'UFO' overflying nuclear facilities. The US Government denied knowing anything about it and France was an ally, but Galley got his air force to pursue the 'blip' and his suspicions were vindicated. It proved to be a US Stealth on a covert mission. He quickly got the Americans to hand over their film of French nuclear capabilities!

However, we cannot forget the real difficulties. Would nobody on Bentwaters have learnt the truth? How could the remains of the craft be removed so quickly? What about the testimony of Burroughs and Penniston? What they saw in the forest at close quarters was no US military aircraft and it took off again, according to their account. No secret aircraft could have done that from a forest.

Once again the theory looks promising – up to a point – but also has problems .

BROWN BEAR PICNIC

Another of the covert messages from the base that came during our investigation was most mysterious. 'Stop looking for UFOs,' the voice informed us. 'You should be looking for a brown bear.'

This meant nothing at the time but we soon established that 'Brown Bear' was USAF code for a Soviet space satellite. This took us right back to the start of this story and the mystery of the burn-up of Cosmos 749, the military satellite that passed over Britain in its death throes and 'fell' somewhere east of Rendlesham Forest. All of the broad hints about the importance of the 'comets in the sky' throughout the rest of that night came to mind.

Gradually, over the years, the pieces of this particular puzzle have slotted together. There have been many sources. Remember all of those stories about green fireballs in the vicinity of Orford Ness, such as the pungent-smelling object that irradiated the postman on the beach at Sizewell. Then there are the local claims about electrical interference on TV sets and the unexplained car stop incidents near Orford Ness. These had been connected with the events at the site where the NSA were conducting secret experiments. But what was the nature of these experiments?

Derek Longman, who had worked at the remand centre at Hollesley, delved into what was happening a mile or so away on the Ness. He says that the 'Cobra Mist' programme was set up in 1971 and locals were told it closed in 1973 but that there were numerous signs of ongoing activity on the island and strong opinion that the project simply went underground after major breakthroughs.

Cobra Mist was, I have discovered, officially an attempt to create a long-range radar by beaming high-intensity energy into the stratosphere and reflecting this back from 'over the horizon'. Because traditional radar beams are limited by the curvature of the Earth to a fairly narrow range, such a scheme would produce a devastatingly effective defensive shield against nuclear attack.

Intriguingly, the official closure of Cobra Mist on the Ness was announced in June 1983 – the very month that the Halt memo was squeezed out under US Freedom of Information.

However, a new and much expanded (as well as hugely funded) programme – Cold Witness – was announced as a replacement and the US defence administration refused to say where it would be located as it was to be top secret. Then, in 1984, papers were dropped by accident by a US scientist catching a plane at Heathrow. These revealed the home of Cold Witness was Orford Ness – as well as the fact that NSA agents, high-level physicists and MoD intelligence staff were working there in unison.

Cold Witness ran until l991, when it was announced that it was to be wound down. The closure of Woodbridge and Bentwaters was occurring at the same time and the two events were probably related.

Were the electrical effects, car stops and green fireballs side effects of this 20-year-long project? Massive beams of energy were being fired into the upper atmosphere. There had to be unexpected side effects and miscalculations. Did one of these occur in December l980? Was the 'jamming' beam that felled two RAF planes in l983 a product of the same experiment? Colonel Halt intriguingly told me, 'Good luck with finding out what the NSA were up to. We had to clean up after them a couple of times'.

One thing we do know comes from a leaked secret memo which I received from a friendly military contact. It referred to a 'NATO warning system' which had been installed on 'Orford Ness in Suffolk'. The report warns military traffic that this is a 'highly sensitive electronic device emanating powerful electrical fields with harmful effects on people in the near vicinity'. It even warned that ships with inflammable and explosive cargo should be steered away from this part of the Suffolk coast.

Clearly something very interesting was underway on this narrow coastal spit.

More information came to me from Stephen Carr, a local man with an electronics background who had decided to get to the bottom of what Cobra Mist and Cold Witness were trying to do. He told me of what he called 'Operation Bear Trap' which he suggested worked in the following manner.

As an unexpected side effect of the Cobra Mist project, the NSA had discovered that some of the high-intensity beams were entering space and not simply bouncing back to Earth. Their electronic interference was actually affecting the controls of orbiting satellites which passed through the beam. By sheer fortune, a prototype 'star wars' mechanism had been discovered – uncontrollable and very crude – but a step towards a weapon that could actually 'kill' orbiting spy satellites or spacecraft conveying nuclear weapons by scrambling their electronics and on-board computer systems. There were military fears that any future world war might be won or lost in orbit.

Carr told me that he thought 'Operation Bear Trap' was a test of this beam, carefully chosen because of the timing of the re-entry of

Cosmos 749. This was predicted to occur on Christmas night. The NSA knew the British media would be at a low ebb, so they could fire the beam and see if they could 'jam' the electronics on the Soviet military satellite and deflect its orbital path causing it to burn up in a controlled fashion. If they succeeded, commentators would assume it was simply following the predicted decay. Any visual phenomena accompanying the event would be written off as 'flying saucers' and doubtless ignored.

Even the name Cobra Mist suggests something more than just a radar system. One can envisage a deadly curtain of energy that can strike with quick effect to 'kill' an opponent.

Was this what happened? Did Cobra Mist fire up that night and interfere with the re-entry path of the Cosmos satellite? Is that why its orbital path changed so dramatically according to astronomers? Was it made to burn up over northern Europe/southern England in such a way that part of its resistant metallic motor escaped the fires of friction and plunged to Earth near Orford Ness? Were the other 'comets in the sky' a result of pieces from Cosmos 749 being 'chipped off' as the natural decay process was severely compromised during several hours of testing?

This is all speculation, of course. But look at all the facts that slot together. The basis of Cobra Mist, as we understand it, suggests it did fire energy beams towards space. They were not intended to down satellites, but that may well have been an unexpected 'bonus'. The various sky spectaculars over East Anglia that Christmas night are strange. The problems astronomers found with the orbital decay of the Soviet satellite and the puzzle of the Paco de Arcos sighting are real – if this was Cosmos 749, it was coming in far too low as if on some kind of semi-controlled descent.

Indeed, if the Christmas holiday was deliberately chosen for a test of the system because of the 'holiday' factor, we must remember (see Chapter 1) how Cosmos 1068 burned up on New Year's Eve in 1978 and another Soviet satellite (Cosmos 2268) on the eve of April Fools Day in 1993. All of these cases involve phenomena burning up en route towards the east coast of England.

Speculation or not, Alan Bond independently came to a similar conclusion from his position as a rocket scientist. If you recall he phoned me in late 1984 to say that he wanted to check out a theory developed after reading *Sky Crash*.

When he did come back, he warned me to drop all research into this area and said that the radiation in the forest might have resulted from the recovery of a nuclear motor from a downed Soviet military satellite. He also said that there were 'problems with the orbital figures' regarding another satellite decay – again a Soviet military mission – this one coded Cosmos 1226. It burnt up on the very day of the Halt encounter in Rendlesham Forest (27 December).

Dr Bond stressed this was simply a theory and said that he was not going to investigate it any further because *if* it was true it was properly a national secret and not our business. I agree with him, but doubt that he realized that others had also reached such an opinion from different perspectives. As a result, the cat was already well and truly out of the bag if, indeed, there *was* a cat or a bag!

Nevertheless, it has always intrigued me that on 29 December, just three days after this incident in Rendlesham Forest, another incredible UFO case occurred 5,000 miles (8,000 km) away – on a country road near Huffman, Texas – not far from the main NASA headquarters in Houston. This case is so bizarre that, like Rendlesham Forest, it has taxed the investigative prowess of UFOlogists ever since. Its main champion has been space-shuttle engineer and UFOlogist John Schuessler who is currently compiling a book about the affair. In November 1983 I drove to the University of Nebraska with Dr J. Allen Hynek to meet this scientist and swap notes on our respective investigations. This proved very interesting indeed.

On that Monday night three people had been for a meal and were returning home. They were Betty Cash, her friend Vicky Landrum and Vicky's grandson Colby. Suddenly, a triangular object appeared on the road ahead, surrounded by fiery light. The terrified youngster was shielded in the car by Vicky who advised him that it was the end of the world and that Jesus would protect them. Betty got out and stood in front of the vehicle to watch the spectacle – a decision with near fatal consequences.

Terrible heat was pouring from the object. Indeed, Betty's wedding ring began to burn as eddy currents were seemingly induced into it by some energy field. (Later her finger swelled up.) She hurried back to the car but the metal of the door had become so hot that she burnt her hand even though holding a coat over it in order to protect herself as she turned the handle.

After long moments it became obvious that the UFO was not flying but was being shepherded, perhaps being carried by a whole flotilla of large twin-rotor Chinook helicopters. They flew off across the countryside and disappeared. However, there were other witnesses to this array of helicopters on their continued passage.

Upon arrival home, all three witnesses became ill. Colby threw up over his bed. He and Vicky were sick for a couple of days with symptoms like bad flu. Betty Cash became far more seriously ill and, within a couple of days, had slipped into unconsciousness. She was hospitalized in a coma and spent weeks in intensive care and undergoing treatment for horrific injuries. Schuessler's photographs of this aftermath are some of the most terrifying I have ever seen.

There is no doubt from the condition of Betty Cash that she was suffering from the effects of radiation exposure. Huge welts appeared on her face. More than half of her hair fell out in clumps. She suffered long-term injuries after that night which required frequent medical treatment at enormous expense. Being closest to the object and out in the open she seems to have taken the brunt of the exposure. But what on earth were these three people exposed to?

It seems inconceivable that if a Soviet nuclear motor *was* retrieved from Rendlesham Forest several days earlier it would have been ferried across the Texas countryside in this way. However, the links between the cases are stunning. The shape is very like that described by Burroughs and Penniston. Then there is the radiation. The NASA-trained Aerospace Rescue and Recovery squadron at Woodbridge links with the main NASA HQ near Huffman.

You do start to wonder what on Earth was going on here.

There are very few places from which so many large helicopters could have come. All of these sources are military and they denied to the US courts having been responsible. Researchers ultimately concluded that, as Huffman is so close to the coast near Galveston, the object could have been picked up from an aircraft carrier and ferried to its destination by helicopters belonging to some highly covert military operation. If something was recovered from Rendlesham Forest in the early hours of 26 December, could it have been shipped to the Texas coast in just under four days? Would a sea passage have been used as opposed to an aerial one? Where was its ultimate destination?

There are many questions that befuddle the mind. However, what is undeniable is that these three witnesses were exposed to a radiating triangular object and suffered dreadfully. Despite legal action against the US Government, who were charged with liability for Betty Cash's medical bills, the origin of this object and the helicopters has never been established and the US Government has evaded censure. But if these witnesses are being truthful – and nobody who has met them seems to think otherwise – then the US Government clearly must take some responsibility for this incident. Either they *knew* what was going on or their defences should have protected the citizens of Texas from it.

However, the story of this theory was not over. The former MoD air commodore and head of the UFO department – Ralph Noyes – chose to write a book about UFOs in 1985. It was, curiously, *not* a factual book but a novel entitled A *Secret Property*. Noyes stressed that this was not based on any specific case, nor did it carry a theory to which he was 'wedded', but set out a hypothesis he wanted to test.

Noyes placed his story in Rendlesham Forest where UFO events involve a landed object near a USAF base he called 'Bentbridge' which had a commander named Colonel Hoyt. Nearby was a secret research facility on an island called 'Blandfordness'. This does sound all too familiar!

The plot revolves around a secret weapon harnessing a natural energy and firing it into space in bizarre fashion. All sorts of political skulduggery is associated and UFOlogists are used as part of the conspiracy – which is cracked by the brave man from the MoD UFO department! One of the early consequences of the use of this Blandfordness 'beam' affects a Soviet space mission.

It is all a good deal more complex than this summary and a most entertaining read, but the fact that this high-level MoD man has 'theorized' along these lines in such a blatant manner is truly fascinating. It is intriguingly similar to ideas which, at the time, Noyes probably could not have known were being researched in reality by the likes of Stephen Carr and Alan Bond .

If Cold Witness *was* involved in the events of December 1980, goodness knows what 'progress' has happened since then, but there are some clues.

In September 1991 the space shuttle D*iscovery* filmed some odd lights at the very edge of the Earth's atmosphere. These were moving at phenomenal speed and scientists were baffled. They appeared to have come *from* Earth and were heading into space at oblique angles. Subsequent footage has been captured by more recent shuttle missions.

Then, on 15 December 1996, in San Francisco, a research team from Stanford announced some preliminary findings into the investigation of a space light it was calling 'elves'. These have been noted for over a decade and occur far above the Earth on the rim of space. Blue jets and streamers of light have been filmed from aircraft high in the stratosphere and from orbital space missions. They emerge from clouds and shoot spaceward. Special equipment was being built to try to understand where these beams of energy were coming from. They assumed these were natural phenomena, but, of course, they could have had an artificial origin via some covert experiment.

Stephen Carr never finished his research into Cold Witness. He died suddenly while still in his forties. Now the once-so-secret island was beginning a new life as a National Trust tourist attraction, it might be a good idea to leave whatever dark experiments had once lurked on Orford Ness well and truly alone.

MINDBENDER

In A *Secret Property* Ralph Noyes imagines an energy beam that was not simply some type of high-intensity radar. It combined sophisticated computer-controlled technology with the power within human consciousness and the natural forces of the Earth itself. Blending both mind and electronics together, it endeavoured to forge a powerful 'psychic' weapon.

In fact, there is real (deeply secret) research into what is known as 'psychotronic' warfare. This uses the known sensitivity of the human brain to strong electrical fields and other bursts of energy (such as microwave radiation) and attempts to create a force that will produce a 'mindbending' consequence on anyone subjected to it. One can readily envisage its offensive capabilities if people can be made to see realistic hallucinations of a terrifying nature.

Dr Michael Persinger, at Laurentian State University in Canada, noticed in 1977 that reports of UFOs, aliens and apparitions clustered in certain locations. As a result he made a long series of investigations and discovered what he called 'transients' – local pockets of strong electro-magnetic energy that were generated by natural processes within the Earth. He speculated that a person who entered this invisible zone of power could experience mind-distorting effects if the energy stimulated certain areas of the brain. As a result these people hallucinated a close encounter, or a sighting of Bigfoot, or other assorted strange phenomena. Persinger felt this might explain many aspects of the paranormal and was not attempting to build a weapon – simply to explore a new threshold of neurological science.

Unfortunately, work like this often comes to the attention of military strategists who see beyond the intentions of the original researcher.

Persinger has since put his theories into practice by developing a machine. This creates an artificial transient inside his laboratory and exposes willing volunteers to its effects. Results suggest that they *do* experience feelings of disassociation from their bodies, which involves an altered state of consciousness and symptoms of distortion of time and space, not unlike those of the Oz Factor as reported by close-encounter witnesses.

Is it possible that such a device has been developed as a weapon for military use and tested in a location where there was a strong USAF presence? The hapless victims would then be used as guinea pigs to see how they responded to the mindbending distortions of the energy field.

If such a possibility were real, then a number of the problems we find within the Rendlesham Forest case would start to make sense. Perhaps even the 'comets' in the sky were atmospheric processes being stirred up by such an electrical field weapon.

Think about it. There *was* an intense electrical field in the forest. All the evidence suggests this. Burroughs and Penniston told of the rush of static charge that washed over them. Bustinza reported seeing an airman's hair standing on end. Radios were filled with static. The light-alls would not work properly. Some of the civilian witnesses 'sensed' the phenomenon before seeing it, as one feels the tingle of an approaching electrical storm. Dogs were especially alert. Local forest wildlife, which would be unbothered by the lighthouse or a meteor, went into a frenzy, upset by something.

If the woods were being swathed in some sort of electrical mist that triggered hallucinations, then those who were the most deeply affected – either because they were the closest to its source or were somehow more susceptible – would have reported severe reality distortions. The susceptibility appears to be within a person's temporal lobe (an area of the brain that seems particularly prone to these energy fields). This effect is just what Burroughs and Penniston did describe. Burroughs even felt 'sensitised' after the encounter as if his brain was still reacting to the effects for a day or two – a not uncommon consequence of exposure to very intense energy fields of this type.

Groups of witnesses together might see something vaguely similar built out of glowing lights that might result from the energy field. But other witnesses in different parts of the forest would presumably see different things. Is this why what Burroughs and Penniston saw is not the same as what Halt and the others witnessed, or why there are the seriously 'weird' reports from people like Larry Warren?

Did he really believe that he was seeing little aliens talking to the base commander?

After all, if we are dealing in stimulated hallucinations here, then *anything* is possible.

Remember also those accounts of wraith-like figures passing through trucks or balls of light going straight through tree trunks. Such physical impossibilities present no difficulty for a hallucination. In fact they are a characteristic – as we all know from the oddities of our dreams.

If this was a covert experiment to test the responses of the airmen it explains the puzzling aftermath that has perplexed witnesses such as Charles Halt. Nobody in the US Government would pursue the UFO report because they knew (even if the witnesses were not to be told) precisely what had provoked it.

We might also now be able to take more seriously the stories of both Larry Warren and Adrian Bustinza about what they saw in the forest. Although the British Government deny any involvement, both men say they were out there in the forest that night. I cannot imagine such a test as this occurring without the co-operation of the MoD, possibly via RAF Bawdsey.

Bustinza says there were British officials in the woods. He also says that film was taken away from the airmen who had cameras. Of course, this may not have been to prevent any visual evidence of the experiment from getting out but, on the contrary, to prevent the *lack* of any physical evidence from becoming apparent. If the stories that I have heard from some of the witnesses are true then some film *did* evade capture. It does *not* show the UFOs that the men thought they were filming. It shows dark sky. Only the fact that these people were hallucinating in a way so vivid that they were convinced that what they were seeing was real could explain that anomaly. Hallucinations would not show up on film.

Warren even says that movie cameras were set up in the woods to record officially what was taking place and that some of the high-level personnel in the forest seemed to be waiting for what was about to happen. Popular UFO legend has it that this is because they were expecting an alien landing, perhaps set up between ET and the US Government. It might also mean that these military observers knew that an experiment was about to be conducted on these unfortunate witnesses.

Only that possibility makes sense of Warren's further claim that these officers were not interested in the aliens or the UFO for themselves, but were instead studying the reaction of the airmen who were watching these fantastic things. Surely even high-ranking USAF personnel would not be so familiar with visiting aliens that they would prefer to look at the goggle-eyed expressions of their entranced juniors and ignore the extraterrestrial wonders unfolding in the forest?

If true, this has to suggest that the whole point of the exercise was to see how the men *responded* to the events. That was what was being filmed – not UFOs.

In fact, Larry Warren told me that he found it rather odd that in the little knot of people in the forest with him that night there were many very junior personnel. It was as if the more inexperienced were purposely selected to take part in this operation. Was that in antic- ipation that they would be the most likely to show maximum response to such an experiment?

The real problem with accepting such a theory is that for it to work we might have to assume collusion from senior officers on the base – for which I have no evidence at all. If Halt, for example, was part of a conspiracy then he is a very good actor and, frankly, I can- not believe that he was.

Of course, it is more than possible that hardly anyone (*if* anyone at all) at Bentwaters at the time knew they were being used as guinea pigs. The observers probably came from more covert opera- tions at Bawdsey or on Orford Ness or elsewhere. If Warren *is* telling the truth then it seems hard to deny that someone from the US and/or British Government *knew* what was going on that night.

Indeed, if this kind of weapon were being tested in the forest, per- haps that was what caused Halt and his team to see the lighthouse in very exotic terms. The lighthouse *must* have been visible all night as Halt stood at the trace site taking measurements. If it was the source of the encounters described on the tape (and some of the evidence certainly fits that premise) then what caused it suddenly to appear in such a fantastic form that it fooled all these men?

It is worth noting that the onset of this sighting coincides with the report that the local 'barnyard animals' were starting to make an 'awful lot of noise'. This was at 1.48 am. Something evidently upset them at the same time as the UFO appeared. If a weapon to trigger hallucinations was creating an electrical energy field in the forest, it may well have equally affected the animals.

Of course, this is all hypothetical, but I have not simply conjured it up out of thin air. I have set out the way in which such a theory might work in direct response to some actual evidence.

In May 1992 I was lecturing at a conference in Lincoln, Nebraska, and renewed my acquaintance with Ray Boeche, the church minister and UFOlogist who has been such a tremendous investigator throughout this case. He was wrestling with his conscience as to whether to reveal a story that had just come his way. It was provided by two men who had some documentation to support their claim and who advised Boeche that they had decided, after months of contemplation, that they had a moral duty to tell him what they knew. They believed that they had the answer to the events in Rendlesham Forest.

These men professed to be agents working for the US intelligence community. They had at one point been with the CIA but had now come into contact with a very secret experiment that was initiated in 1978. This is a device which manipulates the subatomic basis of matter at a quantum level and builds a bridge between mind and physical substance. If I understood it correctly, this supposedly stimulated the mind into having vivid hallucinations but, at the same time, created physical effects in the real world which could take on a semblance of the appearance of the hallucinated images. In other words, what was seen was mostly in the mind – and certainly a product of the subconscious imagination – but it was not entirely without physical form and partially substantial in the same way that a hologram is real, but has no weight or solidity. The result is a terrifying apparition.

Early tests of this technology were conducted on military personnel – some in England around 1980. These men felt sure this was the cause of the nightmare in Rendlesham Forest. In fact this is remarkably like a theory I set out for all strange phenomena in my 1990 book *Mind Monsters*. Here I was proposing a natural mechanism as cause, not a top secret experiment. But secret weapons often start out as someone tinkering with innocuous natural phenomena. The atom bomb is the obvious example.

Checking back through my records, I have found two fascinating cases that may well tie in with this theory. Both occurred at other military bases in Europe during the 1970s. Both involved what appear to be frightening apparitions that were clearly not physically real but which were realistic enough to result in severe physical reactions from the military personnel who witnessed them. In each case the humanoid figure that was seen glowed with a phosphorus-like energy in vivid colours that are not unlike the oranges and greens that accompany laser-projected holograms.

One case occurred at a British base, the Dakeelia Barracks in Cyprus. A soldier on guard saw a brightly glowing form heading towards his room. It was humming and seemed to be charged with electricity, causing its hair to stand on end. In panic, the soldier bolted his door as his fierce wolfhound cowered in terror. The horrified army man fired a bolt from an underwater speargun through the door when he thought the figure was about to enter. This required a feat of strength normally impossible and which was presumably facilitated by the adrenalin rush of sheer terror. Hours later, when the relief guard arrived, the otherwise brave soldier was found still trembling on the floor. The dog never recovered and was 'turned overnight into a devout coward' as the witness told me.

The other case was investigated by Spanish researchers who found supporting military data as proof. It occurred at the air force base at Talvera La Real and involved the repeated hearing of a high-pitched whine on a perimeter area of the base. The guard dog brought in by the patrol covered its ears and responded in pain and terror. Then a floating form with a greenish cast, looking like a monstrous alien, manifested by the base wall. One guard was felled by an electrical blast of energy. The other two emptied several rounds which passed straight through the ghostly apparition. This vanished, along with a sound as if something was being switched off. The felled guard recovered slowly but spent some time in a military hospital suffering disorientation and various neurological problems which suggested that part of his brain had been almost 'fried' by an electrical energy discharge.

Perhaps we should seek other cases in the UFO records where 'holographic' images appear to have been seen. There are some. It is chillingly possible to envisage early tests of a weapon that might have been put to a much greater use in Rendlesham Forest only a couple of years after these incidents.

I asked Charles Halt to comment on theories such as the secret beam weapon and downing of a nuclear satellite. Surprisingly he was willing to admit the possibility. He told me that he had checked with the Aerospace Rescue and Recovery Squadron but their records indicated no involvement with the case. However, as he well understood, the lack of any evidence that such things took place is not proof that they never happened. As he put it, 'I would not be too amazed if something like this might explain part of what occurred that weekend.'

17

AFTERTHOUGHTS

THE ALIEN UNIVERSE

O
F COURSE, all of these rational theories are not what has attracted people to this case. The media have not debated them. The acres of print devoted to this incident by the tabloids came about because of the widespread belief that we had a visitation by aliens.

UFOs certainly exist. I have investigated too many cases over the years to deny that fact. However, it is simply wrong to assume that any event resulting from UFO activity is, by consequence, a result of aliens landing on this planet. It is perfectly possible to believe in UFOs and yet reject the existence of aliens just as vigorously as the most hardened sceptic.

The word UFO covers a broad spread of phenomena. Many of them are naturally occurring events on the fringes of known science. They involve atmospheric processes that are potentially interesting and may lead to technological advances. However, most of them are completely irrelevant to the question of whether we are alone in the cosmos.

Just two illustrations will suffice, although there are others.

The discovery by French UFOlogist Fernand Lagarde, that many sightings congregate around fault lines in rocks, led to experiments by UFOlogist Paul Devereux and geologists such as Dr Paul McCartney. The facilities of the US Bureau of Mines in Colorado, under the supervision of Dr Brian Brady, were then brought to bear. This research showed that, when put under stress – e.g. by large bodies of water or quarrying – the rocks within these faults can release their pent-up energy in an unexpected way. Rather than simply producing a devastating earthquake, this force leaks out more slowly, causing a chain reaction in the surrounding atmosphere and balls of glowing energy that can ride on magnetic currents generated by our planet. These 'earthlights', as Devereux poetically calls them, have been shown to be a real phenomenon to a reasonable degree of scientific acceptability.

However, this completely terrestrial phenomenon has a hidden consequence. If we can understand why a fault line in the Yorkshire Pennines produces a steady stream of lights in the sky and yet the San Andreas fault has the potential to demolish half of California, then maybe we can find a way to defuse the awesome power of killer earthquakes.

Then there are crop circles. Undoubtedly, all of the fancy patterns and the vast majority of circles of any sort are the result of human trickery. However, the need to investigate the matter by serious UFOlogists and scientists, such as meteorologist Dr Terence Meaden and plasma physicist Dr Yoshi-Hiko Ohtsuki, brought about an unexpected discovery.

It is now clear that some atmospheric force has been producing ground traces in the form of swirled circles for hundreds of years. It appears to be a rare and naturally stable form of high-intensity energy screwed up into a ball or tube of rotating light. It is often reported as a UFO but the Japanese researchers at Waseda University are working on reproducing this effect in the laboratory. The work is no academic exercise. If they can tap this energy, it will be of real value to mankind, in the same way that we tamed thunderbolts and now use electricity in so many different ways throughout our lives.

Unfortunately, while the Japanese are investing many yen in the study of these so-called 'plasma vortices', the chances that Britain will make serious progress in this new frontier are almost nil. Alerted to the possibilities, the energy commission of the EC has tried to expand a French project, run by atmospheric scientists in Toulouse, into a European-wide study but several British politicians have openly rubbished the idea by inspiring media reports that Brussels bureaucrats want to waste money chasing little green men.

The very fact that the energy commission sourced this project tells us the nonsense of this idea. Sadly, the media obsession with the view that UFOs *must* be craft flown by visiting aliens means that this significant and sober research has been lost amidst the cackles.

You can be sure that the military forces behind the scenes of the UFO cover-up are not ignoring these matters. Research into these natural energies will be progressing. Irrespective of whether there has ever been a single alien visit to Earth, there are genuine UFO events that remain unexplained and which continue to happen all around us. The vast potential within them is not lost on the powers-that-be.

This may well be a key reason why UFO data are still being collated. The Pentagon and MoD are not collecting sightings like so many stamps for the fun of it. Taxpayers' money is not being flippantly tossed away on wild ideas. Scientific advice to these administrations *must* be that there is something important to be gained from investigation.

Unfortunately, the evidence of history tells us one disturbing fact. Because science is convinced by media frippery that UFOs are nonsense (or rather *aliens* are nonsense – which they assume to be the same thing), these are not issues to be debated at scientific conferences or to which research funds are being channelled. All research that does go on is covert and probably under the control of the military. Consequently, if we do end up with destructive weapons rather than cures for earthquake activity, the blame lies squarely on our own shoulders.

UFOlogists are guilty for not recognizing the responsibility they have. Making extreme claims without evidence may get someone on TV and make money by selling lots of books but it can be an intellectual dishonesty. There is more to the UFO mystery than alien starships (whether these are real or otherwise) and more of us should be shouting that to all who will listen.

The media are also to blame for failing to promote the more modest data and concentrating instead on hyping the little green men stories. Far too often the person with the daftest idea or the wildest quotes will get all the publicity and objective commentary is simply ignored. This reinforces public perception and misconceptions abound about UFOs.

However, scientists are not immune to this necessary censure. Far too often they have failed to look beyond the silly headlines or the vociferous UFO buffs. It only takes a short time to acquaint yourself with evidence that proves conclusively that there are genuine scientific anomalies behind some of the best documented close encounters. The case in this book is a good one but hardly unique. More scientists should stop taking the tabloids and trust to the evidence.

It may well be that some kind of naturally occurring UFO was manifesting in Rendlesham Forest. One or two of the witnesses, such as John Burroughs, have emphasized that possibility to me. A good deal of what went on – from the electrical effects to the lights in the sky – showed common features of the UFO phenomenon and for such data these naturally occurring processes seem likely answers.

This is not to say that the UFO mystery is devoid of any prospect of visitors from beyond. I have never come across any evidence that overwhelmingly supports that fact, let alone proves it, but equally, there are sufficient puzzling cases – of which the events in this book certainly form one – where that option cannot be ruled out.

I suspect that this may well be the opinion of the government agencies who study UFOs and is the real reason for their need to bury the truth. Nobody is quite sure what is going on and that scares them a lot.

The object described by Burroughs and Penniston at very close quarters did not seem like a light produced by atmospheric processes. It appeared in the guise of an aerial craft of fantastic capabilities. This alone does not guarantee that such a thing was present. Witnesses can – and do – frequently report seeing incredible machines when something far less concrete was present. I have seen twinkling stars and airships, silhouetted trees and windblown dustbin bags turned into alien craft by human perception by witnesses who are far from deluded.

However, very rarely do such mistaken witnesses get as close to what they are observing as did these two USAF men. Nor do they have as long to confront the phenomenon at very close quarters as Burroughs and Penniston seem to have done.

That is important. It seems to me that *if* these airmen encountered a UFO that night, as opposed to one of the more terrestrial possibilities set out in this chapter, then it is one of the most probable cases to be a real craft from somewhere else that I have investigated.

By 'somewhere else' it is tempting to leap to the conclusion that I must mean another planet. After all, the universe is teeming with stars akin to our own sun and we have recently discovered that many of them seem to have planets circling round them just like Earth.

Although for a long time science believed that the formation of life on planets was extraordinarily rare (possibly even unique) we now know this is untrue. Primitive fossil microbes perhaps once inhabited Mars. Such low-level life may even still exist. On one of Jupiter's moons, Europa, there is also mounting evidence about a possible liquid ocean and the real chance of marine organisms.

None of this life is likely to be intelligent enough to build space-ships – far from it, in fact. But it means that the *probability* of life at and beyond our own level of intelligence is pretty near certain on the countless planets that are out there in the universe.

At present we have no way of reaching even the nearest star in less than a few thousand years. Interstellar travel is something far into our future. But then barely a century ago powered flight of any kind was a dream and it was widely believed that to travel at speeds above 100 mph (160 kmph) would kill you .Now we send probes into space, which reach speeds hundreds of times greater than those imaginable during the Victorian age. It would be foolish to say that a century from now star travel may not be a reality.

Naturally, if we can imagine success sometime soon, then a more advanced race from another planet (of which there could well be many) might be coming here already. So the idea of some UFOs resulting from alien contact is neither ridiculous nor even scientifi-cally improbable. Scientists would actually be *more* worried if the Earth was never contacted by any aliens – for then we might well ask why they were avoiding us!

However, just because a visit is theoretically possible does not make it happen. To decide whether aliens are behind *any* of the UFO reports requires a study of the evidence for all close encounter cases and the many alleged meetings with aliens .

These cases exist in some abundance but this book is not designed to review the complex questions that they pose. You will find reference sources in Further Reading (page 219) which will steer you in the right direction if you choose to investigate further. My book *Alien Contact* might form a good introduction and *Looking for the Aliens* probes more carefully into the scientific search for proof.

Nevertheless, 50 years of research into thousands of these close encounters has posed more problems than answers. There is a con-sistency behind the data which is quite stunning and suggests that these events are more than just a modern myth or mass hallucina-tion.

I would not be surprised if we *are* being visited but the tangible proof – in the form of any photographs of alien craft at very close quarters, unearthly DNA returned from an abduction, or of any arte-fact that is provably extraterrestrial in origin – has failed to materi-alise.

We cannot ignore this problem if we choose to believe that aliens have landed.

As a result, objective researchers have, for a good while, been exploring other possibilities – examining, for instance, whether unexplained atmospheric phenomena might trigger visions by stimulating certain areas of the brain. However, nobody has successfully proved a rational solution and there are difficulties in accepting that the wealth of evidence for alien contacts results from the human mind alone.

That something is really visiting us seems more and more likely to be correct. The alien possibility therefore remains, even though it is far from established as a fact despite what some UFOlogists might tell you via the tabloid press.

In addition, there is a mood which seems to be asking whether *alien* necessarily means *extraterrestrial*. All of our discoveries about the nature of subatomic physics and the fabric of the universe since Einstein and the splitting of the atom have revealed things that are beyond any of our expectations.

Although we are accustomed to thinking in three dimensions – that things have length, width and height – there is a growing number of scientists who suspect that there may be *many* dimensions and that we only perceive a fraction of the majesty of the cosmos.

Some even suspect that *time* is a dimension and there is now active research which is attempting to build a time-travel device. This is one of the most unexpected transitions from science fiction into science fact but it may become reality before long. If it does – and future historians can travel into their past – maybe we shall discover that these UFO visitors are from Earth, not from space. We may be witnessing our own descendants coming back from the future to observe their distant ancestors.

Other spacial dimensions may also interact with our own reality and we might encounter evidence of this which seems almost incomprehensible. Another universe which literally penetrates our world would always be around but would lie beyond our everyday perception.

You can get some impression of this theory by imagining a creature that lives only in the deep sea and which can have no concept of our human civilization or the unseen reality of the atmosphere beyond the ocean. The limits of awareness of this deep sea creature would be the boundary between sea and air far above its head. This is a barrier between the one dimension that this creature can know and another that it has never seen – this being our world with all of its civilization.

Yet, occasionally, a scuba diver penetrates the creature's universe and may appear as an incredible visitor that 'came down from space' and disappeared again. There would be no proof of the visit. Nobody would be able to find the diver because he would no longer be any-where within the universe of this sea creature. Endless debates might follow as to whether there could be other worlds beyond the dimension of the sea universe but the truth could never be under-stood as it lies outside all possible experience of any seabound en-tity that had never witnessed that other dimension of air.

Such creatures could never possibly appreciate that there is a fur-ther boundary still – far beyond the limits of their world. This is a gateway which leads from our world into the dimension of space. We can see this boundary because we live in a dimension where it is vis-ible to us. The sea creature has never experienced air and so has no hope of sensing the dimension of space beyond.

Now put yourself in the place of that sea creature. If there is a fur-ther 'dimensional gateway' beyond space, which leads, perhaps, into another universe, we will be just as unable to grasp its exis-tence because it is beyond our capacity to do so. However, that would not mean that it does not exist – just as the sea creature's failure to find proof of the diver and his visit to the sea universe would not mean that the diver's visit never happened.

Clifford Stone claims that the top secret government study into the Rendlesham Forest case concluded precisely this. Other dimen-sions exist beyond our own and we cannot imagine them as they lie far outside the parameters of our ordinary experience. However, from time to time something from another dimension passes briefly through our world. These visitors may not be people coming here to see us – just as the skin diver might swim past shoals of sea crea-tures without even noticing them on his way to his destination. Likewise, perhaps to visitors to our world from that 'higher' dimen-sion we may be a mere curiosity or not even noticed as they head on through to wherever they are going.

The truly mind-blowing aspect of the UFO mystery may turn out to be that it tells us just how much we exaggerate our own impor-tance.

Astronauts who have flown to the Moon and back speak of the humbling experience of seeing how our world has but a tiny place in the vastness of space. They realized for the first time that everything does not revolve around our lives and our problems; that we are an almost microscopic speck within an enormously interactive universe. On their return to Earth, some likened this to a mystical transformation.

If, indeed, there is an 'alien' component to the UFO mystery, and in cases like Rendlesham Forest we see it at work, then perhaps we have to go through a similar transformation in our intellectual and spiritual awareness to imagine what lies beyond our simple existence.

A powerful devolution may be required to deflate our human ego. If there are dimensions and life forms way beyond our comprehension and they pass like ships in the night through our reality, then we grasp the limits to human omnipotence.

To passers-by from some other dimension we may be just like ants that we trample underfoot – a life form that is recognized but barely considered worthy of study. If so, the UFO mystery may teach us something deeply profound and far more important than any alien version of a NASA astronaut coming here to pick up rock samples and probe the human race.

Through an understanding of these close encounters we may come to see the true nature of the universe and our humble place among God's creatures. From human arrogance we may finally learn humility.

So what is my opinion about this case after seventeen years of research? My answer is tempered, because I believe there is still crucial evidence to emerge. The photographs have yet to be released. If airmen did view a spectacular craft, even though the film they took depicts blank sky, then that must support the idea that this was some kind of hallucination, probably resulting from a secret electronic experiment. If instead the pictures show fogging, perhaps resulting from radiation exposure, there may be legitimate fears for the long-term health and wellbeing of these witnesses. The British government would also have serious charges to answer for the way they ignored the possible threat to the people of East Anglia.

It is not improbable that a UFO in the traditional sense was involved, I am at best only half-persuaded of that. Some kind of visiting intelligence from another dimension might be the answer, but we are probably best advised not to dwell on that option, because it is a theory that nobody can prove. As such it ought to be our last resort – and there are other options.

We can establish that strange natural phenomena exist. Perhaps this case might even show us that there are times when the laws of physics break down in incredible fashion. Maybe some kind of quantum mechanical doorway between universes can open up through natural means as yet not understood.

Sadly, given the penchant modern society has for doing terrible things, it is at least as likely that the answer to this case will be more down to earth. Yet if it is a testament to the way in which the powers-that-be can treat citizens with such blatant disregard, then it is vital that we recognize that fact and try to prevent if from ever happening again.

I stand by my belief that this case is the most important in British UFO history. Whether the cause was terrestrial, or extraterrestrial, natural or unresolved, it offers major home truths about the greatest mystery of the twentieth century. It shows that even the most outstanding case cannot prove beyond doubt that the earth faces alien contact, but more disturbingly might instead imply that the culprits are not little green men, but cynical humans from some power-hungry administration.

Having had the chance to discuss the evidence at length with key participants during August 1997, I believe that I can now conclude something vital about this case. The same phenomenon was probably not involved on both nights. The events of 25/26 December were, in my view, a genuine UFO – possibly as a result of a rift in dimensional space. This may have been triggered as an accidental by-product of the covert Cobra Mist project being carried out by the NSA. Is it possible that the NSA then 'set up' the second encounter, causing distortion of natural phenomena, as well as projecting laser beams and other visual stimuli into the sky? But why? Was the purpose both to hide their activity on Orford Ness and so confuse the truth that nobody would ever suspect that a real UFO had invaded Rendlesham Forest forty-eight hours before? If so, then they have succeeded brilliantly.

This Appendix contains transcriptions of all the documents which can be found in the picture section of this book.

DOCUMENT 1

Country: MOROCCO
Subject: UFO Sighting at Kasbe
   Tadla, Morocco
D.I.: 28 March 1967
Pl. & Date Acq: Rabat, Morocco
   2 April 1967
Evel: C-3
Source: Local Press

Info Spot: EMS/1s
Distr: EXP

ID MF Rell: 1439
Dpt: 1 865 0069 67
D. R.: 6 April 1967
No. Pages: 1
REF: Project MOON DUST
Originator: USDAO Rabat,
   Morocco
Prep by:

Appr. Auth: C.G. STRUM, CAPT.
   USA U.S. DEFENCE
   ATTACHE, RABAT

Extract of Report

1. This report forwards a translation of an article which appeared in the Potl Morocain, 2 April 1967. This item was not carried in the other daily newspapers, but is significant as it indicates continued local interest in the subject of UFOs.

DOCUMENT 2

REPORT OF UNIDENTIFIED FLYING OBJECT

A. 191945 Jan. (1983)

B. Similar to star or planet, one sight only. Alternating blue and red in colour.

C. From front garden of house in an elevated position, commanding excellent view of Newport, Bristol Channel and Avon.

D. By naked eye, telescope and binoculars.

E. South west.

F. 30 degrees.

G. Unable to state precisely distance, appears similar to other stars.

H. Static.

J. Clear, cloudless.

K. Two aircraft passed below object. Could not be confused with aircraft lights.

(L, M, N, O and P: *information censored from public release by* MOD [*Jenny Randles*])

DOCUMENT 3

24 October 1983
Col. 62
RAF Woodbridge (Alleged Incident)

Sir Patrick Wall asked the Secretary of State for Defence (1) if he has seen the United States Air Force memo dated 13 January 1981 concerning unexplained lights near RAF Woodbridge;

(2) whether, in view of the fact that the United State's Air Force memo of 13 January 1981 on the incident at RAF Woodbridge has been released under the Freedom of Information Act, he will now release reports and documents concerning similar unexplained incidents in the United Kingdom,

(3) how many unexplained sightings or radar intercepts have taken place since 1980.

Mr Stanley: I have seen the memorandum of 13 January 1981 to which my Hon. friend refers. Since 1980 the Department has received 1,400 reports of sightings of flying objects which the observers have been unable to identify. There were no corresponding unexplained radar contacts. Subject to national security constraints, I am ready to give information about any such reported sightings that are found to be a matter of concern from a defence standpoint, but there have been none to date.

DOCUMENT 4

MINISTRY OF DEFENCE
Defence Secretariat Division 8
Main Building Whitehall London SW1A 2HB

Miss J Randles
Somerville
Wallasey
Wirral

Dear Miss Randles

Thank you for your recent correspondence on the subject of UFOs.

As regards your offer to summarise the reports held by this Department, there really is very little to summarise. I attach a copy of a blank report form, showing the type of information we require together with a couple of examples of completed reports (with the name and address of the informant deleted for reasons of confidentiality). I am sure you will agree that, although we hold a large number of reports, each one is indeed very brief.

Turning now to your interest in the sighting at RAF Woodbridge in December 1980, I can confirm that USAF personnel did see unusual lights outside the boundary fence early in the morning of 27 December 1980 but no explanation for the occurrence was ever forthcoming. There is however, no question of the account being a cover-up for a crashed aircraft or testing of secret devices as you suggest, nor was there any contact with "alien beings".

I understand that an article on the Woodbridge sighting has been published in the magazine "OMNI" (Vol 5 No. 6) in which you may be interested.

Yours sincerely

PJ TITCHMARSH (Mrs)

DOCUMENT 5

DEPARTMENT OF THE AIR FORCE
Headquarters Base Combat Support Group
APO New York

13 Jan 81

Attn: CD

Subject: Unexplained Lights

To: RAF/CC

1. Early in the morning of 27 Dec 80 (approximately 0300L), two USAF security police patrolmen saw unusual lights outside the back gate at RAF Woodbridge. Thinking an aircraft might have crashed or been forced down, they called for permission to go outside the gate to investigate. The on-duty flight chief responded and allowed three patrolmen to proceed on foot. The individuals reported seeing a strange glowing object in the forest. The object was described as being metallic in appearance and triangular in shape, approximately two to three meters across the base and approximately two meters high. It illuminated the entire forest with a white light. The object itself had a pulsing red light on top and a bank(s) of blue lights underneath. The object was hovering or on legs. As the patrolmen approached the object, it manoevered through the trees and disappeared. At this time the animals on a nearby-farm went into a frenzy. The object was briefly sighted approximately an hour later near the back gate.

2. The next day, three depressions 1 ½" deep and 7" in diameter were found where the object had been sighted on the ground. The following night (29 Dec 80) the area was checked for radiation. Beta/Gamma readings of 0.1 milliroentgens were recorded with peak readings in the three depressions and near the center of the triangle formed by the depressions. A nearby tree had moderate (.05-.07) readings on the side of the tree toward the depressions.

3. Later in the night a red sun-like light was seen through the trees. It moved about and pulsed. At one point it appeared to throw off glowing particles and then broke into five separate white objects and then disappeared. Immediately thereafter, three star-like objects were noticed in the sky, two objects to the north and one to the south, all of which were about 10 degrees off the horizon. The objects moved rapidly in sharp angular movements and displayed

red, green and blue lights. The objects to the north appeared to be elliptical through an 8-12 power lens. They then turned to full circles. The objects to the north remained in the sky for an hour or more. The object to the south was visible for two or three hours and beamed down a stream of light from time to time. Numerous individuals, including the undersigned, witnessed the activities in paragraphs 2 and 3.

CHARLES I. HALT, lt. col, USAF
Deputy Base Commander

DOCUMENT 6

(1) Directions given to Brenda Butler by witness on the base (directions below given by Brenda)

east gate woodbridge
turn left
3/4 mile
on left hand side
camera
police station

DOCUMENT 7

PRIME MINISTER'S PERSONAL MINUTE
Serial No. M. 412/52

SECRETARY OF STATE FOR AIR
LORD CHERWELL

What does all this stuff about flying saucers amount to? What can it mean? What is the truth? Let me have a report at your convenience.

W.S.C.

28 July 1952

DOCUMENT 8

MINISTRY OF DEFENCE
Main Building Whitehall London SW1A 2HB

D/US of S(AF)/DGT 5173   19 March 1985

Dear Mr Alton

Thank you for your letter of 21 February with the enclosed from Ms Jenny Randles of Birchwood, Warrington.

I should first of all point out that the sole interest of the Ministry of Defence in reported sightings of Unidentified Flying Objects (UFOs) is to establish whether they have any bearing on the defence of the country.

There is no organisation in the Ministry of Defence appointed solely for the purpose of studying UFOs, and no staff are employed on the subject full time. The reports we receive are referred to the staff in the Department who are responsible for the air defence of the United Kingdom, and they examine the reports as part of their normal duties. Unless there are defence implications we do not attempt to identify sightings and we cannot inform observers of the probable identity of the object seen. The Department could not justify the expenditure of public funds on investigations which go beyond the pure defence interests.

The only information we have on the alleged "UFO sighting" at Rendlesham Forest in December 1980 is the report by Colonel Charles Halt, of the United States Air Force, which Ms Randles mentions in her letter. We are satisfied that the events described are of no defence significance. I can assure you that there is no question of attempting to cover up any incident or mishap, nor are we attempting in any way to obscure the truth.

I am also enclosing with this copies of 2 Parliamentary Questions, one of which is that put down by Sir Patrick Wall and which Ms Randles also mentions.

Yours sincerely

Lord Tregarne

DOCUMENT 9

MINISTRY OF DEFENCE
Main Building Whitehall London SW1A 2HB

Ms J Randles
Cheadle Heath
Stockport
Cheshire
SK3 0UP

Dear Jenny

Thank you for your letter dated 28 October, and for sending a copy of "Northern UFO News", which I found very interesting.

I agree that many of the UFO sightings on 30/31 March were probably generated by people having witnessed the re-entry of Cosmos 2238, although there would appear to be some reports that night not explained in this way.

I agree that most of the recent sightings in the Bristol area seem to have been generated by Venus. I believe that there was also a display of lasers or searchlights that night to explain other sightings.

You mentioned two other specific sightings, and asked whether we have any reports that might tie-in; we have no such reports, although I seem to recall that a researcher mentioned a case to me recently which involved a UFO being seen on a security camera.

I have seen the video of the Lockerbie sighting, but it is difficult to come to any firm conclusions. While lights can clearly be seen, it was dark at the time, and there were no other visible features that might have given an indication of the size, speed and distance of the objects filmed.

Finally, I was delighted to hear that "Tony B" is recovering. I think that the handling of this case shows the sort of positive result that can come from cooperation between ourselves and serious UFO researchers.

Yours sincerely

Nick Pope

FURTHER READING

The following books may help you to expand your knowledge of some of the areas that have been explored in this text.

Introduction
Sky Crash, Brenda Butler, Dot Street & Jenny Randles, Spearman, 1984
From Out of the Blue, Jenny Randles, Berkley, 1992
UFOs and How To See Them, Jenny Randles, Collins & Brown, 1992
Left at East Gate, Peter Robbins & Larry Warren, Michael O'Mara, 1997
The Complete Book of UFOs, Peter Hough & Jenny Randles, Piatkus, 1997

Chapter 1
UFO Study, Jenny Randles, Hale, 1981
UFO Reality, Jenny Randles, Hale, 1983
Open Skies, Closed Minds, Nick Pope, Simon & Schuster, 1996

Chapter 2
The Report on UFOS, Ed Ruppelt, Ace, 1956
Project Blue Book, Brad Steiger, Bantam, 1977
UFOs: Psychic Close Encounters, Albert Budden, Cassell, 1995

Chapter 3
When the Snakes Awake, Helmut Tribusch, MIT Press, 1982
The Pennine UFO Mystery, Jenny Randles, Grafton, 1983
Earthlights, Paul Devereux, Turnstone, 1983

Chapters 4, 5, 6 and 7
Strange but True?, Jenny Randles & Peter Hough, Piatkus, 1994

Chapter 8
Clear Intent, Barry Greenwood & Larry Fawcett, Prentice-Hall, 1984

Chapter 11
MIB, Jenny Randles, Piatkus, 1997

Chapter 12
Scientific Study of UFOs, Edward Condon (Ed.), Bantam, 1969

Chapter 13
A *Covert Agenda*, Nick Redfern, Simon & Schuster, 1997

Chapter 15
Lies, Damned Lies, Henry Porter, Chatto & Windus, 1984

Chapter 17
Space-Time Transients, Michael Persinger & G. Lafreniere, Prentice-Hall, 1977
Miracle Visitors, Ian Watson, Grafton, 1978
A *Secret Property*, Ralph Noyes, Octagon, 1985
Mind Monsters, Jenny Randles, Aquarian, 1990
Looking for the Aliens, Jenny Randles & Peter Hough, Cassell, 1991
UFO *Retrievals*, Jenny Randles, Cassell, 1995
Alien Contact, Jenny Randles, Collins & Brown, 1997
Stealth, Lies & Video Tapes, Tim Matthews, Lancashire UFO Society, 1997

USEFUL ADDRESSES

Lancashire UFO Society,
PO Box 73,
Lancaster
LA1 1GZ

New UFO*logist* Magazine,
293 Devonshire Road,
Blackpool,
Lancashire,
FY2 0TW

NARO
6 Silsden Ave
Lowton, Warrington
WA3 1EN

Dr J Allen Hynek Center for UFO
    Studies
2457 W Peterson Ave
Chicago, IL
60659   USA

UFO Australia
Box W42
West Pennant Hills
NSW 2120
Australia

UFO Call (UK only),
weekly news and information
0891 – 12 18 86

If you would like to report a UFO experience or have any
comments to offer about this case (in complete confidence
if you wish) then you may contact the author by writing to:

1 Hallsteads Close,
Dove Holes,
Buxton,
Derbyshire
SK17 8BS

INDEX